Reluctant Revolutionary

Reluctant Revolutionary

The Life and Legacy
of Pastor Andrew Eliot (1718–1778) of Boston

JOHN S. OAKES

Foreword by Kenneth P. Minkema

☙PICKWICK *Publications* • Eugene, Oregon

RELUCTANT REVOLUTIONARY
The Life and Legacy of Pastor Andrew Eliot (1718–1778) of Boston

Copyright © 2025 John S. Oakes. All rights reserved. Except for brief quotations in critical publications or reviews, no part of this book may be reproduced in any manner without prior written permission from the publisher. Write: Permissions, Wipf and Stock Publishers, 199 W. 8th Ave., Suite 3, Eugene, OR 97401.

Pickwick Publications
An Imprint of Wipf and Stock Publishers
199 W. 8th Ave., Suite 3
Eugene, OR 97401

www.wipfandstock.com

PAPERBACK ISBN: 978-1-5326-1337-1
HARDCOVER ISBN: 978-1-5326-1339-5
EBOOK ISBN: 978-1-5326-1338-8

Cataloguing-in-Publication data:

Names: Oakes, John S. [author]. | Minkema, Kenneth P. [foreword writer].

Title: Reluctant revolutionary : the life and legacy of pastor Andrew Eliot (1718–1778) of Boston / by John S. Oakes

Description: Eugene, OR: Pickwick Publications, 2025 | Includes bibliographical references and index.

Identifiers: ISBN 978-1-5326-1337-1 (paperback) | ISBN 978-1-5326-1339-5 (hardcover) | ISBN 978-1-5326-1338-8 (ebook)

Subjects: LCSH: Eliot, Andrew, 1718–1778 | Biography. | Massachusetts—Church history. | Church history—18th century. | Christianity and politics—United States—History.

Classification: BL2525 O33 2025 (paperback) | BL2525 (ebook)

VERSION NUMBER 040925

For Kirsten, my friend, companion, and loving wife of forty-two years, with much love, appreciation, and gratitude for her unstinting support.

"The faithful Minister . . . will therefore labour to convince them of their lost and perishing State by Nature, the Necessity of Regeneration, and that Jesus Christ is the only true Way to Life: And tho' he'll by no Means neglect to preach the Duties of Morality, Yet he will preach them upon Evangelical Principles. . . . A faithful Minister will preach the plain Truth as it is in Jesus, without the Mixture of any new-fangled Notions of his own: He will keep close to the sacred Text; and . . . he will not dare to add any thing to what God has revealed in his holy Oracles."

—Andrew Eliot, *The Faithful Steward* (1742)

"Great Britain may ruin the Colonies, but she will never subjugate them. They will hold out to the last gasp. They make it a common cause, and they will continue to do so. In this confusion, the College is broken up: nothing is talked of but war. Where these scenes will end, God only knows; but, if I may venture to predict, they will terminate in a total separation of the Colonies from the parent country."

—Andrew Eliot, Letter (1776)

Contents

List of Illustrations and Tables | ix
Foreword | xi
Acknowledgments | xiii

Introduction: Face to Face with "Andrew Sly" | 1
1   Dedicated Bostonian | 11
2   Faithful Steward: Pastoral Principles | 20
3   Progressive Minister: Pastoral Practice | 33
4   *Pater Familias* | 51
5   Moderate Calvinist | 66
6   Orthodox Teacher | 82
7   Man of the World | 94
8   Anti-Slavery Libertarian | 106
9   Political and Pastoral Pragmatist | 118
10   Reluctant Revolutionary | 135
11   Finishing the Course | 145
Postscript: Eliot's Legacy | 150

Bibliography | 157
Index | 173

List of Illustrations and Tables

"A South-East View of the City of Boston in North America," by J. Carwitham (active 1720–1740), after an unknown artist. Hand-coloured engraving. Printed for Bowles & Carver, No. 69 St. Paul's Church Yard, London. Source: Paul Mellon Collection, Yale Center for British Art, Yale University, New Haven, Connecticut. Public domain. No known copyright restrictions.

"Locations of Boston Churches on Price/Bonner Map of 1769." Published with permission from Wipf and Stock Publishers, Eugene, OR. Source: Harper, *A People So Favored*, 2nd ed., 2007, ix, based on Price and Bonner. "A New Plan of Boston." Used by permission of Wipf and Stock Publishers, www.wipfandstock.com.

"Eliot's Reported Income in Pounds Sterling: 1749–1774," compiled by the author.

"Mather-Eliot House, 350 Hanover Street, Boston, Mass," photographed by Leon H. Abdalian, July 31, 1930. Source: Leon Abdalian Collection, Arts Department, Boston Public Library. Public domain. No known copyright restrictions.

"Boston, New North Church, Hanover St., 1804," photograph from ca. 1895–1905. Source: Archive of Photographic Documentation of Early Massachusetts Architecture, Boston Public Library. No known copyright restrictions. No known restrictions on use.

Foreword

IN THIS FIRST FULL-LENGTH biography of eighteenth-century Boston minister Andrew Eliot, readers are treated to new insights into this neglected figure that correct longstanding partial and even misleading conceptions of him and his significance. Here, through his manuscripts and the writings of those around him, Eliot is revealed as a family man, a minister, and person of faith, a Bostonian, a British subject, and an American.

Although the Eliots are famous, both in American history and in literature, Rev. Andrew Eliot is not a household name. He came of age and began his ministry at the New North church during the divisive mid-eighteenth-century revivals known as the "Great Awakening." Like the majority of religious leaders in the British North American colonies, he did not subscribe categorically to either New Light or Old Light camps. He was not a supporter of itinerant preachers of the "New Birth" such as George Whitefield. Rather, he shared the sentiment of a Connecticut clerical contemporary who, upon reading Whitefield's published journal, asked, "What is it?" On the other hand, while Eliot's Boston colleague Charles Chauncy became the nominal leader of the anti-enthusiast forces, neither did Eliot go that far. Moderate Calvinist ministers such as him were thoroughly aware that some important shift was underway, but they questioned its nature and potential outcomes, trying to ascertain what exactly it was, and carving a path that joined the old with the new.

So, too, with the coming American Revolution. Eliot is not known for making courageous public defenses of limited submission, as did another Boston colleague, Jonathan Mayhew. However, in a time when increasing numbers of Eliot's fellow clergy (not to mention members of his congregation) were enslaving people, he denounced slavery; and when revolutionary conflict came, he was one of only two Congregational ministers who were not declared loyalists to remain in Boston when it was occupied by the

British army—all of which took a different kind of courage. His devotion to his pastoral calling was first and foremost. In the coming conflict, Eliot avoided the extremes on both sides—thorough-going patriotism or loyalism—because he saw pitfalls in both routes. He valued English identity and liberties, but saw that independence was inevitable because of the inept or heavy-handed ways that British authorities dealt with the colonial problem. As with so many colonists before Lexington and Concord, he was torn, hoping for reconciliation while privately convinced it would not happen.

Eliot lived in an era of religious polarity and political hyperbole in which partisans of each extreme were demanding total allegiance or threatening retribution. In the face of these, he was circumspect, weighed consequences, and sought out what he discerned to be his reasonable duty and moral obligations. In many ways, then, his story is not unfamiliar, and not lacking lessons, for us today.

Dr. Kenneth P. Minkema
Editor, *The Works of Jonathan Edwards*
Director, The Jonathan Edwards Center
April 2024
Yale University

Acknowledgments

THIS FIRST FULL BIOGRAPHY of Boston pastor Andrew Eliot (1718–1778) represents the third of a three-part series of works stemming from my PhD studies. The first was an article on Essex, Massachusetts minister John Wise (1652–1725) for the September 2015 issue of *The New England Quarterly*. The second was my 2016 book, *Conservative Revolutionaries: Transformation and Tradition in the Religious and Political Thought of Charles Chauncy and Jonathan Mayhew*. None of them would have been possible without the help of many individuals and institutions, which I here gratefully acknowledge.

David Hall, my faculty host at Harvard Divinity School (HDS), where I had the privilege of spending more than a year as a Postdoctoral Fellow (2013–2014), has been of great assistance in my recent academic work. I was honored that he read through a complete draft of this study and generously gave his valuable feedback. Since my appointment as a Visiting Fellow at Yale Divinity School in 2012, I have often benefited from the learned expertise of Kenneth Minkema and I am grateful that he agreed to write this book's foreword.

Alan Tully has been of continuing help since I first studied Colonial and Revolutionary American History under him at the University of British Columbia (UBC) in the 1990s. My main dissertation supervisor at SFU, John Craig, has offered sterling support and wise counsel throughout my academic career.

I remain financially indebted to all the institutions which have generously helped fund my studies over the years, including the donors of a St. John's Scholarship, an R. Howard Webster Foundation Fellowship, and an Izaac Walton Killam Memorial Predoctoral Fellowship at UBC, where I was also the grateful recipient of a Social Sciences and Humanities Research Council of Canada Doctoral Fellowship. During my time at SFU, I was awarded two University Graduate Fellowships and a President's PhD

Acknowledgments

Research Stipend. Most recently, I enjoyed the support of two Sabbatical Grants from the Anglican Church of Canada and funding from the W. G. Murrin Fund extended through the Diocese of New Westminster.

No scholar can work effectively without the extensive assistance and resources of libraries, librarians, and editors. Especially helpful in the research and writing of this book have been the libraries of UBC, SFU, Yale, Harvard, Boston, and Toronto Universities, the Massachusetts Historical Society (MHS), and the Boston Public Library. I am grateful for the courtesy of the Harvard Archives and the MHS in allowing permission to quote from their archival sources and to Vaneesa Cook and the editors at Wipf and Stock for their editorial assistance.

No fewer than ten churches in the Anglican Dioceses of New Westminster and Toronto, and the Episcopal Diocese of Massachusetts have graciously supported my studies since the 1990s, including, in chronological order: St. Matthias, Oakridge; St. Anne, Steveston; St. John (Shaughnessy); St. Cuthbert, North Delta; St. Mark, Ocean Park; Holy Trinity, Vancouver; All Saints', Belmont; St. Mary, Richmond Hill; St. Paul, Bloor Street, and now St. Cyprian, Toronto. I am also grateful to the people of Ebenezer Baptist Church in Vancouver, where I recently served for four years. But the person to whom this work is dedicated has consistently offered the most crucial assistance in all my endeavors and ambitions.

Most pastors now work in relative obscurity following an increasingly undervalued and often misunderstood vocation, but such was not always the case. As a minister at one of the largest churches in eighteenth-century Boston for thirty-six years, Andrew Eliot was a prominent figure in a very religious society. Yet history has never properly understood him or given him his due. It is my privilege to contribute something toward rectifying that situation. While making a positive difference in the lives of many around him, the cautious and self-effacing, yet gifted and eminently pastoral Eliot may also offer a helpful example of maintaining ministerial balance and integrity amid competing extremes in a deeply polarized political as well as theological environment.

Any errors or omissions that remain are, of course, entirely my own. *Soli Deo gloria!*

John S. Oakes
September 2024
Wycliffe College
Toronto, Ontario

Introduction
Face to Face with "Andrew Sly"

The Mather race will ne'er disgrace
Their ancient pedigree,
And Charles Old Brick, if well or sick,
Will cry for Liberty
There's puffing Pemb, who does condemn
All Liberty's noble sons;
And Andrew Sly, who oft draws nigh
To Tommy Skin and Bones.

On August 14, 1778, just a month before he died, Andrew Eliot wrote to Harvard President Samuel Langdon about reports of deism at Harvard. He had received a letter from one of his sons, from which he quoted passages, indicating that someone had informed him that "Mr. Jonathan Bird of Hartford," who was "a Candidate for the Ministry" had written that "half, or about half of the members of said College were supposed to be Deists, & also that two ordained ministers not far from Boston were thought to be Deists." Eliot had taken this issue so seriously that he had personally "made enquiry as far as [he]was able and c[ould not] find that there is any Reason for such a report." He recommended that Langdon send a brief letter of clarification to his son, but he also argued that "the less stir is made about the matter, the better, as any public noise would spread the slander, & it is better not to be suspected than to have our innocence vindicated after a slanderous rumor." Eliot then closed his letter with a typically down-to-earth and pragmatic observation: "It is a true as well as trite saying—that if you throw dirt some will stick."[1]

1. Eliot to Langdon August 14, 1778, in Harvard College Papers; "Boston Ministers, Ballad—First and Second Parts."

It is clear from "The Boston Ministers" ballad of the early 1770s that Eliot attracted much attention, including some "dirt," in his own lifetime. Yet his historical significance has not since been fully recognized for two main reasons. First, although he pastored, at New North, one of the most prominent churches in Boston for some thirty-five years and he was one of the most gifted clerical communicators of his age, he did not seek the limelight, especially in public controversy, and he was prepared to yield to those more outspoken. Second, he was a cautious leader, whose restraint was evident in his political, as well as theological, statements and activities. This helps explain why the New North pastor is portrayed as "draw[ing] nigh" to the British Governor, Thomas Hutchinson, who is caricatured as "Tommy Skin and Bones" in "The Boston Ministers," while Eliot's sobriquet, "Andrew Sly," is clearly intended to refer to his care to tread an ambiguous line, as long as he could, between British loyalism and anti-British sentiment.[2]

Yet despite his relative obscurity and the fact that much of his work was undertaken behind the scenes, Eliot's position and participation in some of the most significant religious and political events and debates of his lifetime make him a fascinating historical figure. He was actively engaged in theological controversies surrounding the Great Awakening, the possibility of an Anglican bishop in the American colonies, the extent of human salvation and the divinity of Christ, as well as in political debates reflecting the influence of Whig and radical Whig thought in the pre-revolutionary period. In a series of quite remarkable letters, he also knew and described the harsh realities of pastoral work in Boston under British occupation. For these and other reasons, Eliot deserves fuller biographical treatment than he has thus far received.

Eliot in Historical Perspective—A Study in Ambiguities

The scholarship devoted to Eliot has been quite limited, and he has never been the subject of a major biography. The earliest extended, but limited, account of his ministry is found in his son Ephraim's *Historical Notices of the New North Religious Society* (1822), while the most detailed, but still

---

2. Ibid. "Charles Old Brick" refers to Charles Chauncy, pastor of Boston's First Church, and "puffing Pemb" to Ebenezer Pemberton, minister of "New Brick" church. "Andrew Sly" is clearly Eliot and "Tommy Skin and Bones," Thomas Hutchinson, Governor of Massachusetts from 1771 to 1774 and Acting Governor briefly in 1760 and from 1769 to 1771. The ballad appears to date from 1772.

relatively brief modern treatment is by Clifford Shipton in a compilation based on *Sibley's Harvard Graduates* (1963). Neither Mark Noll in his 2002 overview of American religious history "from Jonathan Edwards to Abraham Lincoln" nor E. Brooks Holifield in his 2003 synthesis of "Christian thought from the age of the Puritans to the Civil War" even mentioned the Boston pastor, for example. But those who have engaged with Eliot's life and thought have emerged over the years with decidedly mixed conclusions.[3]

In the earliest extended account, the minister's son, Ephraim Eliot, drew attention to the increasing "liberality" of church life at New North under his father's leadership. While denying that his father was ever an Arminian theologically, Ephraim's account was quite nuanced. He highlighted the more progressive changes at New North under Eliot's ministry and his reasoned, yet biblically based approach to contentious issues. But he ultimately classified Eliot as "a moderate Calvinist," committed to the reformed teachings of the *Westminster Assembly Shorter Catechism*. Politically, his son and biographer went to some lengths to distance Eliot from charges of factionalism. There were those, he noted, "who disapproved of his prudence in party matters, especially in politics," which he would not introduce into the pulpit. But Ephraim also took pains to defend his father against accusations of being a "tory" and "friend to the measures of Great Britain." By contrast, despite the "circumspection [that] acquired for him the name of Andrew Sly," Eliot "was a firm friend to the rights of his country, and opposed to the claims and measures of Great Britain." In that connection, Ephraim cited an unpublished letter of 1767 to a "Dr. Harris," presumably William Harris (1720–1770), the English biographer and Presbyterian minister, in which Eliot foresaw independence as an "event" which "must take place, in the course of nature, before a great many years are passed."[4]

Writing more than one hundred years later, Alice Baldwin (1928) restated a similar interpretation. She described Eliot as "of great service to the American cause," and a leader "in the revolt against the Stamp Act."

3. Ephraim Eliot, *Historical Notices*; Shipton, *New England Life*; Noll, *America's God*; Holifield, *Theology in America*.

4. Ephraim Eliot, *Historical Notices*, 20–26, esp. 26, 28–29. According to his son's account, Eliot informed Harris: "If the measures of your government are not changed, depend upon it, the colonies will be precipitated into a contest for which they are badly prepared, but which will terminate in their independence upon the mother country. This event *must take place, in the course of nature, before a great many years are passed*" (emphasis added). As per *OED Online*, "reformed" teachings are defined generally in this study as "accepting, espousing, or characterized by the principles of the [Protestant] Reformation," especially of Calvinist theology.

In his Election Sermon of 1765, for example, "he foreshadowed the main lines of argument against England by the colonists." At first, she conceded, "he thought some of the American measures too rash, but by 1769 he had become convinced that vigorous opposition had been necessary. He began then to talk of independence." It was not until Shipton's biographical sketch that such an interpretation was seriously questioned. Shipton largely echoed Ephraim Eliot's assessment of his father's moderate Calvinist theological stance, but argued that he was also part of a more general movement towards Unitarianism. He recognized some "truth behind the idea that the Revolution in Massachusetts was made by the black legion of preachers thundering politics from their pulpits, but Eliot," he stressed, "was not one of them."[5]

Shipton conceded that Eliot was not "without interest in public affairs." He called *Sermon Preached October 25th, 1759* "an excellent résumé of the colonial wars," and described *Sermon Preached before Francis Bernard* (1765), with its quotations from Hugo Grotius, Jean Jacques Burlamaqui, and Charles Montesquieu, as "pure political science." But while Shipton argued that in Eliot's view, "to assert Parliamentary authority over the English settlers after seven generations was absurd," he also stressed Eliot's bitter opposition to "the breaking of the compact by the colonists" and his parallel conviction that "independence would bring anarchy." Shipton noted Eliot's enthusiasm for Whig authors and his opposition to the Stamp Act, to the activities of the Society for the Propagation of the Gospel in Foreign Parts (SPG), and to the appointment of a Church of England bishop for the American colonies. He argued that "Eliot's fears of the church of Rome and the Church of England were purely political," however. Shipton also suggested that Eliot was somewhat naive, for while "his Whiggism was soundly based on a reasonable interpretation of history . . . of the imperial political problems of his own day he had not an idea." By the 1770s, his moderate stand had alienated both English and American Whigs, although Eliot's correspondence gave evidence of a more favourable attitude towards American independence in the last couple of years of his life.[6]

---

5. Baldwin, *New England Clergy*, 111, 90, 112n18, citing Eliot, *Sermon Preached before Bernard*; Shipton, *New England Life*, 408–9. Wherever "Eliot" is listed as author/source without first name, the reference is to Andrew Eliot himself.

6. Baldwin, *New England Clergy*, 409–10, 415, 419–25, esp. 419–20, citing Eliot, *Sermon Preached before Bernard*, *Sermon Preached October 25th. 1759*, and an unpublished letter to Francis Blackburne of December 15, 1767, in Andrew Eliot Letters.

Introduction

The only extended treatment of Eliot's life and thought since Shipton's has been Bernard Bailyn's twenty-three-page analysis of 1970. Although it stands as a piece of scholarship in its own right, it is important to note that Bailyn's work was in great part provoked by the conclusions of Alan Heimert's *Religion and the American Mind* (1966). Eliot was not a major figure in Heimert's central argument that "New Light" Calvinists were leading contributors to the development of American revolutionary ideology. In fact, Heimert only referred to Eliot five times and while noting his "prudence in party matters," his attempts in his 1765 Election Sermon to "minimize the reality of American grievances," and his general lack of outspokenness, Heimert freely conceded Eliot's "legalist devotion" to the seventeenth-century English philosopher John Locke, for example. Nevertheless, a major thrust of Bailyn's brief essay on Eliot was to counter his representation as a member of "Old Light, theologically 'liberal,' clergy" who were "conservatives during the Revolution." Instead, Bailyn argued, "if Eliot was a reluctant revolutionary it was not because of the pull of his religious ideas, which in any case were indecisive, nor of any tepidness in his political thought, which was based on rigorous Whig principles." Bailyn preferred to interpret Eliot's "reluctance to declare for independence" as "temperamental, the reaction of a broadly reasonable, tolerant, instinctively cautious and indecisive person always able to see both sides of the great public issues of his time, ever hesitant to draw his thoughts to thoroughgoing conclusions."[7]

In support of his argument, Bailyn sought to document Eliot's "disposition to temporize" as a consistent theme of his life and work from his first publication, *Faithful Steward* (1742), in which he allegedly wavered over the question of the need for a spiritually regenerate ministry, to his final letters from war-torn Boston. Thus, in his "jeremiad" sermon, *Inordinate Love of the World* (1753), Eliot failed to apply his observations of declension directly to his hearers, Bailyn argued, whilst in his "one high-level intellectual effort," his Dudleian Lecture of 1771, *Discourse on Natural Religion*, Eliot fudged the question of how to reconcile divine sovereignty with human freedom by resorting to an inconclusive quotation from Locke. Among his political writings, Bailyn singled out Eliot's *Sermon Preached before Francis Bernard* and his later correspondence with English Whigs. He rather

---

7. Heimert, *Religion and the American Mind*, 260, 291, 261; Bailyn, "Religion and Revolution," 87–88. The main title of this book, *Reluctant Revolutionary*, is inspired by Bailyn's use of that term to describe Eliot in "Religion and Revolution," 88.

dismissively described the former as "platitudinous throughout," based on "the contract theory of government" and "exemplifying at the outset of the Revolutionary era the substratum of belief that underlay the developing rebellion." In Eliot's correspondence with Thomas Hollis, Francis Blackburne and Thomas Brand Hollis, Bailyn further observed "agreement in general viewpoint . . . sympathy for their dark and progressively despairing interpretation of the tendency of events in England, and, above all, an extreme susceptibility to their conspiratorial, at times almost paranoiac, explanation of the underlying causes of the developing crisis."[8]

Eliot's major problem when it came to "Anglo-American constitutional relations," Bailyn contended, was that he "never followed through the implications of his own thought." In other words, he "never agreed that since . . . England was hopelessly corrupt . . . independence was the only solution." Such procrastinating failure to pursue the consequences or to have the courage of his convictions finally led Eliot to hesitate to leave Boston before the arrival of British troops, and thus to the harrowing years of pastoral detention under enemy occupation after which "he never recovered his former repute." Noting Eliot's continuing ambivalence about his situation even during the crisis of 1775–1776, Bailyn concluded, in effect, that he became a victim of his own tolerance and indecisiveness. Although plainly Whiggish, even radically Whig in his views, Eliot lacked either the intellectual rigor or the moral fortitude to act upon them and fully to embrace the revolutionary cause that was their logical outcome.[9]

Bailyn's interpretation of Eliot was echoed by J. C. D. Clark in *Language of Liberty* (1994), where he viewed Eliot as an example of how heterodox theology fueled Congregationalist revolutionary activism. Clark highlighted Eliot's activities as a correspondent with English Whigs, an opponent of plans for an American episcopate, and an Arian theologically. He noted his "most extreme rhetoric against the Stamp Act" and his persuasion that "a dark conspiracy threatened transatlantic liberties." Clark shared Bailyn's view that Eliot was ultimately caught between the "imperatives" of his radical political worldview, his fear of civil war, and his continuing affection for Britain. But Clark also suggested, without showing how, that the

---

8. Bailyn, "Religion and Revolution," 88–109, esp. 88, 90–95, esp. 90–91, 95–106, esp. 96–97, 98. Bailyn also quoted, 93, a relevant citation from Locke, "Letter to William Molyneux, January 20, 1692/3," in *Works*, 9:305, which will be considered below.

9. Bailyn, "Religion and Revolution," 104–5, 107–10, esp. 109.

evidence did not favor Bailyn's view that Eliot's revolutionary ideas, such as they were, did not flow from his religious heterodoxy.[10]

Eliot as Orthodox Dissenter and Reluctant Revolutionary

The limited availability of primary source materials does not allow for the publication of a thoroughly detailed biography of Eliot. But drawing on his diaries, correspondence, sermons, and other relevant materials, this work offers an overview with many fresh insights into his education, family life and pastoral ministry, in addition to his religious and political thought. To the fullest extent possible, it represents a personal and professional, as well as an intellectual, biography. In the process, it also highlights significant conclusions about the life, as well as thought, of this significant Boston leader during a crucial period of historical change. The main body of this study thus considers Eliot's "legacy" in terms of what he thought and did. Questions surrounding the longer-term influence of his family and the later history of his church are reserved to a brief, concluding "Postscript."[11]

To begin with Eliot's ideas, historians may have been divided over whether he was the convinced patriot characterized by Baldwin, the prudent "Liberal" described by Heimert, or the Whig of "indecisive" religious ideas with a temperamental "reluctance to declare for independence" portrayed by Bailyn. This study will argue that while elements of Bailyn's interpretation remain apposite and insightful, an analysis of Eliot's writings reveals a more traditionalist thinker, both theologically and politically, than has often been portrayed. Eliot's Calvinist theology was more clearly defined than Bailyn has argued and much less heterodox than has elsewhere been suggested. His political thought was firmly grounded in biblically based religious doctrine, and it reflected the ideas of seventeenth- and eighteenth-century Whig and radical Whig thinkers. Eliot's continuing commitment to English national identity, authority and ideals prevented him from becoming an outspoken advocate of the American Revolution until it was already in progress. But he defended notions of liberty that bear many similarities to those of his friend and contemporary Jonathan Mayhew (1720–1766).

---

10. Clark, *Language of Liberty*, 365–66, citing Bailyn, "Religion and Revolution," esp. 88, 95, 97.

11. There are insufficient Eliot sources to yield the kind of detailed biography that has been so well done in Jedrey, *World of John Cleaveland* or Wilson, *Benevolent Deity*, for example—still less in the magisterial, Marsden, *Jonathan Edwards*.

Eliot did not give the same systematic treatment to the topic that Mayhew did, but he presented his ideas in a religiously grounded libertarian discourse that echoed that of his ministerial colleague. In that sense, as others, Eliot's intellectual worldview was shaped by the distinctive contours of the dissenting Protestant traditions of New England Congregationalism that he shared with Mayhew and other like-minded ministers.[12]

As a prominent Boston minister, Eliot enjoyed the kind of personal and professional privileges, of which many of his smaller town or rural counterparts might only have dreamed. He and his large family were not dependent on the town to ensure a living. Eliot was paid relatively well by New North itself and he had other sources of income which left him in a much stronger position to counter eighteenth-century inflationary pressures than most. The Eliots had relatively comfortable accommodations. They enjoyed good health and a lifestyle befitting a family of means and distinction. Although sole pastor of one of the largest congregations in Boston for nearly thirty years, through pulpit swaps and similar arrangements, Eliot was able to arrange his preaching schedule in ways that allowed him to repeat sermons and thus significantly reduce the amount of new material needed to meet his Sunday and other preaching duties. His workload, including pastoral duties and offices, was undoubtedly heavy and his time off very limited, especially by modern standards. But he was still able to combine his church work with major responsibilities at Harvard, for missionary societies and other groups. Notwithstanding such commitments, Eliot's primary vocation remained that of a local church pastor and he pursued it to the exclusion of other possibilities, including the Harvard presidency which he declined at least twice. He was also prepared to pay the price for continuing his ministry in most trying circumstances, not least towards the end of his life, in 1775–1776, when he was one of very few ministers to remain in Boston besieged under British military occupation.

There has been much scholarly debate and discussion over the role of clergy, especially New England Congregationalists, in leading or encouraging revolutionary ideas and impulses among late-eighteenth-century

---

12. Baldwin, *New England Clergy*, 111–12; Heimert, *Religion and the American Mind*, 260; Bailyn, "Religion and Revolution," 85–169, esp. 88. For the most radical account of Eliot's "heterodoxy," see Clark, *Language of Liberty*, 365–66. For an extended analysis of Mayhew's thought and of his views on liberty, see especially, Oakes, *Conservative Revolutionaries*, 111–62. "Biblicism" is here understood simply as commitment to biblical authority and "libertarian" in a very general sense as upholding and/or concerned with human liberty, however defined.

American colonists, as well as over the role of religion in the American Revolution in general. This book does not address such scholarship in detail. But what it does offer is a portrayal of a prominent Boston minister, who was neither a strong advocate of independence nor a consistently committed loyalist. On the one hand, his religious and political positions became increasingly conflicted as the harsher realities of British rule drifted further from the ideals of British rights and freedoms which he cherished so highly as a Protestant dissenter. On the other, once open hostilities broke out in 1775, the cautious and pragmatic Eliot, who had strived long and hard to preserve good relations on all sides, not least to facilitate his pastoral ministry, was led by the practical realities of his situation to champion the Patriot cause which some of his political principles also favored. Eliot's education and prominent position in Boston society undoubtedly made him something of a special case. Despite such peculiarities, a strong argument can be made that his conflicting and sometimes wavering allegiances may have been more typical of the experience of many of his contemporaries than the more fixed positions which have often been front and center in scholarly literature on pre-revolutionary thought and ideology. The apparent realism with which he embraced the revolution after the outbreak of war may also have been more characteristic of his age than has often been recognized. In that sense, Eliot may have been more representative of the kind of pragmatic change of mind and heart that took place in the lives of colonial New Englanders than vigorous advocates of independence or loyalists who have attracted much more attention.[13]

---

13. For helpful summaries of pre-2008 scholarship on the role of clergy in the periods before and during the War of American Independence and on revolutionary causation in general, see Oakes, "Conservative Revolutionaries," 1–25. On more recent works, see Burnard, *Writing Early America*, 173–93. The term "American Revolution" is used throughout this work to refer in a more traditional sense to the 1775–83 War of American Independence. It is recognized, with Gray and Kamensky, however, that "contemporary scholars are inclined to see the American Revolution ... more in terms of the *longue durée*: a swatch of historical time lasting a half century or more, characterized by many of the phenomena and processes attributed to a much narrower Revolutionary time line" (*Oxford Handbook*, 6).

1

Dedicated Bostonian

Shoemaker's Son (1718–1732)

IN 1692, ELIOT'S GREAT-GRANDFATHER and namesake, Andrew Eliot, was one of the jurors summoned to sit in judgement on the so-called "witchcraft" trials in Salem. He was related, but not closely, to the most illustrious Eliot of colonial New England, John Eliot (c. 1604–1690), a Puritan missionary to first nations peoples, whom some called "the apostle to the Indians," founder of the Roxbury Latin School in 1645, and a pioneering Bible translator. The first Andrew Eliot was still a relatively recent immigrant, having brought his family independently from East Coker in Somerset, to Beverly, Massachusetts in 1670. According to William Cutter, he was received as a member of the church there the same year and was "a man of goodly estate, both in property and social position," who, while of some independent means, took on the occupation of "cordwainer" or shoemaker. Eliot also began what became a long tradition of family public service, in his case for the town of Beverly, where he transcribed "the town records into a new book, and in 1690 he himself was chosen town clerk." He served five years as representative to the General Court and in 1686 he was one of the five witnesses to attend the execution of the Indian deed of the town of Salem. His local prominence also qualified him to be part of the twelve-member jury at the Court of Oyer and Terminer, which met from May 27 to October 29, 1692, and condemned twenty people accused of witchcraft to death, including thirteen women and one minister.[1]

Eliot had obviously agreed with the court's initial decisions. But just five years later, he joined the other jurors in offering a public and seemingly heartfelt apology. "We confess that we ourselves were not capable to understand," they wrote, "nor able to withstand the mysterious delusions of the powers of darkness and prince of the air." The resulting problem was that they were,

> for want of knowledge in ourselves and better information from others, prevailed with to take up with such evidence against the accused . . . whereby we fear we have been instrumental with others, though ignorantly and unwittingly, to bring upon ourselves and this people of the Lord, the guilt of innocent blood . . . We do, therefore, hereby signify to all in general (and to the surviving sufferers in especial) our deep sense of and sorrow for our errors in acting on such evidence to the condemning of any person.

This first Andrew Eliot was not to prove alone in his family in his ultimate moderation on contentious issues, as well as in his willingness to serve.[2]

Eliot first married Grace Woodier from a prominent family in East Coker on April 23, 1649. Then following her death in 1652, his second marriage was to Mary Vivion in 1654. His son Andrew, born of his first wife, was made a "freeman of Beverly" in 1683, just five years before he died at sea off Cape Sable Island, Nova Scotia, Canada in 1688 at the age of just thirty-seven. According to Shipton, his son, the third Andrew (1683–1748), was "a pious and industrious cordwainer who moved from Beverly to Boston and bought a house on the present Cambridge Street." He did business as a merchant in Cornhill, "four doors below the corner of State Street," but lost much of his property in the fire of 1711. "In his adopted town he also achieved the social distinction of being appointed to the committee of visitation," Shipton reported, "and of being addressed as 'Mr.'"[3]

1. Cutter, *Genealogical and Personal Memoirs*, 2:1057–59; Walter Eliot, *Sketch of the Eliot Family*, 15–21.

2. Anders, "Real-Life Letter."

3. Shipton, *New England Life*, 97–98; Torry, *New England Marriages*, 246; Hurd, *Representative Citizens*, 300–303; Eliot, *Sketch of the Eliot Family*, 15–26. According to Town and City Clerks of Massachusetts, "Massachusetts," the second Andrew Eliot died "being on board a vessel . . . Of Salem . . . s[ai]d Vessel being then at Cape Sables, by an awful [sic] stroke was violently thrown into the sea and there perished (in the water) to the great grief of s[ai]d father, the penman thereof." His father clearly wrote this as town clerk of Beverly.

It was the latter who eventually became the father of the subject of this biography, the Rev. Dr. Andrew Eliot, minister of New North Church in Boston. Although his family had only arrived in Massachusetts less than fifty years earlier, this Andrew Eliot thus belonged to the fourth generation of his line of Eliots to settle there. He was the youngest of three children to survive infancy, including his older siblings, Ruth (1711–1746) and Samuel (1713–1745). Eliot's mother, Ruth Symonds (1680–1720), had married his father in 1705 in her hometown of Boxford before they moved twenty-five miles south to Boston, where he continued his work as a shoemaker. There, they built a family together. Shipton reported that "the one thing which the Eliot family vividly remembered about Andrew's childhood was the time that he was fished from a tub of water apparently dead and restored only after long labor." He attended the South Grammar or Boston Latin School where he studied under the Harvard-educated Masters Nathaniel Williams and John Lovell.[4]

The Latin School curriculum that Eliot would have followed marked the start of what was to become a long classical education modeled along traditional English lines. As described by Williams in a 1712 letter to Nehemiah Hobart, who was then senior fellow of Harvard, detailing an "acct. of the Methods of Instruction," this was a seven-year course, devoted almost entirely to Latin and Greek classics. Eliot may have been little more than eight-years-old when he began at the Latin School in around 1726. According to John Rexine, prior to 1789, when a minimum age of ten was introduced, admission standards depended entirely on ability. The daily schedule was certainly tough. During Lovell's term, for admission to the School, it was necessary to read a few verses from the Bible. Each of the six or seven classes sat at different benches. Latin and Greek and "the elementary subjects" formed the core curriculum. The morning session began at seven a.m. in the summer and eight a.m. in the winter and ended at eleven a.m. School resumed at one p.m. and classes ran until five p.m. After the eleven o'clock or five o'clock hour or both, students attended a writing school. On Thursdays, the School was dismissed at ten a.m., so that pupils might attend the "Thursday Lecture" presented by leading ministers, a long-standing Boston tradition.[5]

---

4. Shipton, *New England Life*, 97–98.

5. Nathaniel Williams to Nehemiah Hobart, 1712, in Murdock, "Teaching of Latin and Greek." An earlier booklist included Aesop; Cato; Cicero, *De Officiis*; *Orationes*; Clarke, *Corderii Colloquiorum Centuria Selecta*; Culman, *Sententiae Pueriles*; Homer; Lily, *Short Introduction of Grammar*; New Testament; Ovid, *De Tristibus*; *Metamorphoses*;

The first three of seven years at the Latin School were devoted to basic Latin grammar and memorization by heart. In the next three years, pupils like Eliot were expected to expand their classical studies into a wide range of Latin authors, doing translation, composition and even versification exercises until in the last "quarter of the sixth year, they began to learn Greek and Rhetoric." Finally, in their seventh year, according to Williams, they read Cicero's *Orations* and Justin "for the Latin" and the Greek New Testament, Isocrates's *Orations*, Homer and Hesiod "for the Greek in the forenoons," followed by Virgil, Horace, Juvenal, and Persius in the afternoons. In addition, "every . . . fortnight they compose a Theme, & now & then turn a Theme into a Declamation the last quarter of the year."[6]

As Kenneth Murdock has pointed out, perhaps the most striking feature of this curriculum is that Greek and Latin were so thoroughly studied that "there can have been but little time for other subjects." But this was necessary in order to qualify for Harvard, where Latin was the language of instruction and as Robert Middlekauf has noted, the college "Laws" of 1655 stipulated that a scholar should be able to read "'ordinary Classicall [sic] Authors,' understand Greek grammar, speak or write Latin prose, and possess skill in writing Latin verse." Representative authors included Cicero and Virgil in Latin, and Isocrates and the New Testament in Greek. The requirements changed little in the eighteenth century. "After 1734 the examiners became insistent that candidates 'be found Able . . . to write true Latin,'" according to Middlekauf, and in 1767, Xenophon replaced Isocrates as an example of an ordinary Greek author.[7]

Harvard Man (1733–1741)

At Harvard itself, the four-year course that Eliot would have taken represented an expanded version of an earlier three-year format, which, according to Joe Kraus, was "so arranged that all students worked on related subjects each day." The schedule was also designed so that the program

---

Terence; Virgil; "Making of Themes." Williams further listed: Cicero, *Epistolae*; Erasmus, *Colloquia*; Lucius Florus; Garretson, *English Exercises for School-Boys*; Godwin, *Roman Antiquities*; *Romanæ Historiae Anthologia*; Greek New Testament; Hesiod; Horace; Isocrates; Justin; Juvenal; Persius; Walker, *Treatise of English Particles*; and "Turning a Psalm or something Divine into Latin verse." Various editions of classical and other works listed are included in the bibliography.

6. Rexine, "350th Anniversary," 239; Murdock, "Teaching," 21–25.
7. Murdock, "Teaching," 25–26; Middlekauff, "Persistent Tradition," 55.

recommended by French humanist, logician, and educational reformer Pierre La Ramée (1515-1572)—Peter Ramus in Anglicized form—could be implemented. This involved a lecture on each subject, followed by individual study, recitation, discussion, and disputation. Monday and Tuesday mornings were accordingly devoted to logic in the first year, to ethics and politics in the second year, and to arithmetic, geometry, and astronomy in the third year, with study and disputation periods in the afternoons. A similar pattern was followed on Wednesdays for Greek, on Thursdays for Hebrew, on Fridays for rhetoric, and on Saturdays for catechetical divinity. In the mid-seventeenth century, when the original first year's schedule was expanded into two, yielding the four-year course which Eliot and his contemporaries would have pursued, more attention was given to the study of Greek, Hebrew, logic, and metaphysics.[8]

Logic was intended to provide "discipline in the art of thinking as well as an introduction to advanced studies." Anthologies of literary extracts were used in the teaching of rhetoric. Students also engaged in declamations in Latin and Greek before small groups and monthly before the entire school. Except for freshmen, undergraduates translated the Old Testament from Hebrew into Greek at morning and evening prayers. All were asked to translate New Testament verses from English into Greek, an exercise which Kraus has described as "both practical and devotional." Political studies were based on Aristotle's *Politics* rather than on more recent works of political history or science. The study of ethics was more practical, and although biblically based, was conducted separately from formal, theological doctrine.[9]

Theology was studied at undergraduate level along with the Hebrew, and even Aramaic and Syriac languages, and in keeping with the medieval model, it was still very much considered the "queen of the sciences." But as might have been expected in New England, the central texts alongside the Scriptures were strongly Protestant and reformed in emphasis. Thus the Puritan William Ames's (1576-1633) *Medulla Theologiae* and *De Conscientia*, were key texts, as was *Abridgement of Christian Divinitie* by the Swiss reformer Johannes Wolleb [Wollebius] (1589-1629). Indeed, such was the emphasis on deep learning and engagement with such sources that passages were memorized by all classes and recited to the college president at catechetical divinity classes on Saturday mornings. As Perry Miller and

---

8. Kraus, "Development of a Curriculum," 65; Monroe, *Cyclopedia of Education*, 2:63.
9. Kraus, "Development of a Curriculum," 65-66.

other historians have pointed out, it is, therefore, no exaggeration to say that Harvard students of the seventeenth and early eighteenth centuries, including Eliot, were steeped in the reformed, effectively Calvinist theology of the college's Puritan founders.[10]

As Kraus has also suggested, "preparing and reading logical analyses of passages from the Scriptures at morning and evening prayers provided simultaneous training in logic, Greek, Hebrew, and the Bible." Students were further encouraged to present and defend their positions through disputations, which followed the formal rules of medieval universities and were required of all twice each week beyond the freshman year. In order to qualify for a Bachelor's degree, candidates were examined before a local committee. Commencement then included distribution of a printed list of theses prepared by all seniors, as well as oral presentations of a few of them. Three years of post-graduate study were subsequently needed to earn an MA degree, but they could be done individually without any residence requirement. Candidates were, however, asked to give a sermon before the college body, to present a written "Synopsis, or Compendium of Logicke, Naturall Philosophy, morall philosophy, Arithmeticke, Geometry or Astronomy," and to have "thrice problemed, twice declaymed" before the society.[11]

Scholars have debated how much of what Samuel Eliot Morison termed a "Harvard liberalism" moved away from the college's theologically reformed foundations in the eighteenth century. Morison contended that "there was just enough notion of academic freedom to give Harvard a name among strict Calvinists." Yet his account of developments during the presidencies of John Leverett (1708–1724) and Edward Holyoke (1737–1769) shows significant evidence of intellectual transformation.[12]

Norman Fiering demonstrated how late-seventeenth-century tutors Leverett and William Brattle helped shift the emphasis "in nearly every discipline" of Harvard's curriculum away from its "Aristotelian-Scholastic inheritance." Although President Leverett may have made "no important changes" to the substance of what was taught, Fiering also stressed the impact on students of the more "catholic" attitudes that he shared with a

---

10. Ames, *Marrow of Sacred Divinity, Conscience with the Power*; Wolleb, *Abridgement of Christian Divinitie*; Miller, *New England Mind: From Colony to Province* and *New England Mind: The Seventeenth Century*.

11. Kraus, "Development of a Curriculum," 65–66.

12. Morison, *Three Centuries of Harvard*, 53–100, esp. 83.

"moderate group" on the Harvard Corporation, including long-serving tutor, Henry Flynt, and with other influential figures. The Latitudinarianism or "philosophical Anglicanism" of John Tillotson and like-minded Church of England clerics which inspired them did not undermine their commitment to Calvinist doctrine, Fiering argued, but it left them more open-minded. It also facilitated "new forms of integration of reason and religion." The works of Latitudinarians thus joined those of Isaac Newton and Locke in moving Harvard in more critically minded and questioning directions. After Holyoke became president in 1737, the college administration then became more systematically proactive, introducing so much modernization, especially in the teaching of the natural sciences and related subjects, according to Morison, that "the undergraduate course at the end of Holyoke's regime had little in common with that of Leverett's day."[13]

A Classical Education

Notwithstanding such changes, during the years (1733–1740) that he was formally a student there, Eliot's Harvard education must have been very similar to that of an earlier era. As Shipton has noted, he appears to have "entered Harvard in the middle of the Freshman year" of 1733/34, graduating with his BA in 1737. In Eliot's three extant diaries from his years of college study, 1734, 1739, and 1740, he was more concerned to keep track of local church activities than of his everyday Harvard life. But from these and other sources, glimpses of his fairly typical student experience do emerge. A class list which he compiled from 1734, for example, shows that he was placed fifteenth out of some thirty-four, twelve places below John Eliot, whose father was a judge in Windsor, Connecticut. His disciplinary record was relatively light and included just one fine and one private admonition for playing at cards.[14]

Eliot wrote in 1734 of "sa[ying] out Latin Grammar [th]e second time and finish[ing] it" on March 25, of his class completing "Greek Grammar"

---

13. Morison, *Three Centuries of Harvard*, 57, 89; Fiering, "First American Enlightenment," 322, 329, 334. Morison described Leverett as "liberal in his attitude toward religion" (*Three Centuries of Harvard*, 54). See further, Morison, *Harvard College in the Seventeenth Century*, 2:504–65; Fiering, *Moral Philosophy*, 242–54; cf. Fiering, *Jonathan Edwards's Moral Thought*, 227–33 (on Edwards and Tillotson); Wilson, *Benevolent Deity*, 19. Leverett and Brattle became tutors at Harvard in 1685 and 1696 respectively; cf. Oakes, *Conservative Revolutionaries*, 19–20. On Henry Flynt, see *SHG*, 4, 162–67.

14. William Eliot, *Genealogy*, 63–64.

on June 20 and being "dismissed" on July 3. He names the "respondents for [th]e Batchelours" at the Commencement on July 5 and how he began to "learn Hebrew of Mr. Morris" on September 6 and to study Isaac Barrow's *Euclid's Elements* on November 20. Five years later as an MA candidate, Eliot recounted how he "delivere'd a Theological Exercise in Latin in [th]e College Hall" on March 19, 1739 and "another in English" the following day. In July and August of that year, he reported details of Commencement and of a tutorial appointment. On October 31, he "delivere'd an analysis in [th]e Hall" and on November 2, when "the Bachelours began to dispute," he "made the sis" as a Master's student. Eliot spoke as one of the respondents at the 1737 Commencement and graduated MA in the summer of 1740, when graduation ceremonies were delayed until August 27 because of a diphtheria outbreak. Foreshadowing his later political interests, the "*quaestio*" which he presented and discussed publicly was "*An Monarchia absoluta et arbitraria, rectae Rationi repugnet*"—"whether absolute and arbitrary monarchy is repugnant against right reason."[15]

Thanks to a Hopkins Fellowship, Eliot was able to remain in college while pursuing his later studies and first ministerial placement. Indeed, on March 31, 1741, he recorded how he "received key of [the]e Library f[ro]m Mr Marsh." As well as an extension of his years at Boston Latin School, Eliot's Harvard education was clearly foundational to his ministerial training and development. As has been well argued, the college's "curriculum . . . emphasized public discourse and syllogistic debate," culminating in Commencement exercises. Despite its classical and theological focus, Harvard students were also schooled in such a multi-disciplinary fashion that between fifty and two hundred and fifty academic "theses in technology, grammar, rhetoric, logic, metaphysics, ethics, theology, politics, mathematics, and physics," could be debated at the end of their studies.[16]

By modern standards, Harvard was not a large educational establishment. According to statistics culled from the archives by John Burton, 326

---

15. Eliot, Diary, 1734; Diary, 1739 in Papers of Andrew Eliot; *AED* 1740, 1741; Barrow, *Euclid's Elements*; Shipton, *New England Life*, 398; Harvard, Commencement Theses, 1737, box 2, folder 18; 1740, box 3, folder 3. On Commencement exercises generally, see: Harvard College, "Harvard's 1786 Graduating Class." Eliot's phrase "made the sis" probably refers to the process of presenting a "thesis" [summary academic statement] or "analysis."

16. Harvard College, "Harvard's 1786 Graduating Class." According to Burton, "Philanthropy and the Origins," esp. 150, the Hopkins trust supported "four Batchelors of Art to reside at the college and perform publick Exercises in Theology."

people graduated from the college in the 10 years from 1730 to 1739, an average of 33 a year, indicating an overall undergraduate population of about 135, supplemented by Master's students, most of whom, unlike Eliot himself, were non-residential. This was a small, relatively tight-knit community bound together by common participation in an intensive curriculum, as well as by the simple fact of living together. As Youngs has shown, for the most part, the student body also shared a common social and demographic background.

> The two most important determinants of whether a person would go to college were social background and intellect. Simply because of their parentage some children had a much greater chance than others of becoming clergymen. Among Harvard graduates between 1700 and 1740, 63 percent were sons of merchants, physicians, sea captains, innkeepers, clergymen and other relatively well-to-do New Englanders.[17]

As the son of a merchant of means himself, Eliot was thus typical among his peers. In addition to those to whom he ministered at New North and encountered in his neighborhood and other settings, the company that he kept and the contacts that he made during his seven years of studies and ongoing residence at Harvard were also to become a primary social network. But among his fellow ministers, Eliot came to enjoy a more favorable position than most, simply because he was able to remain in Boston, right at the heart of New England clerical life, and live out his vocation as the dedicated Bostonian that he was.

---

17. Burton, "Philanthropy and Origins," 147; Youngs, *God's Messengers*, 12.

2

Faithful Steward
Pastoral Principles

Established at New North

IN 1769, WHEN EDWARD Holyoke (1689–1769), died in office as the ninth President of Harvard, Eliot's son Ephraim reported that the New North minister was "urged to take his place." But he refused to let his name stand for one simple reason. Even after twenty-seven years with his church, "the attachment he bore to his people caused him to decline an election." Then just four years later, after the resignation of Holyoke's successor, Samuel Locke, who served from 1770 to 1773, Ephraim noted that Eliot "was actually chosen into the office, contrary to his earnest request." The Harvard Corporation minutes for a meeting of July 15, which five people attended, including Eliot himself, confirm this account: "Dr. [Samuel] Cooper, who was chosen President on the 7th of Feb[ruar]y last, having declined that office, the Corporation proceeded to bring in their written votes for a President; & it appeared that the Rev. Dr. Eliot was chosen." But again, they continue, "Dr. Eliot, being present, declined that office." Why? "For the same reasons" as before, according to Ephraim. In other words, Eliot chose to remain in full-time church ministry and to contribute only as much of his time and attention to his *alma mater* as those responsibilities allowed. In this case, as in so many others, the pastorate was thus a compelling vocation, as well as career for Eliot. Securing his New North position in the early 1740s certainly required significant patience and attention.[1]

The financial support which enabled him to remain at Harvard for four years beyond his BA graduation in 1737 also opened up greater opportunities for him to engage in supply preaching and networking with local churches and ministers. Even after taking his MA at the Commencement of August 27, 1740, Eliot stayed in residence. He was able, as late as November 26, 1741, for example, to testify before the Harvard Overseers as to "the bad habits of Tutor Nathan Prince (BA 1718)." Beginning in July 1740, Eliot's diaries show him preaching with increasing frequency in different neighboring churches, starting with First Baptist of Boston and the Congregational churches of Natick, Medbury, Menotomy, and Castle William. From mid-November 1740, he began what effectively became a fourteen-month arrangement to preach supply at Roxbury, where the nearly octogenarian Nehemiah Walter was pastor. But throughout that period, his diaries also indicate that he expanded his ministry to other, more prominent congregations, including First Church, Hollis Street, and Old South in Boston.[2]

It was the death of the co-pastor of New North Church, Peter Thacher (1687–1739), on February 26, 1739, that eventually opened the door for Eliot to be called to a permanent position in Boston. The search process was a long and quite arduous one. The New North records show that those to have preached "upon Probation" between mid-1739 and August 1741 included Thomas Prentice and John Burt. Then, after Prentice declined the church's call in August 1739 to become pastor of Charlestown, Aaron Smith, Ebenezer Bridge, Daniel Rogers and Nicholas Gilman followed as supply preachers. When Rogers dithered for eight months without fully accepting New North's offer of the position in September 1740, the church

---

1. Ephraim Eliot, *Historical Notices*, 30; "At a Meeting of the Corporation of Harvard College, July 15th 1774," Harvard University Corporation Records: Minutes 2:404. Samuel Dexter, in his brief biography for John Eliot, *Biographical Dictionary*, 191, suggested that another reason for refusing the Harvard presidency a second time lay in Eliot's sense of "decorum." "When the chair was again vacant by the resignation of another president," Dexter wrote, "he [Eliot] was one of three fellows of the college, elected by the corporation. This he opposed, but his opinion was overruled. It appeared to him, as to many other persons in the province, a deviation from the line of decorum for gentlemen of the same body to choose each other into office, for the sake of the honour, when it was well understood they would not accept it."

2. *AED* 1740-1742; Eliot, Deposition.

eventually withdrew and recommenced its search, picking Eliot and Jonathan Helyer as "candidates for the Evangelical ministry desired to preach with us."[3]

On November 2, 1741, New North voted "by a considerable majority" to retain Eliot alone for the next eight weeks. Then on January 11, he was finally elected pastor by a majority of sixty-three out of eighty-two votes. A committee, headed by the church's founding pastor, John Webb (1687–1750), was "chosen to treat with Mr. Eliot about his settlement with us in this work." Eliot was asked to prepare a "Confession of Faith," which was communicated by Webb on February 21 and was "read and accepted as satisfactory to the Brethren by a unanimous lifting up of their Hands." The acceptance of Eliot's "Confession" signaled New North's final approval of his appointment, which he duly accepted a week later. On March 14, the congregation reported that he had been received as a church member "by dismission from Cambridge" exactly a month before his ordination to pastoral office. One month later, on April 14, he was ordained, with representatives of five Boston churches and First Church, Cambridge participating.[4]

Eliot's candidacy for and eventual appointment to the position of minister at New North thus took nearly nine months from start to finish and, despite the church's strongly stated resolve to exclude doctrinal heresy of any kind, the process was relatively smooth. Given New North's history and the evidence of Eliot's own writings, the obvious conclusion is that notwithstanding his more liberal reputation in some quarters, he began ordained ministry as a thoroughly orthodox Calvinist. Chapter 6 will further demonstrate that an earlier "Confession," which was first published in 1912, supports that view.[5]

Eliot's diary entry for his ordination day was typically brief and factual. "I was solemnly set apart for [th]e Work of [th]e Ministry in conjunction with [th]e Revd Mr Web [sic]. Dr Sewal [sic] began with Prayer, I preached Mr Webb Gave [th]e Charge, & Mr Appleton [th]e Right Hand of Fellowship." Preaching the sermon at his own ordination was not unusual, but in what was also to become his first published work, he expressed some ambivalence about doing so.

3. *NNR* 1:228–38.

4. *AED* 1741.

5. Sharples, *Records of the Church of Christ*, 100. Both the First Church and New North records were reprinted in Eliot, "Profession of Faith."

It would have been much more pleasing to me, and I doubt not, to most in this Assembly; had some Reverend Father now taken this Desk and instructed me in the Duties of the Ministerial Office, informed me from his own Experience of the Difficulties and Temptations which attend it, and warned me of the Danger of an unfaithful Discharge of it. But since, by long Custom, however hard, this Talk is devolved upon me; I shall endeavour, as well as I am able, to evidence the Sense I have of the Nature of this Trust, and of the Obligations all, who take it upon themselves, are under to be faithful in the Discharge of it.[6]

Pastoral Principles

Right from the very beginning of his ordained ministry and his own sermon, *Faithful Steward*, which was published the same year as his ordination in April 1742, Eliot displayed a developed and quite sophisticated pastoral theology reflected in a series of themes that permeate his writings on the topic. This is especially the case in his five ordination sermons: *Faithful Steward* (1742); *Sermon Preached at the Ordination of Joseph Roberts* (1754); *Sermon Preached September 17* (1766); *Sermon Preached at the Ordination of Andrew Eliot* (1774); *Sermon Preached at the Ordination of Joseph Willard* (1773). But his pastoral ideals are also reflected elsewhere, and by comparing his thoughts in print and from the pulpit with his everyday pastoral practice, which will be explored in the next chapter, much can be learned about how this particularly thoughtful pastor lived out his ministry in eighteenth-century Boston. An important point of departure for Eliot's pastoral theology and philosophy is his consistent stress on the priority of Bible preaching. But his oft-stated desire to expound and stay true to the biblical text was combined with parallel emphases on favouring essential "practical" doctrines over those he deemed unduly abstract and/or contentious, on personal "soul care," and on moral education.[7]

---

6. AED 1742; Eliot, *Faithful Steward*, 5.

7. Eliot, *Faithful Steward*; *Sermon Preached at the Ordination of Joseph Roberts*; *Sermon Preached September 17, 1766*; *Sermon Preached at the Ordination of Andrew Eliot*; *Sermon Preached at the Ordination of Joseph Willard*.

Biblicism

Looking back on over thirty years of ministry in 1774, Eliot described his "chief Aim" as "to be a useful Preacher" and in his five published ordination sermons, as elsewhere, he consistently upheld the Bible as the best and most reliable source of doctrine. "The Scriptures," he told the assembled company when he was personally ordained in 1742, "are the only Rule of Faith and Practice" and ministers could only expect to command "submission" from their congregations when they kept "close to the written Word of God." Since the Bible had that exalted status, "and no Schemes of Divinity are to be received, any further than they agree with this Standard of Orthodoxy," those called to the ministry should be "men mighty in the Scriptures," although their preaching would be most "profitable" when they also drew on their own "experience." Speaking at the ordination of Joseph Roberts to his pastorate in Leicester, Massachusetts, in 1754, Eliot saw the "great design of the ministry" as "to promote the Redeemer's kingdom, and the salvation of men" and the minister's "chief business" as "to study the holy scriptures." "Faithfulness" not only required that ministers "preach the truth"; it obliged them to teach "nothing, but what is contained in the sacred oracles." Eliot did not hesitate to offer practical advice about sermon preparation, which was important, and homiletic delivery, which should be "serious and in earnest." Yet because "faithfulness obliges ministers to declare the whole counsel of God," his major focus was on the need for biblical study and exposition.[8]

Similar themes emerge from Eliot's ordination sermons for Ebenezer Thayer (1766), Joseph Willard (1773), and for his son Andrew (1774). "No one can have the approbation of God as a minister," he told Hampton's First Church when Thayer was ordained their minister, "unless he is a good man or a sincere Christian." But study, knowledge and an ability to teach were also vital. "Ministers ought to study clearness, decency, and propriety in the manner of their compositions," Eliot continued. Moreover, "if we leave the Bible and set up any other directory, it will prove an *ignis fatuus* [i.e., a mirage], and lead us into the bogs of error and confusion." The congregation of the First Church in Beverly was given a similar message, when Eliot prepared them for the ministry of Willard with an exposition of 2 Timothy 4:2. The ministry was "an institution of Christ" and "the principal business of a

---

8. Eliot, *Twenty Sermons*, v; *Faithful Steward*, 18, 9, 16, 13; *Sermon Preached at the Ordination of Joseph Roberts*, 5, 13, 32, 12, 22, 29, 24.

minister lies between the study and the pulpit," he argued. Eliot explicitly rejected the Catholic doctrines of apostolic "succession" and "indelible" ordination. He even contended that the laying-on of hands in ordination was "not explicitly enjoined." But on these, as on other issues, his final court of appeal was the Scriptures, which contained "every important truth," teaching "all those doctrines which are necessary to be believed."[9]

Eliot's sermon at the ordination of his son to the church in Fairfield, Connecticut in 1774 focused more narrowly on the issue of conversion, which he plainly described as "a work of Divine power," and was understandably more personal in emphasis. Yet Eliot conceded that "it is not without reluctance, I have consented, that a son so deservedly dear to me should set down in such a distant part of the Lord's vineyard," and as he sought to remind Andrew that "you have a soul of your own to save," he also stressed that "the pure uncorrupted doctrines and motives of the gospel" were most "effectual." Biblical teaching was thus not only ministers' privilege and the source of their own salvation under God:

> This is particularly the duty of ministers; God hath set them in his church, to "watch for souls as they that must give an account."—To warn men of their danger—to enlighten them in the doctrines and duties of Christianity—to lead them in the path of life.[10]

Gospel Essentials

Eliot's biblicism further led him to distance himself from passing judgement on controversial issues which he considered undecided by scriptural teaching. Preaching at the ordination of Roberts in 1754, Eliot addressed the apostle Paul's parting words to the elders of Ephesus in Acts 20:26: "I take you to record this day, that I am pure from the blood of all men." He

---

9. Eliot, *Sermon Preached September 17, 1766*, 5, 17, 14; *Sermon Preached at the Ordination of the Reverend Mr. Joseph Willard*, 6, 13–15, 25. According to *EBO*, "Apostolic Succession," "The Catholic doctrine" teaches that "bishops represent a direct, uninterrupted line of continuity from the first Apostles of Jesus Christ." William Saunders has described "indelible ordination" in the following terms: "The Sacrament of Holy Orders, like baptism and confirmation, is a character sacrament. Each character sacrament confers an indelible spiritual character upon the recipient. These sacraments are not repeated and are not temporary. The spiritual character cannot be lost" (Saunders, "Ordination Confers").

10. *Sermon Preached at the Ordination of Andrew Eliot*, 22, 42, 38, 26, 25, citing Heb 13:17; cf. 2 Tim 4:2: "Preach the word; be instant in season, out of season; reprove, rebuke, exhort with all long suffering and doctrine."

defined ministerial purity as requiring not only an activist commitment to perform "all the duties of that important office," but to "declare all the counsel of God." Biblical study and knowledge and the faithful and earnest exposition of Scripture were thus essential to godly ministry. But it could be just as problematic to be over-reaching or unduly dogmatic in one's theology as to "dwell wholly on those things, which belong to natural religion; and handle them without any regard to their great Master." According to Eliot, "every one, who wears the name of a christian minister, should make Christ the great subject of his preaching." But it was no-one's "business,"

> in declaring the whole counsel of God, to attempt to explain every doctrine of the Gospel.—There are some, in their nature, too sublime for us—Such as, the infinite nature of God; the manner of the Divine subsistence; the doctrine of the Decrees of God; the union of the Divine and human nature in the Person of Jesus Christ, and the like.[11]

Eliot made the same point some twenty years later in his major published collection of *Twenty Sermons*. "My Dear Christian Friends," he wrote in that work's dedication, "it is now more than Thirty-two Years since I devoted myself to the Service of your Souls. From that Time my Studies and Endeavors have been employed to promote your best Interests." He then made a particular point about his teaching:

> In the Course of my Preaching, I have not meddled with abstruse Speculations: And, as far as Ministerial Fidelity would allow, have avoided Subjects of Controversy. I have rather desired to impress on your Hearts and my own a deeper Sense of those great and important Truths, in which good Men are agreed, and which are at the Foundation of all Religion.

The problems with dealing with more contentious matters was that "they, who attempt to be wise above what is written, in those great and mysterious doctrines rather puzzle and confound, than help the minds of their hearers." By contrast, "plain practical truths" were "of the greatest importance, and therefore the scripture insists most upon them."[12]

---

11. Eliot, *Sermon Preached at the Ordination of Joseph Roberts*, 5, 13, 24, 25–26; *Twenty Sermons*, iv; cf. *Sermon Preached at the Ordination of Joseph Willard*, 20, 25.

12. Eliot, *Sermon Preached at the Ordination of Joseph Roberts*, 25; *Twenty Sermons*, iii–iv.

Soul Care

For Eliot then, practical, biblical preaching should be ministers' main concern and such a focus was so vital because the stakes were eternal. "The trust committed to them" was nothing less than "the souls of men, to save them from the damnation of hell; and to lead them to heaven and eternal happiness." In his 1750 funeral sermon for Webb, his surviving colleague went out of his way to praise him as a "Gospel Preacher," whose "great Ambition" was "to dispense the Gospel of Christ in it's native Purity and Simplicity; to bring his Hearers to know God, and Christ, and to walk in Conformity to the Rules of our holy Religion." But what equally impressed Eliot was that Webb showed "a Heart engaged in his Work," which was sometimes, when preaching, "so warmed with the Divine Truths he was delivering, that his Notes seemed a Confinement, and he would, as it were, break loose, and give Way to those devout Sentiments, which crouded [sic] almost too fast into his Mind, so as to render him, to use the figurative language of *Elihu, like a Bottle ready to burst.*"[13]

Webb's passion for the gospel was matched by his fervency in exercising the more directly interpersonal aspects of his vocation. Eliot described him as a prudent moderator in church meetings, who went out of his way to visit those who were troubled or conflicted. "He carefully visited the Sick and Afflicted," Eliot noted, and

> he had a happy Talent of accommodating himself and his Discourse to their particular Circumstances . . . He was a skilful Physician for Souls: Few, if any, have been more frequently applied to by Persons under spiritual Exercises; and they always found him ready to give them such Advice and Direction, as their Circumstances required. Many of you, my Hearers, can testify with what Tenderness he endeavoured to heal the broken; and what unweaned Pains he took to set at Liberty them that were bruised.

Despite pastoring "one of the largest Assemblies in the Town," Webb took time for visitation and "in his Visits he scattered his Alms, where he thought they were needed." He was also "a lover of good Men," and though "a steady Friend to the Order, the Liberties, and the Principles of these Churches," who "openly bore Testimony against every Deviation from them," he did not restrict his care to "any Denomination." Webb was obviously not "a

---

13. Eliot, *Sermon Preached at the Ordination of Joseph Roberts*, 17; *Burning and Shining Light*, 28, 29, 30, citing Job 32:19.

perfect Man." But Eliot could not but "think him one of the best of Christians, and one of the best of Ministers."[14]

In that sense, Webb was clearly a role model, as well as something of a mentor to Eliot—someone who embodied pastoral ideals which he equally espoused. The care of souls was certainly central to Eliot's understanding of what it meant for a pastor to be a "faithful steward" in the sense that he advocated in his own ordination sermon. God had "constituted the Ministers of the Gospel to officiate as Stewards" inasmuch as he had "committed the Charge and Oversight of his Family" to them, as well as the responsibility "to provide and dispense spiritual Provision to those that belong to it"—duties for which they would all be held accountable for at the final judgement.[15]

Gospel preaching and teaching predominate in Eliot's 1742 exposition of pastoral ministry based on 1 Corinthians 4:2. A faithful pastor will

> labour to convince them [his hearers] of their lost and perishing State by Nature, the Necessity of Regeneration, and that Jesus Christ is the only true Way to Life: And tho' he'll by no Means neglect to preach the Duties of Morality, Yet he will preach them upon Evangelical Principles . . . A faithful Minister will preach the plain Truth as it is in Jesus, without the Mixture of any newfangled Notions of his own: He will keep close to the sacred Text; and as he will not dare to add any thing to what God has revealed in his holy Oracles.

But plain gospel preaching should always be accompanied by sensitivity to an individual's spiritual state.[16]

Thus "when any are under Awakenings, he will not immediately apply Comfort, but will search the Wound to the Bottom; lest he be found to daub with untempered Mortar: He will guard against Presumption and Despair, labour to detect the Hypocrite, and encourage the Sincere." It was not enough simply to declaim God's truth from the pulpit. Visitation was also vital:

> Ministers must be faithful in inspecting their flocks. This is more or less every minister's duty. The Apostle Paul "*taught publickly and from house to house.*" And the great end of our ministry requires, that some of our time be improved, in private endeavours

---

14. Eliot, *Burning and Shining Light*, 32–33, 34–38.
15. Eliot, *Faithful Steward*, 7.
16. Eliot, *Faithful Steward*, 18.

> to do good. Some need more particular advice, reproof, and consolation, then [sic] we can give in public; and to know the start of the flock, would be a great help, in our preparations for the pulpit.

For Eliot "fidelity in this part of his work," supposed that a minister was "ever ready to assist those, who apply to him for instruction and advice: or to attend upon those who are under any peculiar spiritual difficulties or temptations when their case is made known to him: and to make private personal application, where it is like to answer any valuable end." Precisely because ministers were "appointed . . . to watch for souls as they that must give an account" and they were "given the ministry of reconciliation," Eliot, who was clearly proud of his son Andrew when he preached his ordination sermon, was at pains to remind him that authentic ministry involved sharing not only "the gospel of God," but also "our own souls, because ye were dear unto us!"[17]

Moral Education

Eliot was also in no doubt about the temptations and evils that believers faced and about ministers' needs to offer their congregations suitable moral education. In his "jeremiad" sermon preached on the occasion of a public fast day on April 19, 1753, *Evil and Adulterous Generation*, Eliot pulled no punches in describing the moral degeneracy of contemporary New England and the resulting needs for repentance and reform. In that sense, as will be argued in chapter 5, Eliot's ethical teaching was clearly morally demanding, even if his overriding emphasis on grace belies any claim that it was implicitly moralistic.[18]

It was, he insisted, ministers' duty to set, as well as to teach the best possible example for their flocks, for "much of a minister's usefulness depends on the holiness of his life."

> The good Steward will be careful to set an Example to the rest of the Family, by obeying his Lord himself, and submitting to the Rules which he has appointed for the Government of his Family. So likewise the faithful Minister will go before his flock in a

---

17. Eliot, *Sermon Preached at the Ordination of Joseph Roberts*, 18, citing Acts 20:20, 19–20; *Sermon Preached at the Ordination of Andrew Eliot*, 33, 34, citing 1 Thess 2:8. All biblical citations in this study, including those quoted verbatim, are from the "Authorized" or "King James Version," which Eliot and others used.

18. Eliot, *Evil and Adulterous Generation*.

holy and blameless Conversation. The Apostle tells us, "*The Bishop must be blameless as the Steward of GOD*"; there can't be a greater Inconsistency than a vicious Minister: With what Face can he reprove others for their Sins, who lives in the allowed Practice of them himself?[19]

When it came to moral instruction, Eliot was equally dogmatic that "the faithful Minister will teach what CHRIST has commanded and nothing else." Ministers should, therefore, "fetch spiritual Provision for the Nourishment of CHRIST'S Family" from Scripture, even when biblical standards proved offensive to their hearers:

> However these may disgust the carnal Part of his Audience, and the polite taste of the Age; yet the faithful Minister dare not omit to preach with Warmth and Earnestness, those Things which CHRIST has so plainly commanded, and upon which so much depends. Besides, as he has felt the Power of Divine Truths upon his own Soul, he can't be easy till others have experienced the same; He will therefore labour to convince them of their lost and perishing State by Nature, the Necessity of Regeneration, and that JESUS CHRIST is the only true Way to Life: And tho' he'll by no Means neglect to preach the Duties of Morality, yet he will preach them upon Evangelical Principles.[20]

This concern to balance "the duties of morality" with "evangelical principles" is perhaps most evident in *Twenty Sermons*, which address such topics as "the connection between the duties and comforts of religion" (Sermon XI), "the obligations to family-religion" (Sermon XII), and "the usefulness and importance of religious education" (Sermon XIII) alongside "Jesus Christ: the only source of rest and happiness"(Sermon III) and "the blessedness of those who have not seen and yet have believed" (Sermon XX). Moreover, as Eliot consistently argued, especially in his third sermon in the collection, growth in Christian character was itself the clearest evidence of God's grace at work in people's hearts.

> We are to enquire, whether we have universal benevolence to mankind, and a special reason to those who bear the image of God, and walk agreably to his commandments. Further we are to enquire, whether we are meek and patient, forgiving and forbearing;

---

19. Eliot, *Sermon Preached at the Ordination of Joseph Roberts*, 32; *Faithful Steward*, 25, citing Titus 1:7.

20. Eliot, *Faithful Steward*, 17–18.

whether we do justly, love mercy, and walk humbly with our God (Mic 6:8); whether our affections are placed on things above and not on things on the earth; whether we grow in grace, in our love to God, in our regard to Jesus Christ, in a devout, humble, serious, Christian temper. These are some of the marks which the scripture gives of the true christian; and if our conscience bear witness that they are to be found upon us, we may safely determine that this character belongs to us.[21]

In that sense, as others, Eliot's pastoral theology and principles were consistently Bible-centred and practical. He understood his primary calling as pastor to be that of a gospel preacher who focused on the central themes of his faith, and educated and cared for his people in such a way that they came to genuine faith and lived it out with Christian integrity.

---

21. Eliot, *Twenty Sermons*, 247.

Eliot's Reported Income in Pounds Sterling: 1749–1774

Year	Salary	Help/Addition	Wood	Marriages	Presents	Rings	Gloves	Rent	Interest/Estate+	Other*	Total
1749	£1040		£175	£32 10s.	£374 13s.	£40	£71 04s.	£8	£11 5s.	£107 10s.	£1860 11s.
1750	£1040	£162	£160 5s.	£76 9s. 6d.	£520	£44 13s.	£112 15s.	£8	£47 12s.	£226 14s.	£2398. 6s.
1751	£1040	£390	£168 1s. 3d.	£97 10s.	£375 7s.	£30	£76 3s.	£8	£60	£110 12s.6d.	£2355 13s. 9d.
1752	£1040	£390	£162 10s.	£66 18s.	£231 18s. 3d.	£36	£82	£8	£51	£369 4s. 6d.	£2437 11s.
1758	£1040	£390	£173 16s. 3d.	£87 5s.	£181 10s. 6d.	£27 17s.	£69 6s.	£10	£100	£28	£2049 16s. 9d.
1759	£1040	£390	£209 18s. 9d.	£66 6s. 3d.	£238 5s.	£22 5s.	£67 7s.	£40	£144 18s. 9d.	£68	£2287 5s.
1760	£1040	£390	£198 15s. 3d.	£190 3s. 3d.	£162		£128 3s. 4d.		£263 15s. 7d.	£70	£2627 16s. 4d.
1765	£1040	£390	£207 10s.	£117 10s.	£182 19s. 6d.		£93 5s.		£296 18s. 3d.		£2328 2s. 9d.
1768	£1040	£390	£196 8s. 5d.	£159 12s.	£228 18s. 3d.		£40 16s. 6d.		£302 10s.7½d.	£174 11s. 11¼d.	£2532 6s. 8¾d.
1770	£1430		£200	£43 7s. 6d.	£214 0s. 1d.		£32 10s. 6d.		£370 0s. 7d.	£187 19s. 4d.	£2477 18s.
1772	£1430		£237 5s.	£81 6s. 3d.	£239 15s 1d.		£29 7s. 3d.		£376 3s. 11d.		£2393 17s. 5d.
1773	£1430		£212 11s. 6d.	£71	£266 2s.		£32 1s. 6d.		£684 3s. 6d.		£2695 18s. 6d.
1774	£1430		£215 1s.	£47 5s.	£169 7s. 3d.		£8 9s. 8d.		£915 11s. 11d.	£54	£2839 15s. 6d.

Source: *AED*.

Notes:
+ The "interest/estate" category includes interest received on investments and income listed from Eliot's estate.
* "Other" income includes all sources beyond those specified or identified under other categories.

3

Progressive Minister
Pastoral Practice

Pastoral Collaboration

ON THE MORNING OF April 22, 1750, when Eliot gave the funeral sermon for his senior colleague, Webb, who had died just six days earlier, there was much to celebrate, as well as to grieve. Webb had served as founding pastor of New North since 1714, following his election by a group of influential former members of Old North Church. They had been planning a new church since 1712. They had secured the permission of Old North's pastor, Cotton Mather, and elders and had constructed a new building at the corner of Hanover and Clarke Streets. On October 20, 1714, Webb was duly ordained after the congregation's founding members formally subscribed to their church covenant. Over the next six years, New North grew rapidly, with 301 baptisms and forty-nine covenant renewals, and such growth soon resulted in the church's decision to elect a second pastor to assist with the needs of the church. Peter Thacher, who was ten years older than Webb, joined New North in 1720 and subsequently stayed until his own death in February 1739. He had previously served as pastor of Weymouth, Massachusetts from 1707 to 1719, and although he had already left that position, his appointment to New North led to significant internal dissension, as well as external opposition from other ministers. But Thacher's ministry at the church eventually led to a highly fruitful collaboration with Webb and to a further period of major congregational growth.[1]

Eliot still went out of his way to explain why his funeral homily was somewhat different from what he might normally deliver on such an occasion. Webb, who had apparently suffered a stroke years before and whose health had not been strong, had been in the pulpit himself as recently as April 8. But by the day of his death on April 16, Eliot noted in his diary that his congregation "had a solemn assembly to ask of Heav'n [th]e Continuance of Mr Webb's Life who is bro't very low. Dr Sewall began w[i]th Prayer. Then we sang. Then Mr Prince prayed. I preached Mr Checkley concluded w[i]th Prayer." Webb was clearly much loved by his people, but Eliot recognized that it was still unusual to devote seventeen of the forty-two pages of his funeral sermon to the deceased, and he said as much. "It is not my Inclination nor has it commonly been my Practice to enlarge in funeral Panegyricks," he said. "But the Relation I stand in to you, Gratitude to the Deceased, and the Respect I have for distinguishing Merit, incline me to make a more particular Mention."[2]

And what were Webb's greatest "distinguishing merits"? First,

> He was bless'd with valuable natural Endowments, which he improv'd by applying himself with Diligence to Reading and Meditation. He was well acquainted with the more polite Branches of Literature, but Divinity was his favorite Study; in this his Soul was engaged; and to this he chiefly bent his Mind: And such was the happy Effect of his Application, that few have a more comprehensive View of the Method of Salvation by Jesus Christ; or attain to a clearer Understanding of the Doctrines and Duties of our Holy Religion. Nor did his Knowledge end in Speculation; he felt (to use a favorite Expression of his) the Power of Divine Truths upon his Soul; He found the Doctrines of the Gospel had a most happy Tendency to conform his Mind to the Blessed God, and to

---

1. *NNR* 1:6–11, 201–10; Wells and Fanning, *New North Church*, 10–18; Harper, *People So Favored of God*, 182. For a biography of Thacher, see *SHG* 4:303–8. For other accounts of the disputes over his appointment, see Wells and Fanning, *New North Church*, 15–18; Drake, *History and Antiquities*, 545–48; Ephraim Eliot, *Historical Notices*, 10–17. In 1722, members who departed New North on Thacher's appointment were part of founding Boston's New Brick Church with which Eliot came to work quite closely years later.

2. *AED* 1750; Eliot, *Burning and Shining Light*, 25–26. Eliot reported that Webb had suffered a "paralytic Shock, which he received some years since; by which (as I am told) his Powers both of Body and Mind were greatly enfeebled" (28).

influence him to that universal Holiness, which is the Honour and the Happiness of a reasonable Creature.

From his days as a Harvard undergraduate, Webb had thus "devoted himself to the Service of that God, who had called him by his Grace." Webb was also "an able faithful Minister of the New Testament," whose "great Concern" was that "he might be instrumental to build up the Redeemer's Kingdom among you." Among Webb's strongest qualities was that he was a "Gospel Preacher," who "rightly divided the Word of Truth, giving every one their Portion in due Season." In fact, he was so committed, Eliot reported, that "when urged on the last Sabbath of his Life, not to spend himself by too much speaking; he replied, 'this is the Day on which I have been won't [sic] to speak for God, a Work in which I always delighted, let me therefore speak this last Sabbath I am to live; possibly I may be instrumental to do good to some poor Soul." Webb had thus "died as he had lived, burning with the most ardent Desire of doing good in the World."³

Webb was also a model pastor in that he was "greatly concerned for the Peace and good Order of the Church," faithfully visited "the Sick and Afflicted," and had "a happy Talent of accommodating himself and his Discourse to their particular Circumstances." "It may with Truth be said of Mr. Webb," Eliot concluded, "that he was an able and faithful Minister, a zealous and laborious Servant of Jesus Christ; and in a great Measure deserved the Character of a burning and shining Light," attributed to John the Baptist in his text from John 5:35. Such was Eliot's considered judgement of the man with whom he worked for the first eight years of his pastorate at New North.⁴

Theologically, both Webb and Thacher clearly upheld traditionally orthodox positions. Webb came from a family of some wealth and social prominence and joined the church after a successful career at Harvard and as a Reading Grammar School teacher. He seems to have owed his New North appointment in great part to the influence of Increase Mather (1639–1723), pastor of Boston's Old North church for sixty-two years and former President of Harvard (1685–1701). It was Mather who persuaded, according to competing candidate John Barnard, the group of "substantial mechanicks," largely from Old North itself, who were responsible for building New North, to reject Barnard in favor of Webb. Certainly, at his

---

3. *AED* 1750; Eliot, *Burning and Shining Light*, 25–26, 28, 29, 32.
4. Eliot, *Burning and Shining Light*, 32, 34.

ordination on October 20, 1714, the Mathers were very much front and center. According to Samuel Sewall, who attended the service,

> He [Webb] Preached from John 5th. 35, That part, He was a Burning and a shining Light. Dr. C[otton] Mather Prayed first then the Old Dr. [Increase Mather] Read the Covenant which the Church upon their Gathering Entered into, and gave him his Charge, and Dr. C. Mather the Right hand of Fellowship. The Two Drs. and Mr. Bridge with Mr. Pemberton laid on Hands, A Great concourse of People being Auditors.[5]

Right from the start, then, Webb enjoyed the support of the most influential members of Boston's traditionalist theological establishment. Over the course of his thirty-six-year ministry at New North, he was largely to stay true to that heritage. Shipton described the New North minister as "stepping into the place made for him as the champion of the old and conservative parsons, the Mathers and Thomas Bridge," although he also suggested that Webb went "further to the ecclesiastical right and the political left than . . . his patrons." Eliot's irenic spirit, as well as his deliberate avoidance of more contentious or speculative teaching, must have helped facilitate the pastoral collaboration with Webb, which was a practical necessity during the earliest years of his ordained ministry.[6]

Preaching and Pastoral Duties

> Eliot the great, whose doctorate,
> Was surely well applied,
> To sermonize is wondrous wise;
> He is the people's pride.
> New North would sink, they rightly think,
> If he should them forsake;
> If he were sent as a President,
> Their hearts would sadly quake.[7]

The judgement of the author(s) of the Boston ministers' "ballad" in the early 1770s is clear evidence that like Webb, one of Eliot's major gifts and

---

5. Barnard, "Autobiography," 214–15; Sewall, "Memoranda," 298, where Sewall wrongly listed the text as from "John 4th. 35," not as corrected in the above citation.

6. "John Webb," in *SHG* 5:463–71, 465–66.

7. Boston Ministers, "Ballad, Advertisement," 131. "If he were sent as a President" is clearly a reference to Eliot's possible appointment as President of Harvard.

appeals as a minister was his preaching. Judging from his own diaries, this was the major focus of his ministry right from the start. From August 1734, when he was not yet sixteen years old, his earliest journals show him taking careful note of who occupied the pulpit at Cambridge's First Church, which he attended while he was a student in residence at Harvard. Nathaniel Appleton, who pastored the church for a remarkable sixty-seven years (1717–1784) thus features prominently. Throughout the three years prior to his ordination, Eliot later kept a record of preachers at First Church, Boston, his "home" congregation, as well as at Cambridge, of those who spoke at the weekly Boston ministerial lecture, and of speakers and other participants in various fast, thanksgiving and other special days of religious observance. It is no exaggeration to say that Eliot's diaries are consumed with details of the church life of Cambridge, Boston, and the surrounding areas.

Eliot's own preaching seems to have begun regularly from July 1740, when he started to offer supply at different congregations while seeking a permanent position, and his records indicate that he had already given thirty-three sermons before the year of his ordination. Probably throughout his ordained ministry, which began on April 14, 1742, but certainly for at least the first twenty-eight years of his preaching, Eliot kept detailed notes of the biblical texts on which he spoke and of how many separate sermons he composed. There is also evidence that he numbered his handwritten sermons in keeping with that list.[8]

In his ground-breaking and definitive study of unpublished New England sermons through the seventeenth and eighteenth centuries, Harry Stout stressed the social and cultural impact of biblical preaching in a society where "the average weekly churchgoer (and there were far more churchgoers than church members) listened to something like seven thousand sermons in a lifetime, totaling somewhere around fifteen thousand hours of concentrated listening." The Yale scholar also pointed out the "demands" on ministers of preaching at least two, one- to two-hour discourses weekly, which would have involved preparing close to twenty thousand words of text. Moreover, Sunday sermons were not pastors' only preaching responsibilities. There were special days of prayer, fasting and thanksgiving several times a year, each of which required its own address, sometimes two, and especially in Boston, there was a variety of lecture series, centering

---

8. See *AED* 1741–1742; Eliot, Unpublished Sermon on Luke 22:19. The list of Eliot's sermons is contained in his annotated diary of 1752.

on the weekly Thursday Lecture, which featured most of the major town ministers.[9]

On Sundays alone, as Charles Hambrick-Stowe has pointed out in his excellent study of seventeenth-century New England "Devotional Disciplines," "New Englanders worshiped publicly in both the morning and the afternoon of the Lord's Day" and "services were long, about three hours each, so in effect the day was spent in church," allowing for a one-hour lunch break at around noon. There is little reason to believe that such practice had changed significantly by the 1740s or that a typical service order was very different from that compiled by Hambrick-Stowe:

<u>Morning</u>		<u>Afternoon</u>
Opening prayer		Opening prayer
Scripture reading		Scripture reading
Exposition of Scripture		Exposition of Scripture
Psalm singing		Psalm singing
Sermon		Sermon
Prayer		Prayer
Psalm singing		Psalm singing
Lord's Supper	[monthly or bimonthly]	Baptism
	[occasionally]	Collection for needy saints
		Admission of new members
Blessing		Blessing[10]

Ministers were expected to lead church services all day Sunday, including extended prayer *ex tempore*, often for at least an hour after each one- or two-hour sermon. They briefly expounded the day's Bible reading(s) before launching into their formal sermons and effectively led every other aspect of Sunday services. Pastoral responsibilities in connection with weddings and funerals were initially quite limited in colonial New England. Alice Earle wrote of early Puritan ministers that although they had "such powerful influence in every other respect, they were not permitted to perform the marriage-service nor to raise their voices in . . . exhortation at a funeral." In the seventeenth century, she observed, "the office of marriage was denied the parson and was generally relegated to the magistrate. In this, Governor Bradford states, they followed 'the laudable custom of the Low Countries.'"

9. Stout, *New England Soul*, 4.
10. Hambrick-Stowe, *Practice of Piety*, 99, 103–4.

However, Earle also noted that "it was plain that the benediction of religion would not long be withheld at weddings, and by the close of the seventeenth century the Puritan ministers solemnized marriages."[11]

According to Steven Bullock, who cited an account from the 1640s, early Puritan funerals adopted "the restrained practices of Reformation Geneva," and were very simple affairs, where "nothing is read, nor any Funeral Sermon made" at a burial. Instead, the neighbors "carry the dead solemnly to his grave, and there stand by him while he is buried." Over time, funerals grew to such a point that "with the possible exception of the weekly church service . . . [they] were eighteenth-century New England's most common, most substantial, and most highly developed public ceremony. They were also, for the region's wealthy elites, its most expensive." But this growth had more to do with what happened before and after, than at the burials themselves.[12]

The early simplicity of funerals reflected the fact that "Puritans rejected the use of ritual reading" and the exclusion of clerical leadership which "left no other group with the power to impose" any type of formal ceremony. As a result, "New England burial ceremonies were regulated by custom as mediated through the families of the deceased." What especially grew over time, particularly in more elevated social circles, were the extent and elaboration of funeral processions, gift-giving and social gatherings before and after burials, which could include significant meals. According to Bullock, "the repertoire of gifts within the large funeral was not definitively fixed until the 1720s. Scarves were central to turn-of-the-century ceremonies; rings and gloves became more popular later. Once the 1721 ban on scarves took effect, however, no other object emerged afterwards." Moreover, as with weddings, the religious role of ministers also seems to have expanded over time. In addition to being prominent guests at funerals, they were often asked to pray at home gatherings or briefly at the graveside. As one expected to minister, as well as to attend such events, especially those of congregants and local notables, Eliot's time commitment to funerals and weddings would certainly have been considerable. But he was amply rewarded, as shall be seen, receiving significant gifts, as well as income, from the subsequent sale of gifts of rings and gloves. Although they would have been delivered on Sundays or perhaps lecture days after burials, rather

---

11. Earle, *Sabbath in New England*, 266, citing Bradford, *Bradford's History*, 84; Earle, "Old-Time Marriage Customs," 102.

12. Bullock, "Often Concerned in Funerals," 187, 182.

than on the days of funerals themselves, he also preached funeral sermons, including one of his published works.[13]

Preaching Priorities

Eliot regularly ministered from the pulpit over one hundred times a year, according to the carefully maintained records in his diaries. During the decade between 1750 and 1760, for example, he preached no fewer than 119 times in 1750, 116 in 1752, 124 in 1758 and 112 in 1760. However, the unique circumstances in Boston, where there were eleven Congregationalist churches and two Baptist churches by 1750 and pulpit exchanges among the town's ministers were quite common, meant that Eliot's situation was very different from that of a more isolated rural minister who needed to preach at his own church every Sunday. In 1752, for example, Eliot recorded that he preached just twenty-one full Sundays at his own church of New North. He was only completely absent from church work for one, when the co-pastors of New Brick substituted for him. On the other Sundays, preachers from four other Boston congregations and five from elsewhere did either a half- or full-day pulpit exchange, filled in during Eliot's absence, or helped out in other ways.[14]

Similar numbers emerge for 1758 and 1760, with pulpit exchanges with ministers from New Brick, New South, Old South, Hollis Street, and Brattle Street congregations featuring strongly. Eliot also regularly collaborated in this way with Joseph Jackson of Brookline and Amos Adams of Roxbury among other ministers, and the scheduling could become even more complicated when Eliot swapped an exchange commitment with another pastor. Eliot's general practice was to serve at at least one service at New North every Sunday, to cover all the preaching some twenty times a year, and to administer the sacraments of baptism and Communion regularly at his own church. But his strong relationships with other Boston ministers, and with many passing through town, enabled him to have a rich

---

13. Bullock, "Often Concerned in Funerals," 199, 206, 201; Eliot, *Burning and Shining Light*. See further the unpublished Sermon on the Death.

14. In addition to the eleven Congregationalist and two Baptist congregations, according to Weis, *Colonial Clergy*, 241–42, there were two Episcopal churches and a French Huguenot congregation by 1750. The Boston churches whose pastors exchanged with or helped Eliot in 1752 were New Brick, Brattle Street, Old South, Hollis Street and New South. Ministers from Roxbury, Brookline, Mansfield, Barnstable and Mansfield, CT, also worked with Eliot.

and varied Sunday and weekday preaching ministry. Eliot did not need to preach a new sermon on every occasion but could recycle existing material in different congregations, and there is clear evidence that Eliot repeated homilies, sometimes years apart.

In keeping with his pastoral principles, Eliot's sermons were entirely biblically based. He generally focused on just one or two Bible verses at a time, and he listed no fewer than 824 sermons composed and delivered in the twenty-eight years between 1740 and 1768. In addition, ten more published and one unpublished remain among his extant works, including three which he does not list before 1768 and eight printed subsequently. This represents an average of roughly thirty new sermons annually by comparison with the 110–120 times that he preached. Judging from the fewer than 4 percent of Eliot's total known sermons remaining (31 out of 835), he clearly spoke for at least an hour at every service. The texts varied widely. About 65 percent of his homilies were based on the New Testament and nearly half of those on the four Gospels. Eliot also preached 249 sermons on the Epistles. In his Old Testament sermons, Eliot clearly favored the Psalms and "Wisdom" literature, on which he delivered just over half. In keeping with his stated intention to avoid more abstruse or controversial texts and issues, his preaching on the prophetic books was limited to just 10 percent of his total output.[15]

In his study of "religious leadership in colonial New England, 1700–1750," William T. Youngs noted that "the composition of a sermon was usually a time-consuming task. It was considered unusual" for a minister to "write a discourse in seven or eight hours." Stout has further observed that "to meet the demands of preaching at least two, one- to two-hour discourses weekly, [ministers] typically organized their sermons into larger blocks of thought to extend over many weeks or months in the form of 'sermon series'" and that "they preferred to take a chapter or a book of Scripture for long-term study, a verse at a time." "Sometimes," Stout wrote, "a single verse would occupy their attention for many weeks" and it was fairly standard practice to keep extensive sermon notes "in leatherbound volumes that closely resembled printed treatises." If he ever kept one, no such notebooks have apparently survived in Eliot's case; nor is there clear evidence of sustained series in his list of sermons. But it is plain from the number devoted to the Sermon on the Mount in Matthew 5–7, to other

---

15. *AED* 1752. The most definitive evidence of Eliot repeating sermons comes in the form of different dates listed on a few of Eliot's extant manuscript sermons.

major Gospel passages, and to Romans texts central to reformed salvation theology (e.g., Rom 8:28–35), for example, that Eliot's primary concerns in his preaching centred on the "sin-salvation-service" thematic triad which Stout has rightly defined as consistently central over the first five generations of New England ministers.[16]

In addition to extensive Sunday preaching, like other ministers, Eliot was also responsible for lecture, fast, and thanksgiving sermons. During the 1750s, when he kept regular lists of his annual preaching, for example, Eliot recorded himself speaking at fifteen lectures in 1750, at thirty lectures and charity or society meetings in 1754, at twelve in 1756, eighteen in 1758, and nineteen in 1760. Except for a period beginning in the early 1740s, when New North held its own Tuesday lecture, Eliot mostly gave lectures at other congregations, especially at the Boston ministers' Thursday Lecture, which was a fixture throughout almost his entire ministry, and at a Friday lecture with a sacramental focus at New Brick.[17]

Peter Thacher of Malden church, the namesake of Eliot's predecessor at New North, who preached the published and somewhat hagiographical memorial sermon after Eliot's death in 1778, described Eliot's "genius" as "solid, penetrating and extensive." In terms of his preaching style, Thacher contended, despite his advanced education and dedicated studies, the New North minister had "a remarkable facility in communicating his ideas." He was deeply committed in his faith and it was that and "a regard to the souls of men," which primarily motivated Eliot's ministry. Eliot's "public performances" in the pulpit "were always excellent" and "universally admired." For he "possessed," Thacher continued,

> a most happy talent of arranging his thoughts and expressing them in a plain, elegant, nervous manner: when a man heard him preach, he would always think that this is the very way in which he would have wished to express himself, had he been called to speak upon the same subject: he discovered no design to work upon the passions; his discourses were plain, pathetic, and animated, without those strained descriptions and intemperate expressions which nauseate the serious mind; and yet such was his manner

---

16. Youngs, *God's Messengers*, 56; Stout, *New England Soul*, 34. On "ministerial generations," see Stout, *New England Soul*, 5, and for "sin–salvation–service" as a cluster of common homiletic themes for Congregationalist ministers in the seventeenth and eighteenth centuries, notwithstanding theological differences, see 37, 41–43, 92, 148, 180.

17. In *AED*, Eliot keeps notes of Tuesday lectures at New North from January 1742 to June 1745.

as that many have observed, no man could sooner move their affections.[18]

Thacher stressed Eliot's gospel focus, avoidance of "controversial subjects" and "catholic" openness to those who shared his fundamental convictions. His preaching held people's keen attention, Thacher contended, and "this might be owing in a degree, perhaps, to the dignity, the gracefulness and unaffected fervor of his delivery." But "that it was not wholly so is evident from the effect of perusing many excellent discourses which thanks be to God, he hath left published behind him; by which. being dead, we may yet, as it were, hear him speak." Leaving aside their theological content, which will be discussed separately, Eliot's extant sermons are certainly typical in their form, with carefully developed argumentation and textual focus to the general body of work described by Stout, Youngs and others. Hambrick-Stowe has offered a particularly helpful summary:

> Every sermon began with a reading of the text, followed by the opening or exegesis of the text, the extraction from the text of the doctrine to be propounded, the discussion of reasons for and refutation of objections against the doctrine, and finally the application of the doctrine to the lives of the listeners.[19]

Eliot largely followed this pattern, and when it came to his public prayer and underlying devotional life, Thacher encouraged his former congregants to think back on

> with what an elevated devotion, with what a grateful variety of pertinent expression he would address the throne of grace at some times, especially when celebrating the peculiar mysteries of our holy religion, he would seem as if the veil was taken from before his eyes, as if heaven and its glories were bared to his view and he wished for the wings of a dove that he might flee away and enjoy the sum of that bliss whereof he had here the earnest! Unconfined to forms, let the occasion be what it would, he would pray with such pertinency, fluency, and fervency as evidenced plainly that he was no stranger at the throne of grace, but that he maintained a daily, intimate converse with God his maker.[20]

---

18. Thacher, *Rest Which Remaineth*, 27–30.
19. Ibid., 29–31; Hambrick-Stowe, *Practice of Piety*, 118.
20. Thacher, *Rest Which Remaineth*, 29.

Visitation and Soul Care

Unlike most rural ministers, who also farmed and/or pursued other "secular" occupations, Eliot could devote himself fully to his pastoral work. There was much to do. Alongside their preaching and worship leadership duties, which were obviously considerable, eighteenth-century New England pastors were also expected to conduct regular visitation. Some of Eliot's "extra-curricular" activities will be explored in chapter 8, together with his political engagement. But his responsibilities to live an exemplary life of Christian integrity, to teach beyond the pulpit, and to lead and counsel his flock in more direct ways first deserve consideration in their own right.

Youngs has usefully highlighted how in colonial New England, it was not enough for a minister simply to "pronounce doctrine on the Sabbath and then wait for the people to apply religion to their own lives." Instead, he argued, the ideal pastor "reinforced his sermons with four kinds of pastoral instruction: setting a good example, catechizing, giving counsel, and reprimanding." Moreover, "setting a good example, was the *sine qua non* of the minister's work." In the small towns where ministers lived and worked—even in Boston with a population still under sixteen thousand—a pastor's weaknesses would clearly have been difficult to conceal and serious moral failings were potentially fatal to his career. But biblical commandments to follow the example and teaching of Christ provided Eliot and those like him with the prime motivations for living a godly life, as he repeatedly stressed in his ordination sermons. To quote just one example from his 1754 *Sermon Preached at the Ordination of Joseph Roberts*,

> True religion, or a work of grace in the heart, is necessary to constitute a good minister, or to render him *pure from the blood of all men*. Knowledge is good; it is very necessary for the ministers of the gospel. But it is not all that is necessary. They must be good men, men of inward piety and holiness; they must, in the language of scripture, be *men in Christ*, and *born of the spirit*.[21]

Thacher was predictably unstinting in his praise of Eliot's Christian behavior and example. "His conduct in discharging the more private duties of his ministerial function, caused him to be revered by all his people," Thacher recalled.

---

21. Youngs, *God's Messengers*, 46; *Sermon Preached at the Ordination of Joseph Roberts*, 13, citing Acts 20:26, John 3:6.

> In his private visits he maintained the dignity of the minister, while be discovered the politeness of the gentleman and the affability of the friend: he carefully avoided stiffness on the one hand and levity on the other; his piety sat easy upon him, he discovered no ostentation of this nor of his abilities, but would steal instruction upon us in a way so gentle and yet so prevalent that we felt he had done us good e're we perceived the method he took to do so.[22]

A reader of the *Boston Gazette* newspaper made similar observations on Eliot's passing, expressing "his Grief and Astonishment, that the immemorial Custom of embalming the Memories of those illustrious Persons who have been the Ornaments and Blessings of the Community should, for the first Time, be, violated in the Neglect shown to the Character of that great and good Man, the Rev. Dr. Eliot." He especially regretted that "so striking, so amiable an Example of Piety, Purity and Charity, should pass off the Stage of Action entirely unnoticed." This correspondent further noted a long list of qualities which had not received enough attention, he thought, even from fellow-ministers. They included Eliot's:

> Progressive Improvements in Knowledge and in Virtue—the Sincerity and Fervour of his Devotion—his Integrity of Heart and Simplicity of Manner—his Benevolence, Candor and Condescension—his penetrating Genius and Precision of Thought—his extensive Erudition—his Fortitude and Prudence under peculiar Trials—his Assiduity in the Duties of a Christian Minister—the serious and affective Matter of his public Addresses—the Fullness, Perspicuity, Elegance and Purity of his Compositions—his pathetic and attractive Elocution, and Command of an Audience—his Patronage of Learning—his Sympathy with the Distress'd, and Beneficence on every Occasion—his Love of Liberty and his Country—his domestic Virtues.[23]

In the person of Webb, Eliot worked with and for a minister who provided a strong example as one whom George Harper has described as "always vigorous in the practice of pastoral visitation." In his funeral sermon for his colleague, Eliot himself recalled Webb with "Condescension and Goodness" going "from House to House" and "especially . . . willing to spend and to be spent for the Good of your Souls." He described it as "a constant Principle" with Webb, "as he sometimes express'd himself, rather

---

22. Thacher, *Rest Which Remaineth*, 31–32.
23. *Boston Gazette*, Supplement, Sept. 28, 1778.

'to wear than to rust out.'" According to Harper, "the payoff for such strenuous efforts was striking." As Eliot noted, "God peculiarly honoured him, by encreasing the Number of his Hearers: So that for a long Time he has had one of the largest Assemblies in the Town and Land. But, which is vastly more desirable, God was pleased to crown his Faithful Labours, with remarkable Success: Great Numbers were awakened, under his Ministry . . . No small Number have owned to me that he was their spiritual Father." Eliot himself kept no extant visitation records, either of the sick and suffering, or for the purposes of catechizing, giving counsel, and reprimanding his congregants. In his earliest days at New North, he noted visits to a number of households in his diaries—perhaps by way of self-introduction or welcome as pastor. As Youngs has observed, catechism classes were also considered an important aspect of pastoral care in eighteenth-century New England, and with some ninety catechisms printed in New England before Eliot's death, available resources were ample. Yet there is no evidence of Eliot's activities in this area.[24]

Harper quoted from Eliot's 1754 ordination sermon for Roberts in support of his argument that he was not as committed to pastoral visitation as Webb and that this practice accordingly "died the death of a thousand cuts" at New North. But the evidence does not support his decision to read Eliot's 1742 observation concerning the difficulty "in the present situation of things, to manage pastoral visits to any valuable purpose," or his statement that "people are apt to expect too much from their ministers in this respect" as indicative of the New North pastor's practice over thirty-six years of ministry. Nor does the statistical analysis that Harper offered in support of his far-reaching judgment justify his contention that "whatever Eliot's deficiencies as a pastor, plainly Webb was quite effective." Eliot's view was pragmatic. He thought that "[t]he duty of a minister, with respect to private inspection, depends on so many circumstances, that it cannot easily be determin'd." Yet the recollections of someone who knew him very well, his son Ephraim, indicate that Eliot was a very sociable man who visited often with members of his congregation and others. "As a friend and companion," Ephraim wrote, his father was "sought after. Although his avocations were many, he husbanded his time in such a manner, as allowed him opportunity to visit among his parishioners more than any other minister in the town." Moreover, as Harper himself conceded, "figures for first-time

24. Harper, *People So Favored*, 110–11; Eliot, *Burning and Shining Light*, 32–34; Youngs, *God's Messengers*, 47–49.

admission to membership in Fifth [New North] Church" showed "an underlying pattern of slow growth followed by equally slow decline," while those for "covenant renewal . . . trend[ed] upward fairly steadily" after Eliot's arrival. At the same time, "baptismal statistics reflect an upward trend as well, peaking in 1741 and stabilizing after 1750."[25]

Over the course of his years there, Eliot also took a lead in introducing quite specific changes which arguably served to make New North more widely accessible to congregants. As Shipton noted, "under Eliot's administration . . . the public confession of sin was less frequently exacted, and two non-church members were added to the Standing Committee to represent the congregation." Following Webb's death on April 16, 1750, the church voted "under their p[re]sent bereaved Circumstances & after mature Deliberation . . . That for the present our Pastor be desired to provide for the supply of the pulpit"—a task which remained Eliot's for the rest of his time at New North without the appointment of an associate. At the same meeting, after accepting the gift of a "handsome Folio Bible" from Nathaniel Holmes, the congregation unanimously decided, according to the New North records neatly kept in Eliot's own handwriting, "that the Scriptures be publicly read in our assemblies for Divine Worship on the Lord's Day in such Portions as the Pastor shall see meet."[26]

On August 18, 1755, the church then voted to allow "a collection of Hymns" to be added to a new Psalm Book and "introduc'd into our public Worship." Further changes approved at church meetings on May 27 and August 22, 1759, "after considerable debate," were to adopt a more contemporary method of singing the Psalms, using the Tate and Brady Psalm Book, and to institute a later start time [of two forty-five p.m.] for the afternoon service. In 1763 a steeple was added to the meetinghouse, and ten years later, the church voted that "whereas it hath been the practice of this Ch[urc]h, when any one hath been admitted to full Communion to demand a Relation of Experiences . . . for the future it be left to the choice of the person to be admitted, whether to make such a Relation or only to make a public profession of Christianity by assenting to the Covenant in use in this Chh." As Shipton further noted, "about the same time the rules for baptism were liberalized." The net effect of all these changes was thus to

---

25. Harper, *People So Favored*, 113–14, 117, 181–82, 185; Eliot, *Sermon Preached at the Ordination of Joseph Roberts*, 18–19; Ephraim Eliot, *Historical Notices*, 30. For New North congregational statistics, see also Worthley, *Inventory*, 53–54, 59, 63, 70, 72–73, 75, 77, 81, 84.

26. Shipton, *New England Life*, 402; *NNR* 1:251, 255, 258, 270–71.

relax traditional Puritan practice, as well as to make New North's membership, as well as its worship more accessible.[27]

Under Eliot's leadership, as well as Webb's, the church was among the largest in Boston. In 1761, Ezra Stiles reported that Eliot told him that "the Episc[opalians] were estimated at not a Quarter of the Town; and reckoning about 2,000 fam[ilies] . . . they were not above 500, nor so many." Eliot further divided the church-attending population of Boston by major congregations as follows:

[Episcopalian]	Number of Families
King's Chapel	150
[Christ Church] Dr. Cutler	100
Trinity [Church]	250
	500
Congregationalist	
[First Church] Dr. Chauncy	150
[West Church] Dr. Mayhew	150
[New North] Mr. Eliot	300
[Brattle St.] Mr. Cooper	280
[Old South] Dr. Sewal[l]'s & Cumming's	200
	1,080

Such numbers obviously exclude a number of smaller churches, including the Old North, New Brick, New South and Hollis Street Congregationalist congregations and First Baptist Church, with all of which Eliot collaborated over the years. Even so, there seems little doubt that Eliot was claiming to Stiles in 1761 that New North was the most popular church in the city. Available statistics would certainly indicate that of a total population of 15,631 in 1760, at least 2,000 could be said to attend his congregation.[28]

---

27. *NNR* 1:251, 255, 258, 270–71; Tate and Brady, *New Version*.

28. Stiles, *Extracts from Itineraries*, 100–101. Stiles further noted that "I think Mr. Gumming told me he thot his Meeting hardly 200." See also Pierce, *Records of the First Church*, 39:xliii: "The First Church held an honorable place throughout the century but, if the information supplied in 1766 to Ezra Stiles by Dr. Andrew Eliot, minister of the New North Church, is correct, the Old Brick had by now taken fourth place among the congregational churches with only one hundred-fifty families, while the Old South, the Brattle Street and the New North had two hundred, two hundred-eighty and three hundred respectively." The New North attendance estimate is based on numbers in Eliot's 1752 diary. The 1760 population figure is taken from Kennedy, *Planning the City Upon a Hill*.

All this seems indicative of a healthy congregation in which Eliot labored fruitfully as well as vigorously in pursuit of his life-long calling, with very little time away. Quite apart from his everyday labors over decades in Boston, as shall be seen in chapter 10, Eliot's selfless decision towards the very end of his years to remain there under British occupation in order to minister to those temporarily trapped behind enemy lines provides one of the strongest pieces of evidence of the depth and intensity of his commitment to the vocation that he effectively pursued for the whole of his adult life.[29]

---

29. Eliot's diaries show that he generally worked every Sunday and had a wide range of midweek commitments, with limited absences due to illness. He often traveled locally on church and Harvard business. Evidence in Eliot, *AED* and Annotated Almanacs, 1740–1784, of longer journeys, when he took extended breaks from New North, is found in 1743, 1744, 1746 and 1748, when he was still working with Webb. He also traveled further afield in 1754, 1756, 1763, 1771 and 1774 and 1776, for example, often in the months of June to September, when he visited friends and family. Even then, however, he filled in to preach and offer other ministries on numerous occasions.

Map 1: Locations of Boston Churches on Price/Bonner Map of 1769[1]

1 = First Church (1630)
2 = Old North (1650)
3 = Old South (1669)
4 = Brattle Street (1698)
5 = New North (1714)
6 = New South (1719)

7 = New Brick (1722)
8 = Hollis Street (1732)
9 = West Church (1737)
10 = Bennet Street (1742)
11 = Eleventh Church (1748)

---

[1] Published with permission from Wipf and Stock Publishers, Eugene, OR. Source: Harper, *A People So Favored*, 2nd ed., 2007, ix, based on Price and Bonner. "A New Plan of Boston."

4

Pater Familias

AT THE TIME OF Eliot's birth, Boston was the largest city in colonial America, but its population, at an estimated twelve thousand, would not even qualify it as a small town in modern-day terms, according to the US Census Bureau. As the son of a merchant and especially as a Congregationalist minister, Eliot was one of its most prominent citizens. After he became senior minister of New North on Webb's death in 1750, Eliot was also sole pastor of perhaps the largest and best-attended congregation in the city. In a very religious society, he was a major Boston leader and his activities beyond pastoral ministry only served to increase his prominence. But Eliot was also a devoted husband and father, who provided amply for his wife and many children.[1]

Eliot married his wife Elizabeth (née) Langdon in the year of his ordination on October 5, 1742, when she was twenty-one years old, and theirs was to be a long and fruitful marriage. His diary typically reveals nothing about his courtship and offers just one entry for the wedding day itself. Following a report that Pastor John Burt of Bristol, Rhode Island gave the Tuesday evening lecture at New North, Eliot simply recorded that "I was married in [th]e Even[in]g." As a daughter of Josiah Langdon, who was an elected and eventually ordained deacon of New North from 1736 until his death at the age of fifty-five in 1742, Elizabeth clearly had the kind of background and upbringing that might have been expected of a suitable ministerial wife. Salem minister William Bentley later wrote in his diary

---

1. Pirulis, "What to Consider."

that she was "exactly the prudent wife for a minister." Over the years, the Eliots built a large family together, with no fewer than eleven children surviving childhood. In a time and place where infant mortality was about one hundred and fifty per one thousand births, and average life expectancy was just thirty to thirty-five years, that in itself was quite exceptional.[2]

The Eliots' children included five sons and six daughters, born between 1744 and 1765, who collectively enjoyed a well-above-average lifespan of fifty-one years. Their son Josiah and daughter Elizabeth both died single. The others all married "well" in eighteenth-century Bostonian terms—three of the daughters to sea captains, for example, and one to a Yale graduate. Three of their sons, Andrew, John, and Ephraim followed in their father's footsteps to Harvard and were perhaps the highest achievers. The two others, Josiah and Samuel, were merchants in Boston. After a period teaching school in Boston, Andrew was appointed minister in Fairfield, CT, in 1774 and enjoyed a long and productive ministry there until his death. John succeeded his father as a pastor at New North and went on to become an important figure in the founding years of the Massachusetts Historical Society. Ephraim was a prominent pharmacist, who became first President of the Massachusetts College of Pharmacy in 1822. Their mother outlived their father by seventeen years, eventually dying on June 14, 1795.[3]

The house in which Eliot's family grew up on the northeast corner of Hanover and North Bennet Streets had been first built in 1677 to be the home of Increase Mather, pastor of Old North Church from 1661 until his death in 1723. According to Shipton, "the Eliots rented until 1756, when they bought [the] house." With two floors, as well as a cellar and an attic, 350 Hanover Street was a relatively spacious home by prevailing standards, and it was very close to New North. But it would still have been a tight fit for a family of thirteen, especially given the need to set aside room for Eliot's study, including his personal library. A family of the means that the Eliots enjoyed would also normally have had domestic help of some kind, and there are clear references to concerns over a maid in one of his letters and to the employment of wet-nurses in his accounts.[4]

2. *AED* October 5, 1742; Kunitz, "Mortality Change," 561–64; Bentley, *Diary*, 4:151.

3. On Ephraim, see Basquin and Walsh, "Ephraim Eliot." The Eliots' children were: (1) Andrew (1744–1805); (2) Josiah (1746–1796); (3) Elizabeth (1747–1780); (4) Samuel (1748–1784); (5) Ruth (1749–1803); (6) Mary (1750–1810); (7) John (1754–1813); (8) Sarah (1755–1799); (9) Susannah (1759–1832); (10) Ephraim (1761–1827); (11) Anna (1765–1799). Their mother died on June 14, 1795.

4. Shipton, *New England Life*, 400. For a floor plan of a similar-sized home, see "Floor

As Alexander Keim has noted, when the Eliots lived there, the North End, which was Boston's oldest neighborhood, was right at "the center of the town's thriving economic, social, and political life." This was due in great part to the area's location, which also shaped its streetscape.

> The proximity of the North End to parts of the waterfront deep enough to accommodate ocean-going vessels made it ideally suited as a residence for prosperous merchants and mariners looking to keep an eye on their livelihood. Middle-class craftsmen, mechanics, and artisans built their homes and businesses in the North End as well . . . During the mid-eighteenth century the urban landscape of the North End would have been crowded with people and buildings and filled with the sights, sounds, smells, and tastes of the ocean and the maritime trades. The physical landscape would have been a mixture of wooden structures and brick buildings—including some mansions belonging to the political and merchant elite—interspersed with gardens and other green spaces.

Eliot was thus well placed geographically, as well as culturally, educationally, and socially, to socialize with, as well as to minister to people of all social backgrounds and to exercise a major influence in one of colonial and revolutionary America's leading cities.[5]

Prosperous Pastor

Even in the eighteenth century, as Stephen Botein rightly observed, "most Congregational ministers were maintained by compulsory public taxation." Eliot was among the favored few exceptions in Boston, "whose affluent congregations could support them by voluntary contributions." But between 1700 and 1750, inflation led to a fall in the real value of clerical salaries of some 50 percent over the worst decades. Based on figures gathered from negotiated contracts, Botein calculated that, "the average graduate of Harvard obtaining a pulpit in the 1720s could expect to receive an annual salary worth less than £45 by turn-of-the-century standards, which was about

---

Plans," Paul Revere House. In Eliot to Thomas Brand Hollis, April 28, 1775, "Letters," 181, he writes from British occupation in Boston, "What to do with our poor maid I cannot tell."

5. Keim, "Boston Inside Out," 112–13.

35 percent below normal [i.e., £70]." Equivalent figures for the 1730s and 1740s were about £35 and a little above £40.⁶

Soon after Eliot's ordained ministry began in 1742, inflation, which was already a problem, grew exponentially during King George's War (1743–1748). The main reason, according to Owen Humpage, was that "to finance the conflict, New England's colonies . . . resorted to huge issues of paper currency" and "with *specie* no longer circulating in New England, inflation was the inevitable consequence." Another scholar has referred to this period as New England's "great inflation." Although he noted that ministers' average annual salary did rise, from £68 4s. to £131 16s. between 1700 and 1760, James Schmotter made a similar observation that "available figures do not always take into account the changing value of colonial currency."⁷

Schmotter also pointed out that while inflation ravaged New England's economy, not all ministers were paid in the same currency. Some received pounds sterling, others depreciated Old Tenor notes, and others "country pay," or "provisions at the current going rate." As a result, he suggested that his own figures for rising average salaries between 1700 and 1760 indicated only that "ministerial incomes moved in the same direction as the general economy." Salaries were supplemented in other ways, as Eliot's was. Schmotter reported, for example, a great increase in churches offering "ministerial settlements" or cash gifts at ordination from 12 percent of ordained Congregationalist clergy in 1700 to 52 percent in 1750. But given that other means of supplementing income, such as "plots of land, houses and yearly allotments of wood for heating" actually declined over the same period, Schmotter's overall conclusion was that "consistently more than half of New England's Congregational pastors had no contractual protection against inflation." This only became less of an issue after the passage

---

6. *AED* 1749-50, 1753, 1760, 1772, 1774; Botein, "Income and Inequality," 397, 399–400. Ephraim Eliot described the funding of ministerial salaries at New North: "The expenses of supporting the ministers had been defrayed by a voluntary contribution made every week," he wrote, but "the contributions often fell short, and frequent calls were made upon the generosity of the members of the society, to make up deficienc[i]es." As a result, it was decided on December 14, 1749, that "a committee should be chosen to assess the pews in a sum sufficient to defray all the expenses of the society that could be calculated; and that they take into consideration the circumstances of the occupants, as well as the situation of the pews. This did well enough at the time; but as the occupants changed it was necessary to alter the rates, which seldom were satisfactory, and caused altercation and uneasiness" (*Historical Notices*, 21).

7. Humpage, "Paper Money and Inflation," 3; Schmotter, "Ministerial Careers," 257.

of the 1751 Currency Act, which led to the redemption of paper bills in silver, leaving those outstanding only legal for payment of taxes. As a result, Massachusetts prices stabilized significantly and "New England's economy waxed strongly."[8]

Given such general economic trends, what stands out about Eliot's financial situation is that his income was clearly sufficient to support him and his family relatively well, despite quite heavy expenses. When comparing Eliot's position with that of other ministers, it is important to note, as Sylvester Judd did in a nineteenth-century history of Hadley, Massachusetts that some farmers, tradespeople, and others, maintained accounts in "Old Tenor" until as late as the 1770s. Eliot was among them, as can be seen from his diaries, although he sometimes noted values in "lawful money" based on the price of Spanish silver, using the 1747 exchange rate of "seven and a half for one." At the same time, because some assets, income, and expenses are reported in "lawful money," disentangling his accounts can be a complex and sometimes impossible exercise.[9]

Schmotter noted that the majority of Boston ministers were paid weekly, but the examples he gave were not in "Old Tenor." Among those which he quoted were Benjamin Wadsworth of First Church from 1690, who was paid £3 5s. a week [£170 per annum], and Thomas Prince of Old South from 1718, who received £2 a week [£104 per annum], rising to £6 a week [£312 per annum] to meet inflation. By comparison, Eliot's base "Old Tenor" stipend of £1,050 in 1749, which remained unchanged for twenty years, was worth roughly £140 in equivalent terms, rising to £190 in 1770. But his base stipend was supplemented from such a wide array of other sources that his total income was actually worth much more.[10]

---

8. Schmotter, "Ministerial Careers," 259; Wright, "Lessons from America's First Great Inflations." *OED Online* defines "fiat" money as "US money (such as an inconvertible paper currency) which is made legal tender by a 'fiat' of the government, without having an intrinsic or promissory value equal to its nominal value." "Specie" is defined as "actual coin."

9. Judd, *History of Hadley*, 312; AED 1765, 1777; cf. Schmotter, "Ministerial Careers," 259. The true scale of Eliot's expenses is particularly unclear, since he rarely specified the currency in which they were listed. He seems to have based any conversion from "Old Tenor" to "lawful money" on the official rate established after passage of the 1750 Currency Act. See *Exact Table*. Massachusetts still used the English monetary system of pounds sterling, shillings [twenty to the pound], and pence [twelve to the shilling]. Hence the use of £, s. and d. symbols in the following pages.

10. Schmotter, "Ministerial Careers," 265n14, citing *SHG*, 4:86; 5:348; AED 1749, 1770. As noted below, Eliot, Andrew Eliot Diaries, 1777, listed a total income in "lawful

Shipton observed that Eliot "accepted as normal the friendship of members of the old and wealthy families," despite his "comparative poverty." But Eliot came from a respectable family, and although his father's fortunes varied over the years, he had an established business as a shoemaker. Eliot also derived a significant income from New North and other sources over the course of his career. According to figures meticulously, but only periodically kept in his diaries, his base salary of £1,040 remained unchanged between 1749 and 1768. But this was steadily supplemented by allowances for "help," "salary plus" or "addition," and wood, which had the effect of boosting his income from £1,215 in 1749 to £1,608 1s. 3d. in 1751, £1,603 16s. 3d. in 1758, £1637 10s. in 1765, and £1,645 1s. in 1774.[11]

Eliot's basic church income was also increased very significantly by funds received through gifts, rent, and interest. Although there were high and low years, over time, income derived from performing weddings rose steadily from £32 18s. in 1749 to £117 10s. in 1765 and £159 12s. Eliot kept a list of all the weddings in which he participated, which added up to 785 between 1742 and 1778, and earned him nearly £2,600 in gift income. He understandably received more in his busier years and progressively more over time for such services. The average figures come to roughly twenty-one weddings a year, for which he earned a supplemental income of just short of £70 annually. Eliot received further funds through "presents" or gifts, and these ranged in value from £374 13s. in 1749 to £520 the following year, when Webb died and he became sole pastor of New North, to £238 5s. in 1759, £117 10s. in 1765 and £266 2s. in 1773. According to a detailed list of £262 11s. worth of "presents," which Eliot kept in his 1773 almanac-diary, for example, the latter consisted of food, beverages, including tea,

---

money" of £750 2s.2d in that year alone. Ephraim Eliot, *Historical Notices*, 33–34, reported different salary figures and they cannot be reconciled with Eliot's own accounting, given how Ephraim converted sterling values into contemporary "Old Tenor" and later dollar amounts.

11. Shipton, *New England Life*, 401–2; AED 1749–51, 1758, 1765, 1772–73. Shipton noted that by contrast with other Massachusetts Congregationalist pastors, who depended on town support raised through tax income, "the Boston ministers had always been maintained by voluntary contributions, but even in the flourishing New North these were no longer large enough to support two clergymen. Consequently, when Webb died in 1750, the parish asked Eliot to carry the entire burden, and sweetened the request with a substantial raise. Fortunately he was a powerful man as well as an industrious one, quite able to do the work alone."

coffee and alcoholic drinks, tobacco, and clothing materials, and they were given primarily by church members.[12]

Other significant earnings came from the sale of gloves and rings that Eliot received from conducting or attending baptisms, weddings, and funerals. As Alice Earle reported, Eliot "kept a full list of the gloves he received, the kid gloves, the lambswool gloves, and the long gloves" and "in 32 years he received 2,940 pairs." There were also plenty of occasions for such gifts. Between 1742 and 1760 alone, there were no fewer than 1,570 baptisms at New North, or about eighty-three a year. Again, the annual amounts varied. In 1749, for example, Eliot received £111 4s. in rings and lamb and kid gloves. Ten years later, the total figure was £89 12s. 8d., but in 1772 just £29 7s. 2d. The same years, other income from rental income, earned interest, or gifts intended for his children amounted to £46 15s. (1749), £206 18s. 9d. (1759) and £376 3s. 11d. entirely from his own "estate" (1772).[13]

The net effect of Eliot's reliance on different income sources was that while his earnings stayed strong, especially after 1750, they periodically fell, even as the overall trend was upward. Thus in 1751, while his total income was £2,355 13s. 9d., and that figure rose as high as £2,627 16s. 4d. in 1760, Eliot's earnings in 1772 amounted to just £2,393 17s. 5d., before they rose again to £2,839 15s. 6d. in 1774. In total, however, Eliot's income increased some 53 percent between 1749 and 1774 and judging from comparative figures summarized by Botein, even if that increase did not entirely compensate for the negative impact of inflation, Eliot remained among the favoured "few prominent clergymen in Boston, like the Mathers," who could count themselves "reasonably prosperous."[14]

Exacting Expenses

Although his diaries offer fascinating insights into some of his major costs, as well into the sources of his extra income, which he periodically listed in extensive detail, it is impossible to get a full picture of Eliot's expenses. The

---

12. *AED* 1749–51, 1759, 1765, 1768, 1772, 1773. Eliot, List of Weddings by A. Eliot from 1742 to 1778, is found in Andrew Eliot Papers.

13. Earle, *Sabbath in New England*, 304–5; Harper, *People So Favored*, 185–86; *AED* 1749, 1759, 1772. In *AED* 1758, Eliot listed the sources of all the gifts of rings and gloves received at funerals over a two-page spread, together with details of the deceased, including names and ages of adults.

14. *AED* 1751, 1760, 1772, 1774; Botein, "Income and Inequality," 399–401.

numbers appear incomplete and it is unwise to compare them strictly with earnings figures, given uncertainties over the types of money being counted. But recorded accounts for 1765 show, for example, £335 14s. 11d. in expenditures on food, clothing, and home materials. In March and April of 1765, Eliot reported spending £45 1s. on clothes for two of his teenage sons and in October and December £11 15s. on shoes for several of his growing family. Other expenditures noted include £40 4s. 9d. on his house for repairs and maintenance and £86 16s. 6d. on winter stores, mostly advance purchases of food. By contrast, the numbers reported in 1773 contain £265 2s. 2d. on food, clothing, and other household expenses and much higher amounts of £276 7s. on winter stores and £291 7s. 11d. on house repairs and maintenance.[15]

Another major cost to emerge from diary records is for Eliot's sons' Harvard education. In 1759, for example, he reported expenditure of £239 18s. 8d. plus another £51 18s. 9d. in miscellaneous expenses for his son Andrew. In 1772, he tallied up "An Account of John's Expenses at College" over the four years of his Bachelor's studies at Harvard and arrived at a total of £803 7s. 10d., including costs surrounding his son's Commencement. More than 85 percent of these expenses were for "College Bills." The remainder was for "other charges." He also noted an additional £319 7s. 3d. on clothing alone. By 1776, Eliot reported his expenses in terms of "lawful money," as well as "Old Tenor," and his diaries do not seem to contain a full accounting. But his income could clearly cover them amply. Other fascinating details to emerge from Eliot's records show that he was so meticulous that he noted the dates he went to the barbers in 1741, for example, and all the names of the eighty-two people to whom he gave a copy of his published Election Sermon in 1765. He reported travel costs by carriage. There is also clear evidence of his pipe-smoking and alcohol consumption, especially of cider and wine. From such evidence, the overall picture is clearly that of a well-to-do gentleman with a prominent position in Boston society, who enjoyed a lifestyle befitting his social station.[16]

Evidence of Eliot's relative prosperity perhaps most clearly emerges from another income source. In 1765, he reported £296 18s. 3d. in "estate income" in "Old Tenor," much of which came in the form of interest on

15. AED 1765.

16. AED 1759, 1772, 1741, 1765; Eliot, Andrew Eliot Diaries, 1776. There is none extant of Eliot, but other contemporary portraits clearly show that wig wearing was still widely expected among Boston ministers. In his 1773 diary, Eliot reported paying a tradesperson £2 10s. on February 3 for "dressing wigg [sic] last year."

loans or investments. He made a separate listing of "money [he had] due in Bonds & Notes," which totaled £2,741 10s., or the rough equivalent of a year's income. Eliot also scrupulously listed £374 6s. as owed to nine of his children, presumably in funds received as gifts or left as legacies to them, plus a further £89 14s. 6d. "belong[in]g" to his then ten-year-old daughter Sarah, including interest. By contrast, he recorded his own debts as limited to "ab[ou]t £30 in 1765.[17]

Figures from Eliot's 1777 diary confirm the scale of his resources. He listed a total income of £750 2s. 2d in "lawful money," including a basic salary of £190 13s. 4d, supplemented by amounts for wood and from "presents," marriages, and earnings from his own estate of more than £107. In a nineteenth-century transcription of the diary, his grandson John F. Eliot later valued his grandfather's interest-bearing "private property" as of January 1, 1777, at £1,634 11s. 1d. John F. also reported that he "owned the house he lived in at the corner of [North] Bennet St."—a major asset in and of itself. In an old 1722 almanac, which Eliot used to keep such records as the weddings he conducted between 1742 and 1778 and the income received from them, as well as the "presents" given to him between 1742 and 1766, he recorded that £1,228 19s. 3d was "given towards my house in cash" plus £141 16s. 6d. in "work" on it. In 1778, which was to prove the last year of Eliot's life, he noted down an account of his estate, which included £293 10s. 8d in "silver & gold in the hands of Mr. Williams of Bradford," £1,269 9s. 1d in interest-bearing loans to others, £132 15s. 8d in "interest due," and £86 13s. 4d in "paper money." He further listed the "back part" of a house, three shops and a "place at Concord" as rental properties, from which he derived income. The total value of his assets, if well below that of the richest men of Massachusetts, was apparently well over ten times "the average physical wealth" of a free man in New England, which Alice Jones and Boris Simkovich have estimated at some £169 in 1774.[18]

---

17. AED 1765. Eliot first listed "money... due in Bonds & Notes" in "lawful money" before converting it to "Old Tenor at an exchange rate of exactly 1 to 7.5."

18. Eliot, Andrew Eliot Diaries, and Andrew Eliot Diaries Copies, 1777; Eliot, Andrew Eliot Diaries, 1778, 30. On average wealth statistics, see Hanson and Simkovich, "Wealth of Women, 1774," 253–54.

Family Relationships

Eliot's records certainly show him providing for his family, educating his children, enjoying an affluent lifestyle, and even dressing himself, including a suitable wig, like one "to the manner born." His family was also quite close. Remaining correspondence shows warm communications with his sons and strong expressions of feeling for other family members. Eliot's letters to his sons John and Samuel in the 1770s are particularly revealing. John graduated from Harvard in 1772 and spent a couple of years teaching at the Feofee Grammar School in Roxbury and in Dedham, after which he returned to Harvard to read theology with the faculty. He then spent time in several towns, including Milton, Braintree and Dover, New Hampshire, and did some supply preaching before taking over the pulpit at New North soon after his father's death. Eliot's extant letters to him and his brother from Boston during his ministry in occupied Boston in 1775–76 are sometimes quite moving. On May 4, 1775, soon after the British occupation of the town began, the New North minister informed John of the departure of six members of his household from Boston to Salem and Fairfield and his response to his son's own question about plans for the future was practical and helpful. "You ask me what you shall do. My dear child, what can you do?" he wrote. "Can you get business of any sort? . . . Can you get a school? Can you preach? Possibly, in this strait, a few of my sermons might be of advantage. You shall have them, or money if you need it." He concluded with words of promise and blessing. "Any thing I can do for you I will do. God bless you, my son."[19]

Just five days later, Eliot wrote to John, who was then in Milton, in a similar vein, but this time, his concerns were decidedly spiritual, as well as practical:

> You must endeavor to spend your time to as much advantage as you can. Especially let the present troubles lead you to God. I wish you had joined to the church. I would have you do it at Milton, if you tarry there, and labor after sincerity. O my son, my principal concern for you is that you may know God and Jesus Christ, whom to know is life eternal. If you could procure any way of subsistence, I should be glad; in a school; or if you had any opportunity to

---

19. "Eliot, John," in *SHG* 18:55–68; Eliot to John Eliot, May 4, 1775, in "Letters," 282–83.

preach, I would have you embrace it. Whatever you want of me that I can supply you with, you shall have.[20]

In four further letters sent between May 12 and June 5, Eliot continued to express paternal anxiety about John's plans and to urge both spiritual devotion and professional pragmatism. "I hope the difficulties and trials you meet with will be sanctified to you," he wrote on May 12, amid a wealth of other family concerns. "Trust in God and do good, and verily thou shalt be fed," he advised on May 19. "Let it be your first care to walk with God, and maintain a constant intercourse with heaven," Eliot told John on June 5, "and let your whole conversation be as becometh the gospel." He was pleased to hear of John going to spend time in Dover with his friend Jeremy Belknap (1744–1798) and continued to urge a ministerial future. "I hope you will soon make the dedication of yourself to God in public," he continued. "See to it that your heart be right. I would have you preach as soon as you find yourself prepared for it. Study to be an Evangelical preacher, and to win souls to Christ." On August 1, Eliot was pleased to hear of John's time with Belknap but continued to urge spiritual concerns above all. "Let it be your particular concern that you may have a sense of the importance of religion. This will make you earnest that others may have an acquaintance with it," he wrote. "Determine to know nothing but Christ Jesus and him crucified, and let it be your sedulous endeavor to make your hearers good men and sincere Christians."[21]

Four weeks later, Eliot worried about John's health, fearing that "keeping school and preaching will together be too much for you." His suggested remedy was that "at present, [John] had best preach but seldom; and, if some time hence (I should not choose it very soon) [he] should be engaged in constant preaching, [he] must quit the school." On September 16, Eliot informed John that he "lately heard that [his] mother and family were well." Recognizing that John had "seen a good deal of the instability of earthly things," his hope was that his son had "made it [his] great concern to secure an interest in a better world." On January 18, 1776, Eliot informed John, who was now in Braintree, how his "heart ache[d]" for his wife, "my faithful companion, whose absence is my daily distress." His paternal advice remained spiritual in emphasis. "Be so much the more careful of yourself," he wrote. "Make God your friend, and he will never leave you. Study to

20. Eliot to John Eliot, May 9, 1775, in "Letters," 283.
21. Eliot to John Eliot, May 12, May 19, June 5, August 1, 1775, in "Letters," 283–86, 294.

preach Christ Jesus and him crucified." But his fatherly concern was clear. "Whether you hear from me or not," he told John, "you are ever on my mind. I pray God to take you under his protection, to bless you and make you a blessing." Finally, on February 19, he wrote again "that you may not think I have forgotten you. I wish it were possible for me to see you," he advised John. "Since this is denied for the present, I can only express my earnest desires of your best good. Let me hear from you as soon as may be, and let me know whether you officiate statedly in any place." Eliot closed with a touching reminder that "your happiness lies very near the heart of your affectionate parent."[22]

Eliot's correspondence with his third son Samuel (1748–1784), who was a Boston merchant, but left the town during the period of its British military occupation, is primarily practical in emphasis. But he still took the opportunity to offer him spiritual counsel. In an undated letter sent after Samuel's departure, for example, he wrote how his son saw "the emptiness of this world, and by what an uncertain tenure we hold the things of it." And that prompted him to urge Samuel to "make sure of a better portion. To see you a good rather than a great man is the desire of your affectionate parent," Eliot concluded. His letter of August 19, 1775, was full of family concerns. Having reminded Samuel that "you live in a troublesome time," he urged him to "remember this is not your resting-place," but to "make sure of an inheritance beyond the grave," for "wisdom is the principal thing: get wisdom." He asked that his son "remember" him to his wife "Betsey" [Elizabeth Greenleaf, whom he had married five years earlier] and sent fond wishes to others: "Kiss the pretty lambs for me. May God bless them! Compliments to your father Greenleaf and his family."[23]

Eliot wrote again on September 6. He had personally been refused a pass to leave Boston and again his thoughts were with his wife and wider family. "I commit myself to my heavenly Father," he told Samuel. "I am greatly distressed for your dear mother, who will be inconsolable when she hears that there is like to be a longer separation. May she have divine support!" He wrote how he longed "to hear of Betsey's safe delivery [of her daughter Myra]. She has my best wishes and prayers. Remember me to her with the tenderest affection. May God bless you and her and your dear children!" Eliot's letters of October 20, November 20, and December

---

22. Eliot to John Eliot, August 28, September 16, 1775; January 18, February 19, 1776, in "Letters," 297, 299, 303, 305–6.

23. Eliot to Samuel Eliot, undated, August 19, in "Letters," 292, 295.

9, 1775, and January 2, January 18, and February 16, 1776, reflect similar preoccupations. His words of February 16 are typical of his ongoing familial concerns:

> My situation is full of cares and anxieties, and yet I bless God I have many mercies. I hope you and yours are in health. Remember me to your dear wife, and kiss the pretty babes for me. Present my respectful compliments to Mr. G[reenleaf] and family. Your uncle and aunts are well, and charge me to mention them with every expression of love and regard. I rejoice with our cousin at Haverhill. May God preserve the life of their babe, and bestow every blessing upon them pertaining to this life and that which is to come.[24]

Eliot's war-time correspondence with his son Andrew in Fairfield, Connecticut, is perhaps most notable for the details which they shared about revolutionary developments. But Andrew Jr.'s forty-two letters to his father are also replete with affectionate family detail. Eliot's own earlier letter to Andrew of June 17, 1774, from Weatherfield, which Bernadine Fawcett included in her interesting collection of mostly revolutionary-era correspondence from Andrew Jr., is consistent in tone with other letters. "Your Mamma is well & in good spirits," he wrote. "Everything is pleasant so far—except that we want to hear from home... I suppose Sukey & Nancy are at Mr. Woodward's. You will take all the care you can that things may be right. Remember me & your Mother to your Brother & Sisters & to your Cousin Samuel & wife. I can say nothing about my return till I get to Fairfield," he concluded as "your affectionate Parent." In his October 5, 1777, letter from Boston to his son John, he ended in similar terms:

> Your Mamma says you must kiss the children for her. You must bring her word how they look, what they wear & how they are employ[yed] & whether they love Uncle John. Josiah has been at Dartmouth ever since your Brother has been here. The people at N[ew] South have been inquiring for you. I have nothing from Dedham. Betsy is with us. She & your other sisters desire to be remembered to you. I wish you every blessing & am your affectionate parent.[25]

---

24. Eliot to Samuel Eliot, September 6, October 20, November 20, December 9, 1775; January 2, January 18, February 16, 1776, in "Letters," 297–98, 300–4, 305.

25. Eliot to Andrew Eliot, June 17, 1774, in Fawcett, *Missing Links*, 247–48, 264–65. "Sukey" is probably a reference to Eliot's daughter Susannah, who would have been fifteen at the time of writing.

Andrew Jr. expressed similar sentiments in his letters to his father. To quote just a few examples, on January 29, 1777, he closed his letter with a "dutiful son['s]" domestic picture, suggesting that "Perhaps Mama & the girls would just know the situation we are in at this time of writing. Polly is mending her stays—Peggy spinning—Little Poll in her little arm Chair with the hand Brush in her arms hugging kissing & talking to it as to a Baby—little fat good natured quiet Betsy in the Cradle asleep—all well—wife & children send duty & love as does Peggy." On June 26, he reported that "It is also a time of Health—tho' the small pox & measles hover about. I hope my little ones will be preserved. Here they sit each with their Mother. Poll with a needle & thread—and Betsey chomping a handle of a penknife between her gums . . . Tony is under reproof for not cleaning the Tongs well—industrious Peggy is twisting thread to knit me stockings." "We are all in health," he informed his father on July 18. "Polly joins me in dutiful & affectionate regards to Mama & little Polly & Betsey are thriving. I asked little Poll whether she will send her duty to Grandpa & Grandma & she says, 'Es Sir.'" By way of a final example, on January 22, 1778, Andrew Jr. was especially forthcoming about one of his young daughters:

> We have a few families, visited with the measles but in a very light manner. For grandma's comfort I will inform that the two little girls are a couple of as pretty, sweet lively rogues as ever she saw in her life. Poll desires all kind of plays & childish pastimes with which she initiates her little sister. I often turn my eyes from my Book & with complacency behold them, amidst their little innocent enjoyments. I have an action against the roguish Poll, for which she hardly escaped the Rod. She got into Pa's study—ascended his chair, got the pen and ink—opened his preaching Bible & then fell to "eiting" as she calls writing she had scrawled over two pages before she was discovered. Peggy's courtship goes on with warmth.[26]

---

26. Andrew Eliot Jr. to Eliot, January 29, June 26, July 18, 1777; January 22, 1778, in Fawcett, *Missing Links*, 9, 19, 23, 49. Fawcett's transcriptions have sometimes been corrected based on the original text copied in *Missing Links*, 247–48, 264–65, 83–227. "Polly" seems to refer to Andrew Jr.'s wife, Mary, "Little Poll" to his young daughter of the same name, "Betsy" to his then infant daughter Elizabeth.

Pater Familias

The Mather-Eliot House, 350 Hanover Street, Boston, photographed by Leon H. Abdalian in 1930

"Boston, New North Church, Hanover St., 1804"
N.B.: When this photograph was taken, c. 1895-1905, the building already belonged to St. Stephen's Roman Catholic Church.

5

Moderate Calvinist

Admission Questions

ON AUGUST 13, 1738, when Andrew Eliot was formally admitted to Communion at First Church, Cambridge, just across the street from where he was continuing his studies at Harvard, he was nearly twenty years old and had graduated BA the previous year. His 1739 diary shows that Eliot had moved from his family church of Old South to attend First Church, Boston, whenever he was there on Sundays. But First Church, Cambridge, had been his primary church home since at least his second year at Harvard. Since there is no mention in its records that Eliot was officially released by "dismission" from another congregation, it is reasonable to assume that he had not been admitted to Communion previously. He was also of an age when this was unlikely.[1]

As part of the process of qualifying for full membership in Cambridge, Eliot would have been expected to make a "relation"—a personal testimony both of the authenticity of his spiritual experience and of the orthodoxy of his faith. In the earliest years of Puritan New England, anyone seeking to join a Congregationalist church was required to give oral,

---

1. Sharples, *Records of the Church of Christ*, 100; Eliot, Diary, 1739, in Papers of Andrew Eliot. "Sir Eliot Andrew—Student" was admitted to Communion at First Church, Cambridge, on August 13, 1738. The reversal of first and last names is clearly a mistake. See chapter 2 for a much more detailed account of Eliot's Harvard years. Release by "dismission" was normally done by letter when a person left one congregation to move to another.

public declarations of personal conversion and doctrinal soundness as part of an extended process of congregational discernment. But even in the seventeenth century under founding minister, Thomas Shepard, First Church had adopted a more streamlined procedure, which allowed the two statements to be combined. By 1738, a handwritten account would also have sufficed, to be read and tested privately by the minister, Nathaniel Appleton, rather than delivered openly before the whole church. Exactly what process Eliot underwent in August 1738 is not entirely clear from the records, although an early profession of faith has survived.[2]

In releasing this document to the Colonial Society of Massachusetts in 1912, its then owner, Henry Edes, declared himself incapable of determining whether the work dated from Eliot's admission to First Church, Cambridge, or to New North, Boston, four years later in 1742, when he was received by dismission just before his ordination. Shipton had grounds for assuming the latter. The New North Church records show that congregation's resolve, in early 1742, to honour an earlier decision of July 9, 1739 that:

> Since the settlement of a Pastor, is an affair wherein the Honour of our Lord Jesus Christ, and the salvation of precious Souls is most nearly concerned; and since for these Reasons, it is the indispensable Duty of every Church to introduce no man in the Pastoral office over them, but one that, with other Definable Qualifications, is sound in the Faith of the Gospel, and of a good conversation in Ch[ris]t Jesus: It is proposed that the Person upon whom the Lot may fall, be strictly examined concerning his Principles in Christianity, both doctrinal and disciplinary, and that proper care be taken to enquire into his Christian conversation: and that the Ch[urc]h receive reasonable and Christian satisfaction in the promises, before they fully confirm said choice.

After Eliot was overwhelmingly elected New North's new assistant or colleague minister to Webb on January 11, 1742, a committee was thus

---

2. Eliot, "Profession of Faith." On early Puritan church admission procedures and how First Church, Cambridge somewhat departed from them, see Shepard, "Thomas Shepard's *Confessions*," 1–28, esp. 18–21. For procedures at Cambridge from 1697 onwards, see Sharples, *Records of the Church of Christ*, 122–23, reporting resolutions on admissions to Communion made at church meetings on March 11, 1697 and May 4, 1697. On the general relaxation of such policies from the late-seventeenth century onwards, see, for example, Hall, *Faithful Shepherd*, 205; Youngs, *God's Messengers*, 83–85.

appointed to examine his personal and doctrinal qualifications and they found no problems with either.³

But there are significant problems with dating Eliot's extant profession to New North in February 1742 rather than to First Church, Cambridge, in August 1738. The document's handwriting, spelling, and grammar are much more untutored than entries in his diary even a year later, and its style much less sophisticated than that of his first published work, *Faithful Steward* (1742). The profession's content also extends well beyond a statement of the soundness of his faith or his Christian "conversation." Its combination of personal conversion testimony with basic doctrinal affirmations is consistent with what was required at First Church as early as the mid-seventeenth century, and in making very deliberate reference to his desire "to come to the Lord's table," Eliot was clearly requesting admission to Communion. His account of his journey of faith is also so extensive that it would likely have been superfluous to obtaining a simple admission by dismission at New North.⁴

Eliot's profession is more appropriately read as that of a nineteen-year-old Harvard Master's student rather than that of a twenty-three-year-old ordinand. Whatever its dating, the document's theological content is its most striking feature, especially from one sometimes linked with far less traditional views. On first publication, Edes quoted the opinion of contemporary scholar William Fenn that "the writer was evidently a Calvinist believing, however, in 'means' and in a limited atonement." But historians have not always shared that assessment of Eliot's theology, especially in light of his later writings.⁵

None has offered a comprehensive analysis, but scholars have differed quite significantly in their interpretations of Eliot's doctrinal positions. Among those echoing—and in his case, actually long foreshadowing—Fenn's

---

3. Eliot, "Profession of Faith," 234–41, esp. 234–36; NNR 1:230, 240. The original "profession" is entitled "Essay," in Papers of Andrew Eliot, folder 4. According to New North Church, *New North Church*, 41, Eliot was "Adm. To church by dis. From Cambridge" on April 11, 1742, three months after he was chosen to be the new assistant minister and three days before his ordination to that position.

4. Eliot, "Profession of Faith," 234–36; Diary, 1743, in "Diaries, 1740–74"; cf. Eliot's handwriting in his "Essay," in Papers of Andrew Eliot.

5. Eliot, "Profession of Faith," 235–36. The most significant passage in favor of an earlier dating includes the words, "[I] desire to come to the lords table." In order to demonstrate the "relatively untutored" style and content of this document, citations have not generally been edited at all to meet modern stylistic conventions, but in the most obvious cases unusual spellings are signaled by [sic].

view was Eliot's youngest son, Ephraim in his 1822 history of New North. In matters theological, he described Andrew as one who held "the doctrines laid down in the [Westminster] Assembly's Shorter Catechism . . . in high estimation." Although he did not deem himself qualified to judge the issue, Ephraim rejected the notion that his father was an Arminian. Instead, he preferred to view Andrew as steering a rational, but scriptural *via media* amidst the doctrinally contentious minefields of his day:

> The creed commonly called the Apostles' he assented to . . . About the time of his settlement it was supposed by some, that he favoured the doctrine of the New Lights. But they would not acknowledge him . . . If he was so inclined, he fully got over it, and was a warm opposer of [James] Davenport, [William] Hobby and other itinerants. He thought Whitefield a good man, and attended his preaching, especially on his last visit. But he disliked him as being an enthusiast, and was fearful that he would do injury, by diverting people from their business several times in a day, to attend upon his lectures . . . In the pulpit he was a favourite. His discourses were plain and practical, seldom on controversial points.[6]

The first modern historian to pay serious attention acknowledged Ephraim's perspective. Shipton also maintained, with surprisingly little substantiation, that "in his openness to logic and Biblical criticism," Eliot "was sailing full in the course which in another generation was to carry the [Harvard] college into Unitarianism," and he has not been alone in that view. By contrast, Bernard Bailyn took a more personal, even psychological approach. A ministry characterized by cautious indecision rather than bold innovation was consistent with a careful hesitancy that he found throughout Eliot's life and writings. Even in his most intellectually ambitious work, *Discourse on Natural Religion*, Bailyn saw Eliot failing to solve the tensions between God's sovereignty and human free will by quoting an inconclusive passage from Locke. Eliot's heavy reliance on other sources, especially those of "eighteenth-century latitudinarian rationalists," further betrayed the derivative nature, inherent rationalism, and emergent liberalism of his thought.[7]

Bailyn's interpretation was seconded, but also extended by Jonathan Clark, who adduced Eliot as an example of a central thesis in his work, *Language of Liberty*, that theological and, specifically, Christological heterodoxy

---

6. Ephraim Eliot, *Historical Notices*, 28–29.
7. Ibid., 20–26, esp. 26, 28–29; Shipton, *New England Life*, 408–9.

helped activate revolutionary engagement among eighteenth-century New England Congregationalists. Clark stressed Eliot's English Whig connections and his opposition to plans for an American episcopate, as well as the contention that the New North minister was an "eager student (and silent plagiarist) of the English Arian Samuel Clarke." He shared Bailyn's view that Eliot was a "reluctant revolutionary." But he also suggested that "the evidence marshalled by Bailyn tells against his unsupported claims . . . that Eliot's political ideas and revolutionary sympathies were *not* a result of his religious beliefs." The major problems with Clark's analysis are that he neither showed how, nor offered any independent evidence in support of such a claim.[8]

Chapters 5 and 6 will test conflicting views of Eliot's theology. Insofar as he was clearly open to new ideas and keen to stress the ethical implications of his faith, it will confirm more rationalist and moralist themes and sources. But it will also demonstrate how both his published and unpublished works from 1742 to 1776 show strong elements of continuity with a traditionalist, even Puritan, New England heritage that continued to inform Eliot's basic theological stance. In that sense, he remained true to the firm, but moderate Calvinist position which his son, Ephraim, followed by Fenn, rightly ascribed to him, and to which he gave vivid personal testimony when first seeking admission to Communion.[9]

Consistent Calvinism

Eliot's moderate Calvinism is quite easily demonstrated. His career may have coincided with one of the most tumultuous periods of early American theological change. Yet despite the storm of religious enthusiasm and the torrent of doctrinal questioning and reformulation unleashed by the Great Awakening from the early 1740s, Eliot negotiated a mediating position that allowed him to distance himself from the excesses of revivalism without

---

8. Bailyn, "Religion and Revolution," 85–169, esp. 87–88, 92–94; Clark, *Language of Liberty,* 365–66, citing Bailyn, "Religion and Revolution," esp. 88, 95, 97. In his first publication, *Faithful Steward,* Bailyn contended, Eliot wavered over the question of the need for a spiritually regenerate ministry and in *Inordinate Love,* Eliot failed to apply his observations of declension directly to his hearers. Among English "eighteenth-century latitudinarian rationalists," Bailyn, "Religion and Revolution," 92, listed John Tillotson, William Wollaston, and especially Samuel Clarke as particularly influential on Eliot.

9. "Moralism" is defined, following *OED Online,* as a "preoccupation with moral teaching or morality" that can result in "religion . . . reduced to moral practice."

betraying long-standing personal convictions or sacrificing relationships with its key leaders. More to the point, despite the rise of Arminianism and of rationalist currents of thought that led contemporaries like Charles Chauncy (1705–1787) and Mayhew further down the path of heterodoxy into proto-Unitarianism and/or full-fledged universalism, Eliot was also able to embrace new ideas without casting aside long-held convictions. A strategic sampling from his works over a period of thirty-four years clearly shows, for example, that he never decisively departed from the five core tenets, or "points," of Calvinist belief first defined by the Synod of Dort (1618–1619) and so well summarized by Daniel Walker Howe:

1. All men are totally depraved . . .
2. God has unconditionally elected a few to salvation.
3. The Atonement of Christ is limited in its applicability to those few.
4. They receive the Grace of God, which they cannot resist.
5. True saints persevere without ever falling, even for a moment, from Grace.[10]

In one of his earliest extant writings, Eliot's early profession of faith not only establishes his Calvinist theological credentials, but shows how his doctrine was grounded in profound, personal, religious experience which he interpreted through its lens. The document opens, for example, with the story of Eliot's faith journey, which he structured using key elements of a classic, but quite dramatic Puritan conversion narrative. The first was Eliot's "conviction" of his own sinfulness:

> [I]t pleased the Lord to work upon my heart by the convictions of his spirit and to shew me that I had something to doe [sic] in order to my own souls eternal salvation and blesednes [sic] in a nother [sic] world but I went on contrary to convictions and stifled them

---

10. Howe, "Decline of Calvinism," 306–27, esp. 307. On New England Calvinism, see, for example, Miller, *New England Mind: Seventeenth Century*, 92–97; Holifield, *Theology in America*, 25–55, esp. 38. The Calvinism encapsulated by Dort is employed here as something of a litmus test or benchmark for Calvinist "orthodoxy" on the ground, as Holifield argued, that early "New England preachers subscribed" to its "tenets." It is recognized, however, that Calvinism was a far from uniform belief system and that it encompassed a significant diversity of views from the sixteenth century onwards. "Rationalism" is defined in general terms throughout this study. As in *OED Online*, a "rationalist" is understood as "one who emphasizes the role of reason in knowledge," including theological knowledge.

very much for a long time but at length I was so much awakened and terifyed [sic] in my self that I could not resist any longer then I complyed [sic] in some measure with these convictions that I had in me by the spirit of god and thought with my self I would not any longer stand out and fight against god but after some time I fell much from my resolutions and became cold and careless in the ways of godliness.

There followed a process of "humiliation," whereby Eliot was reduced to the recognition that only God could ever save him from sin and death and impart or "impute," through Christ, the righteousness that would properly equip him to face the Day of Judgement without fear:

> [B]ut it pleased the lord to stir me up again and to bring me to consideration of what adreadful [sic] condicion [sic] I was in while I thus continued in a state of coldness in the ways of religion and then I was brought into dreadful doubts and fears about my sincerity in the ways of religion but I have great hopes that it was in love to my poor soul that god dealt with me after such a maner [sic] and that it was to humble me and to shew me that my own strength and all my own righteousnes [sic] was but as filthy rags and worse than nothing and that the righteousnes of the lord Jesus christ was that in which I must apear [sic] in at the day of Judgment . . . but now by these fals [sic] that I have mett [sic] with I have seen in me a mear [sic] fountain of sin and iniquity and a wrethed [sic] body of death within me so that from what I have experinced [sic] of it in me I can cry out with the apostle who shall deliver me from this wrethed [sic] body of sin and death and by these fals [sic] I have been almost brought to dispair [sic] of any hopes of my sincerity.[11]

Finally, having reached such a spiritual nadir and recognizing his own powerlessness, Eliot was ready to receive the "illumination" of spiritual regeneration or rebirth leading to salvation by grace through faith in Jesus Christ. Interestingly enough, the profession speaks less explicitly of this than of the two previous stages in his conversion, but his affirmation of God's sustaining power, his request to be admitted to Communion, and his ultimate profession all clearly assume it:

---

11. Eliot, "Profession of Faith," 234–35, alluding to Rom 7:24. Marsden, *Jonathan Edwards*, 26–29, offered a helpful summary of Jonathan Edwards's father Timothy's typical, three-stage, Puritan theology of conversion, for example, and, in attached endnotes, of modern scholarship on the topic.

> but god by his infinite power and through his infinite wisdom has keept [*sic*] me in a little hopes all along and by this hope that was in me I was kept [*sic*] from laying down my duty totaly [*sic*] though it was keept [*sic*] up in much coldness and indiferency [*sic*] and now desire to come to the lords table and to pertake [*sic*] of the benifites [*sic*] that christ has purchased for his chosen and hope that I shal [*sic*] receiue of the benifites [*sic*] that christ has to giue to all those that wait upon him there in sencerity [*sic*] because he has apointed [*sic*] it for weak and doughting [*sic*] christians and desire the prayers of all gods people for me that I may have all my wants supplyed [*sic*] and my doughts [*sic*] resolued att [*sic*] this holy ordinance of the lords super [*sic*] and that my life and conuersation may shew forth that I doe adorn the profesion [*sic*] that I now make before the lord this day.

It was only after Eliot had described this spiritual experience and stated such necessary preliminaries, that he went on to outline key elements of a faith that would have been familiar and non-controversial in any mid-eighteenth-century New England Congregationalist minister.[12]

The basic tenets of Eliot's creed thus embraced standard beliefs in the Trinity, in Christ's incarnation, death, resurrection, and ascension. He affirmed the ministry of the church and its two sacraments of "baptism and the lords supper," and he looked forward to Christ's second coming to judge the world, when he expected eternal rewards for the "righteous" and punishments for the "wicked" in the after-life. Eliot's profession became more distinctively Calvinist through some of the unmistakable distinctions and qualifications to basic doctrines that he made along the way. He clearly expressed his belief in the "limited" atonement of Christ, for example, whereby he "dyed a miserable and cruel death" solely "for the sins of the elect," not for those of all humanity. He likewise saw the primary purposes of the church as being "for the edifying and comforting of his chosen"— not, again, of humankind—"and to s[o] unite their hearts in love to god and also to one another for the strengthing [*sic*] and establishing of them in the ways of holynes [*sic*] and comfort and building them up in their most holy faith." Last but not least, he conceived of the divine election of these "chosen" church members as an event that resulted from divine decree before humanity had ever sinned and fallen from grace. There was, he stated, a select "number of elected ones chosen in christ before the foundation of

---

12. Eliot, "Profession of Faith," 235.

the world for which number Christ dyed [sic]" in fulfilment of a "covenant between the father and the son from the dayes [sic] of eternity."[13]

The theological conservatism surrounding New North's founding has already been noted and it is clearly reflected in the Church's founding covenant, which was formally subscribed to by Webb and 15 other church leaders in October 1714. From the very beginning, the subscribers stated their total dependence on the grace of God even to make a covenant together. They declared their admiration for "that free & rich Grace of his [God's] which triumphs over so great unworthiness" and their "humble Relyance [sic] upon the aids of Grace . . . promised to them," recognizing "their Inability to do any Good Thing" and their need "humbly [to] wait upon him for all." It is in that context that they "thankfully lay hold on this Covenant, & wou'd Chuse [sic] the things that please him." The subscribers then stated their "serious Belief of [th]e Ch[ris]tian Religion, as contained in [th]e Sacred Scriptures, and as exhibited in [th]e Confession of Faith received in our Churches," by which they clearly mean *The Confession of the New England Churches* (1680). The covenant continued with a clearly Trinitarian affirmation of "[th]e Lord Jehovah, who is [th]e Father, Son & Holy Spirit," with a strong commitment to "the Blessed Jesus, who is the Lord Jehovah . . . Head of his People . . . our Prophet, & our Priest, & our King," and with pledges "to glorify our God in all the Dutyes [sic] of a Godly, Sober, & righteous Life" and "to walk together as a Church of [th]e Lord Jesus Christ in [th]e Faith & Order of [th]e Gospell [sic]." But promises of godly conduct were again qualified by recognitions of the necessity of God's enabling grace. Finally, the subscribers commended their children to God's care, promising appropriate "Religious Education," and concluding with a powerful affirmation of their dependence on "[th]e Blood of [th]e everlasting Covenant for the Pardon of our many Errours [sic], & praying that the glorious Lord . . . would prepare & strengthen us for every good Work."[14]

Selected examples from key works clearly show that Eliot could not only endorse such a covenant, when he assumed office, but never subsequently departed from fundamental elements of a reformed theology in which divine grace was consistently paramount. In other words, he remained firmly committed to the distinctive five points of Dortian Calvinist

---

13. Eliot, "Profession of Faith," 235–36. Eliot's doctrine of election was thus "supralapsarian" in the sense it entailed Christian salvation by divine decree before the biblical Fall of humankind, as portrayed in the Book of Genesis.

14. *NNR* 1:10–11; *Cambridge and Saybrook Platforms*.

orthodoxy—"total depravity," "unconditional election," "limited atonement," "irresistible grace," and "perseverance of the saints." Preaching in markedly "jeremiad" terms on *Inordinate Love of the World* (1744) to the Thursday Lecture in Boston just two years after his ordination, for instance, Eliot left no-one in any doubt that he affirmed the key Calvinist doctrines that human nature was totally depraved and that Christian salvation could only result from irresistible divine grace.

> There is naturally in our Souls a Principle of Enmity to the blessed GOD, which results from this Consideration, that he is holy, just and true, and that we are odious to his Holiness, obnoxious to his Justice, and expos'd to the Execution of his Threatnings: This Enmity therefore can never be removed, 'till the Cause is taken away; which must be by a Change both of our State and our Nature: Which Change is effected when God is pleas'd effectually to call us by his Grace. Our State is then changed by GOD's free justifying Act on Account of the Righteousness of CHRIST imputed to us on our receiving him by Faith; our Nature is changed by the Operation of the blessed Spirit working all his Graces within us.[15]

In his 1750 eulogy of his New North ministerial colleague, Webb, Eliot was even more specific in commending the full panoply of five-point Calvinism that his now departed senior colleague had consistently defended. Webb addressed "the great Doctrines of Christianity," Eliot argued, including:

> the State of Sin and Guilt to which Man was reduced by the Apostacy of our first Parents: The amazing Love and Grace discovered in the glorious Scheme for our Redemption, which was formed in the Divine Mind in the Days of Eternity, and accomplished by the

---

15. Eliot, *Inordinate Love*, 21–22. McNeill provided an extended definition of "five-point Calvinism," as upheld by the Synod of Dort: "The canons of the synod assert: (1) that election is founded on God's purpose 'before the foundation of the world' [unconditional election]; (2) that the efficacy of Christ's atonement extends to the elect only [limited atonement]; (3) that the Fall has left man in a state of corruption and helplessness: his gleams of natural light are of no value for salvation [total depravity]; (4) that regeneration is an inward renewal of the soul and of the will and is wholly a work of God, 'powerful, delightful, astonishing, mysterious, and ineffable' [irresistible grace]; (5) that God so preserves the elect, ever renewing their repentance, patience, humility, gratitude, and good works, that, despite their sins, they do not finally fall away from grace [perseverance of the saints]" (*History and Character,* 265). Miller, *New England Mind from Colony to Province,* 27–39, still offers the best account of the development of "jeremiad" sermons lamenting the sinful decline of New England. Among more recent work on more general themes, see also Bercovitch, *American Jeremiad.*

Incarnation, Obedience and Death of Jesus Christ: The Doctrine of Justification by Faith alone: The Necessity of Divine Influence, in order to begin and carry on a Work of Grace in the Souls of Men: The Certainty of their Perseverance to the End, who were once effectually called by Divine Grace.

Webb had "chiefly insisted" on these "Doctrines in the Sense in which they are understood by the Generality of Calvinistical Divines." Hence, in great part, Eliot's praise of him as a biblically orthodox preacher.[16]

Twenty-four years later, when Eliot's compilation of *Twenty Sermons* (1774) was published, the consistently reformed nature of his views was still very much in evidence. He wrote, for example, of "a depraved nature ... conveyed from Adam to his posterity," of "the apostacy of man; which hath debased our nature, and degraded us among the creatures of God," and of sin being "the greatest evil to man since it hath brought upon him death in this world, and exposes him to perdition in another." Eliot defined "Christian faith" as "a belief of the truth of the religion of Jesus Christ, or an assent to the testimony which God hath given of his Son, who hath now in the end of the world appeared, to put away sin by the sacrifice of himself," and he plainly advocated an understanding of Christ's atonement as an act of penal substitution. It was "the death of so glorious a person [i.e., Jesus Christ]," he argued, "being by God himself substituted, instead of the death of the offender," that "answered all the purposes, that could have been answered by our punishment." Eliot expanded on such a theology in his sermon on "Redemption by the Blood of Christ," and on the principle that "the more we grow in grace, the stronger is the proof that we have grace," he later sought to encourage his readers to rest secure in their faith. A few years later and just four before his death, Eliot gave an equally strong affirmation of his persisting belief in the "perseverance of the saints." "That which secures a good man from a total defection from religion," he told the congregation of First Church, Fairfield, in a sermon preached at the 1774 ordination of his son, "is not any impossibility in the nature of things that he should apostatize." Instead, it was "the power and grace of God, which a sincere Christian is assured will be employed to secure him."[17]

Eliot thus consistently upheld the Calvinist principles of his heritage. While he never produced a systematic defence of the "New England Way,"

---

16. Eliot, *Burning and Shining Light*, 28–29.

17. Eliot, *Twenty Sermons*, 452, 51, 453, 109, 67–68, 205–26, 259; *Sermon Preached at the Ordination of Andrew Eliot*, 19.

there is equally strong reason to believe that his positions on Congregationalist church polity were also impeccable. In his major defense against the threat of Episcopalianism, "Remarks on the Bishop of Oxford's Sermon" (1766/67), his main target was a sermon preached some twenty-five years previously, when Bishop of Oxford, by the future Archbishop of Canterbury, Thomas Secker. Secker had defended the record and ministry of the Church of England's SPG and offered a negative interpretation of the state of religion generally in the American colonies. In response, Eliot not only offered a vigorous response to Secker's factual allegations, he made a strong case for the retention of American religious liberties. The missionary society's ultimate "design," he argued, was "to episcopize the colonies." History taught that the consequences of such Anglican influence would be costly both financially and politically. "Wherever she [the English church] gains the ascendancy," he wrote, "all must be taxed for her support, but the members of that church must never be taxed for the support of any other minister."[18]

It was central to Eliot's understanding of history that "the glorious errand" of "those excellent and heroick men, who first settled New-England" was ultimately a quest for freedom of religion. These "noble predecessors" had "left their native land, and ventured into the American deserts, that they might enjoy that religious liberty, which was denied them there." So it was incumbent on their latter-day descendants to "stand fast in the liberty, wherewith Christ hath made them free." Eliot's view of the "fathers of New England" was not totally uncritical. While sharing their opposition to religious "subscriptions" of any kind, he elsewhere expressed the view that "they did not understand religious liberty," because "there was too much of an intolerant spirit among them." But precisely because he thought that "the principles of liberty and Christian candour have gradually obtained in New-England, as in other places," Eliot warned his contemporaries to guard their freedoms with care. He opposed all forms of state church establishment as "contrary to the natural rights of mankind, and to the religion of Jesus

---

18. Eliot, "Remarks on the Bishop of Oxford's Sermon," 196, 209; Secker, *Sermon Preached*. "Remarks on the Bishop of Oxford's Sermon" was undated in the *CMHS* reprint of 1814. However, a reference within the work itself, 196, to "the late excellent Dr. Mayhew" having "given a just representation of facts in his writings, which have been published in England" indicates that it was composed after Mayhew's death in July 1766. Another mention in Eliot's letter to Thomas Hollis of December 10, 1767, "Letters from Eliot to Hollis," 418, further clarifies that he had already completed "Remarks on the Bishop of Oxford's Sermon" by that stage and passed it on to Charles Chauncy.

Christ, whose kingdom is not of this world" and feared that "an American bishop will be like other prelates; he will aim at power and pomp." In a 1767 letter to the English Whig Hollis, Eliot expounded on the full dimensions of his anti-episcopal anxiety:

> They who plead so strongly for an American bishop, have other ends in view; to make a more pompous show, by which they hope to increase their faction; to add to the number of Lord Bishops; to extend their episcopal influence; to subject the American dissenters to their yoke; . . . and—as Dr. Blackburne judiciously observes in the letter I had the honor of receiving from him—to prevent any reformation at home. God prevent the execution of their pernicious designs![19]

Faith over Works

Eliot was thus as committed in his Congregationalism as his Calvinism. He was also so consistently forceful in urging the primacy of divine grace over human effort in the Christian economy of salvation that his teaching was far from moralistic. Bailyn has critiqued Eliot's *Evil and Adulterous Generation* (1753), for having "blunted the edge of the ritual attack" of this traditional "jeremiad" homiletic trope on social and moral degeneracy. But in his treatment of four major themes of "Impiety towards God.—A prevailing Neglect of Jesus Christ.—A great Contempt of the Holy Spirit.— and Vice & Immorality of almost every Kind," Eliot made clear that he saw his society's declension as requiring a prior and thoroughgoing remedy of spiritual regeneration and transformation that would far transcend Bostonian efforts to elevate moral standards by sheer force of will. Compared with the shining virtue of New England's first founders, he argued, "we are guilty of great Apostacy; we have broken the Covenant, which, as we are a

---

19. Eliot, "Remarks on the Bishop of Oxford's Sermon," 197 (citing Gal 5:1), 209, 204, 202, 210; Eliot to Francis Blackburne, May 13, 1767, cited in Shipton, *New England Life*, 416; Eliot to Thomas Hollis, November 13, 1767, in "Letters from Eliot to Hollis," 408–12, esp. 411. Cf. Eliot to Hollis, October 17, 1768, in "Letters from Eliot to Hollis," 429–34, esp. 431, where Eliot states, "I dread a Bishop of the Church of England, in any shape." In his letter of January 23, 1767, included in Eliot, Andrew Eliot Correspondence Transcripts, 127-29, esp. 128, Francis Blackburne argues that, "The scheme of Episcopizing the Colonies . . . could not fail, had it taken place, to have blocked up all prospect of any reformation in this country in those things where it is most evidently wanted." On Hollis, see esp. Robbins, "Strenuous Whig"; Marshall, "Thomas Hollis."

professing People, subsists between God and us." Thus in "impiety towards God," Eliot noted "an observable Degeneracy with Respect to the Sabbath," "Irreverence and Indecency" even in "religious Assemblies," the omission of both family and "secret Prayer," and too many taking "the sacred name of God in vain." Among "the Immoralities which abound in our Land," he listed "Intemperance," "Uncleanness," "Oppression and Injustice," "Pride," "Luxury, or that Propensity there is in us, to gratify our sensual Appetites," "Slander and Calumny," and "the encreasing Rudeness, and Ungovernableness of Children and young People." A universal problem was that "these Kind of Vices are too much connived at; at least, they are not sufficiently branded and put out of Countenance."[20]

As a result, Eliot thought New England's position both "dishonourable" and "dangerous." Yet he was equally sure that the solution would require more than hard work. "'Tis only by Repentance, we can avert the Judgments which are impending over us," he contended, and this needed to begin in people's homes. But true repentance and reformation could not be self-generated; they would ultimately depend on "the Effusion of the Holy Spirit on this ungrateful, sinful People," for which all should be praying. Thus rather than issuing a moralistic call to reform, Eliot closed by emphasizing that vital condition with a citation from Isaiah 32:15–17:

> If we are once, by the Influence of the Spirit of Grace, brought to a sincere and thoro' Repentance; God, even our own God, will delight to dwell among us, and to bless us. Things will go well with us. If "the Spirit be poured [upon us] from on high, [and] the Wilderness" shall "be a fruitful Field; Then Judgment shall dwell in the Wilderness, and Righteousness remain in the fruitful Field: And the Work of Righteousness shall be Peace; and the Effect of Righteousness, Quietness and Assurance for ever."[21]

Such an emphasis on the sovereignty and priority of divine grace, even in moral improvement, which he had also stressed when speaking of "the Neglect of Jesus Christ and his Salvation," was only to be expected given the consistent Calvinism of Eliot's thought. His avowedly Arminian colleague and friend, Mayhew of West Church, argued two years later, in 1755, that "this quality is essential to a true justifying faith; viz. that it is operative, and productive of good works," and so "faith justifies, only considered as

---

20. Bailyn, "Religion and Revolution," 90; Eliot, *Evil and Adulterous Generation*, 8–9, 10, 11, 12, 16, 17, 18, 19, 20, citing an unidentified work.

21. Eliot, *Evil and Adulterous Generation*, 23, 26.

having that property; i.e., on account of the obedience involved in the idea of it." But Eliot upheld the much more conventional, reformed position that "Faith in God, in Christ, and in a future State, is necessary to produce that Holiness & Goodness, which, we all allow, is necessary to Happiness." Among the major doctrinal problems of his age, Eliot saw not only the elevation of "Natural Religion . . . above the Religion of Christ," the denial of Christ's atonement and the marginalization of "Faith in the Mediator, and in a future State." He also lamented that "Morality is spoken of, as being all that is necessary in order to our Acceptance with God." While he was prepared to own, in the words of James 2:17, that "Faith, if it hath not Works, is dead," he consistently went on to affirm that "Works without Faith . . . will be a mere lifeless Carcase."[22]

A similar approach to the faith/works dilemma is found elsewhere in Eliot's writings. As early as *Faithful Steward* (1742), he argued that the "faithful Minister" would "teach that good Works are the Effect of Faith and the Evidence of it, and not the Cause of Justification, that they proceed from Grace in the Heart and don't produce it." Some thirty years later, in a sermon apparently delivered at the express wish of a prisoner, Levi Ames, who was subsequently executed for burglary, Eliot's main concern was to stress the overriding mercy of God even to those *in extremis*, like the penitent thief on the cross at Christ's crucifixion. Calling his hearers to "repair to our blessed Redeemer for pardon and salvation" and holding out the possibility of salvation even to a duly repentant Ames, Eliot emphasized the omnipotence and sovereignty of divine grace. But he also expounded a classically reformed understanding of the relationship between justification and sanctification in *Christ's Promise to the Penitent Thief* (1773):

> The way in which God makes it evident to his saints and people, that they are to have a place in his kingdom, is by implanting a principle of holiness, and making them like his own blessed self. It is by their sanctification he makes it clear that they are justified.[23]

Eliot regularly stressed human responsibility to make use of all available means not only to grow in grace in the Christian life, but to come to faith in the first place. In that sense, his theology contained familiar Puritan "preparationist" themes. "God expects something from us," he told the congregation of First Church, Fairfield at his son's ordination in 1774,

---

22. Eliot, *Evil and Adulterous Generation*, 13–14; cf. Mayhew, *Sermons upon the Following Subjects*, 247.

23. Eliot, *Faithful Steward*, 18; *Christ's Promise*, 20, 25–26; Luke 23:32–43.

and "if we carefully and seriously wait on Him in the use of his appointed means, we may reasonably hope that he will produce this great and necessary change [i.e., spiritual regeneration] in us." Likewise, "every direction to unregenerate sinners supposes some power existing in them, which they ought to improve, and in the improvement of which they may hope for a blessing." Nevertheless, spiritual regeneration and salvation could never be dependent on human preparation. Boston's Old South minister Thomas Prince had rightly observed that "every command to do a duty . . . implies an offer of grace to enable us to do that duty," but in the final analysis, "Conversion" was "a work of Divine power." That same year, as he continually called upon "those who profess the religion of Christ" to "be careful to evidence their sincerity to the world, by an answerable conservation," Eliot's ethical teaching was clearly morally demanding. But his overriding emphasis on grace belies any claim that it was implicitly moralistic. Like the true, albeit moderate Calvinist that he was, the New North minister saw "the exercise of grace" as "the proper scripture evidence that we are in a state of grace," but saw that initial state as entirely the work of God.[24]

---

24. Eliot, *Sermon Preached at the Ordination of Andrew Eliot*, 23, 19–20, citing an unidentified work by Prince, whom Eliot described as "a great man of our own" (22); *Twenty Sermons*, 77, 139. On Puritan "preparationism," see Pettit, *Heart Prepared*.

6

Orthodox Teacher

Great Awakening Revivalism

On April 15, 1745, Eliot wrote to Richard Salter, a fellow minister in Mansfield, Connecticut, giving his latest assessment of the English revivalist, George Whitefield, who so dramatically impacted New England and elsewhere with his revivalist ministry, beginning in the early 1740s. "As to Mr. Whitefield's being the ringleader of these things of bad and dangerous tendency which have prevailed among us," he observed, "I am really at a loss what to say." He went on to make quite a nuanced argument:

> In one sense he seems to be the accidental cause, as he was an instrument of stirring up a religious concern in the minds of great numbers, which concern the devil has unhappily improved to lead many astray, and give them a false and enthusiastical peace. But you'll say, has he not been the direct cause? Has not a vein of enthusiasm run through his writings, his preaching, and his conduct? . . . [T]o call him a rank enthusiast, is, I think, carrying the matter too far . . . The modest expression which the united ministers used in their *Testimony* against Mr. Davenport, suits me better—that he is "tinctured with enthusiasm."

Here, as elsewhere, Eliot's position resists simple labeling. It does not seem appropriate to describe him either as a "New Light" advocate or as an "Old Light" opponent of Great Awakening revivalism. Instead, he supported Whitefield's ministry in very practical ways in Boston and there is no record of him ever having personally spoken out against it. But he did so, even as he saw the dangers and carefully resisted them, where possible.[1]

An obvious factor was that Eliot's senior colleague Webb was a keen supporter of the ministry of Whitefield and New North was fully engaged. But Eliot's interest was more than simply pragmatic. In September and October 1740, he recorded his attendance at a number of Whitefield's preaching events during his first tour of itinerant ministry in New England. An even clearer indication of Eliot's early interest in revivalism was that he also reported hearing the more outspoken Presbyterian revivalist Gilbert Tennant on January 27, February 3, 4, 11, 12, and March 2, 1741. As one of the signatories of the 1743 *Testimony of the Pastors of New England*, Eliot opposed the associated excesses, but he also shared the view that "where there is any special Revival of pure Religion in any Parts of our Land, at this Time, we would give unto God all the Glory." When Whitefield returned to Boston to preach on November 26, 1744, Eliot kept a more thorough record of his preaching engagements, including visits to New North on December 1, 5, 7, and 12. Whitefield spoke further at the church on January 9, 14, 16, 18, 23, and 25, 1745. January 9, when Eliot reported "a great Disturbance in [th]e assembly" seems to have been a particularly dramatic occasion. Then when Whitefield returned to Boston in April of 1745, New North effectively became the major site of his revivalist preaching, hosting him no fewer than fourteen times in that month alone.[2]

The church was also actively engaged in Whitefield's later trips to New England, both before and after Webb's passing in 1750. In 1747, he spoke at the church three times during a visit of just nine days. In 1754, Eliot recorded four visits by Whitefield in September and three in October, and during a 1764 tour, he reported the date of the evangelist's last sermon on June 5. Finally, in the year of Whitefield's death in 1770, Eliot again kept track of his preaching in August and September, including six visits to New North. Two indications of the continuing closeness of their relationship may be gleaned from the fact that Eliot traveled to Cambridge with the evangelist on August 28, and in a series of diaries, which typically noted

---

1. Eliot to Ruchard Salter, April 15, 1745, cited in Sprague, *Annals*, 1:417–18; Ephraim Eliot, *Historical Notices*, 28.

2. AED September and October 1740, January–March 1741, December 1744–April 1745; Convention of Congregational Ministers, *Testimony of the Pastors*, esp. 13. On Webb, see, for example, his *Christ's Suit to the Sinner*.

few wider events, he made sure to record Whitefield's death at Newbury on September 30, 1770.³

Given his continued welcome and obvious practical support for Whitefield over so many years, Shipton's observation that "he disliked the revivals" is plainly false. What he really disfavored, as Shipton more aptly pointed out, was the enthusiastic excesses of extreme revivalism and of certain revivalists, including William Hobby and James Davenport. In this, as in other areas, his views defy simplistic categorization because he was pragmatic, as well as nuanced and irenic, in his approach to ministry and issues of theological contention.⁴

At the same time, while Eliot showed no sign, even towards the end of his public ministry, of discarding the Calvinist Congregationalism of his youth, he was an inherently cautious man, whose relative moderation on some issues betokened a clear desire to avoid unnecessary controversy. He demonstrated a strong concern—clearly evident in *Inordinate Love of the World* (1753) and extending well beyond *Discourse on Natural Religion* (1771)—to present a cogent account of the Christian faith as an inherently rational religion that served to promote higher moral standards in society. Yet however moderately and reasonably he presented his teachings, as has been seen, Eliot remained a fundamentally biblicist thinker, whose consistent and oft-stated desire was to stay true to his text without indulging in unnecessary and unhelpful speculation.⁵

Revelation over Reason

Eliot's doctrinal moderation, together with his parallel belief in the inherent rationality of his faith, which he supported with frequent citations from philosophical sources, might easily encourage his portrayal as a rationalist. Yet such was Eliot's conception of the primacy of God's sovereignty in revelation, as well as redemption, that this is equally problematic. For while he devoted much time and attention, especially in his lecture on natural theology, *Discourse on Natural Religion* (1771), to demonstrating the inherent reasonableness of his beliefs, Eliot ultimately regarded theological

---

3. *AED* August 1747, September–October, 1754, June 1764 and August–September; 1770.

4. Shipton, *New England Life*, 402–3.

5. Eliot's "biblicism" should not be confused with "fundamentalism" of any kind.

conclusions derived from human reason and observation as inherently inferior to those of dogmatic theology based on divine revelation.[6]

Like Mayhew and many others of his age, Eliot repeatedly stressed the reasonableness of Christianity. In his Election Sermon of 1765, for example, he defined religion as "that . . . which Jesus Christ taught . . . It is a belief of the truth and a temper of mind correspondent to it." Just two years later, his academic credentials were honored at the heart of Scottish Enlightenment rationalism, when Edinburgh University awarded him an honorary doctorate. Sprague observed that "it was common, at that period, to purchase diplomas from the Scotch Universities; and that of Mr. Eliot was paid for by John Barrett, a particular friend and a deacon in his church." What may say more about Eliot's reputation among American colonial intellectual leaders is Shipton's report that "Benjamin Franklin in 1767" was already "moving distinguished Europeans to help him to obtain an S. T. D. for Eliot at Edinburgh or Glasgow."[7]

In *Twenty Sermons*, which was published seven years later, Eliot highlighted the duties flowing from the fact that "God hath given us living souls, and endowed us with reason and understanding." This entailed, among other things, that "we are under the highest obligation, to use our reason, and to act reasonably." The capacity for rational thought and questioning would also mean that "there may be doubts about the truths of religion, where there is real sincerity of heart." If even the disciples could question Christ's resurrection in John's Gospel, "every error" clearly did not "proceed from a wicked mind, and it is not for us to say, how far a good man may fall into wrong sentiments in religion." The potential for human error also reinforced Eliot's doctrinal caution. "It becomes us to be very cautious," he noted towards the end of his final collection of published sermons, "how we determine any point to be fundamental, which God hath not determined to be so." Yet allowance for legitimate doubt and scepticism did not detract from Eliot's belief that "the christian's joy is . . . a sober rational thing, and may be defended upon all the principles of reason and religion." He no longer thought miraculous spiritual gifts operative in the church and he decried "enthusiasm" of any kind, including the "Presumption" that one could receive "those qualifications which are necessary for a Gospel Minister by immediate Inspiration." But such convictions were based, in great

---

6. Eliot, *Discourse on Natural Religion*.

7. Eliot, *Sermon Preached before His Excellency*, 26; Sprague, *Annals*, 1:418; Shipton, *New England Life*, 417.

part, on his underlying premise that "there is nothing in Christianity that is contrary to reason. God never did, He never can, authorize a religion opposite to it, because this would be to contradict himself."[8]

The ethical corollary of such an assumption was that "if our minds were in a right state, we could not have the least hesitation about any part of Christian practice." The major hindrance to such unhesitating, rational obedience—and without the atoning mediation of Christ, this was obviously insurmountable for Eliot—was human depravity, whereby "man had by sin exposed himself to punishment." Yet in *Discourse on Natural Religion*, Eliot was initially less concerned to stress the sin-sourced separation between God and humanity that featured so prominently in his published sermons, than the inherent rationality of belief in God and of "natural religion" in general. In so doing, he drew heavily, as Bailyn noted, on the works of British seventeenth- and eighteenth-century theological and philosophical luminaries, including Samuel Clarke, James Beattie, Thomas Halyburton, John Howe, Locke, Robert Riccaltoun, Matthew Tindal, and William Wollaston. Yet even when he began with the latter, biblical ultimately trumped philosophical considerations.[9]

In first arguing that it was rational to conclude that "the universe is the effect of some powerful cause" which must be "intelligent, wise and good," Eliot relied heavily on an influential "proof" of the existence of God *a posteriori* produced by the latitudinarian Church of England cleric and philosopher Clarke in his 1704–1705 Boyle Lectures. Given "the structure and constitution of the world, the accurate adjustment of its various parts, and the uses and ends to which they are mutually adapted," Eliot further contended, following the Scottish philosopher Beattie, especially in his *Essay on the Nature and Immutability of Truth* (1770), that only "a Being possessed of . . . perfections [of wisdom, power and goodness] in the highest possible degree could have created this stupendous universe." Having established the "Being and Perfections of God" on the basis of such inherently rationalistic arguments, Eliot thought it "not hard to prove that there

---

8. *Twenty Sermons*, 45–46, 470–71, 244; Eliot, *Sermon Preached at the Ordination of Joseph Willard*, 9; *Burning and Shining Light*, 14; *Discourse on Natural Religion*, xxxvii; *Twenty Sermons*, 4, 210. Eliot's theology of *charismata* was "cessationist," inasmuch as he held that "extraordinary [i.e., miraculous] gifts ceased in the church" around the completion of the biblical canon.

9. Eliot, *Twenty Sermons*, 4; Bailyn, "Religion and Revolution," 91–93.

is such a thing as Religion," in the sense that "there are duties incumbent on man towards the Deity, which God hath a right to require of us."[10]

Underlying Eliot's approach to religious responsibilities was a key assumption that "man acts freely" and in support of such a premise, he marshalled a range of citations not only from Beattie, but from the English clergyman and scholar Wollaston, from Oliver Cromwell's Puritan chaplain John Howe, and, decisively, from Locke. Given that primary supposition, Eliot did not hesitate to argue that "it is fit and right that we should act in conformity to the will of an all-perfect Being, whose will is rectitude itself, and who requires nothing of us, but what tends to make us like himself, who is the standard of excellence." He also went considerably further, contending that God's "moral government" gave rise to the "just and unavoidable" conclusion that God would reward or punish people according to their individual behavior, and that there would be a "future state" when God's justice would be fully displayed and vindicated. Yet when Eliot attempted to describe the character of natural religion in more detail, his concern for the primacy of biblical revelation ultimately gave rise to significant caution.[11]

Bailyn has been critical of Eliot's lack of originality in *A Discourse on Natural Religion*, rightly stressing his dependence on the arguments of eighteenth-century "rationalists" such as Clarke, as well as his reliance on a quotation from Locke to decide the thorny issue of divine providence and human free will. But even when upholding them, Eliot refused to allow the claims of natural religion to override those of biblical revelation, and he was quite prepared to support the priority of the latter with citations from the works of otherwise quite divergent thinkers. Right from the outset of his disquisition on "in what sense . . . Religion is called Natural," Eliot contended, for example, that

> it is thus denominated, not because men discover it in the sole exercise of their natural faculties and powers; but because it hath its

---

10. Eliot, *Discourse on Natural Religion*, vii–viii, citing Clarke, *Discourse*, 23–24; x–xi, citing Beattie, *Essay*, 119. Beattie's work was a response to Hume, *Treatise of Human Nature*. The 1711 edition of his Discourse was the first in which Clarke's Boyle Lectures of 1704–5 were published together. Bailyn, "Religion and Revolution," 92, also noted the influence on Eliot of Clarke's "Answer to a Sixth Letter" and "Answer to a Seventh Letter, Concerning the Argument A Priori," which were republished in the full edition of his *Works*, 2:751–58.

11. Eliot, *Discourse on Natural Religion*, xviii, xv, xvii–xviii, xviii–xxi, citing Wollaston, *Religion of Nature*, 5; Beattie, *Essay*, 367–68; Howe, *Works*, 2:502; Locke, "Letter to William Molyneux, January 20, 1692/3," in *Works*, 4:278.

foundation in the Perfections of God, and in that constitution of nature which he has established, or which arises from the mutual relation between God and His creature Man.

Just as "the Christian Religion is contained in the book we call the Bible," so "the religion of nature is written in the book of nature, in the works of God." Eliot accordingly cited the reformed Scottish Presbyterian minister and theologian Halyburton in support of his argument that "this religion, which is taught by the natural order and constitution of things, all men are capable in some degree of knowing, of embracing and practicing."[12]

The major problem, when Eliot tried to discern the limits of possible human knowledge and practice of principles arising from natural religion was the plain truth that "man is evidently at present in a state of degradation." As a result, if left to their own devices, without the benefit of special divine revelation, people "would certainly attain to very little knowledge of God or of [their] duty." Having adduced the authority of the Calvinist Halyburton in support of the accessibility of natural religion, Eliot then went to the opposite end of the theological spectrum, the English Deist Tindal, to preface his claim that it was "impossible to determine, how much or how little acquaintance man would have had with moral truths, by his own natural light, without instruction." Moreover, such were Eliot's doubts "whether according to the present constitution of our natures, any abstract ideas of the fitness or unfitness of things would produce a right moral conduct," that he devoted a significant part of the closing pages of *Discourse on Natural Religion* to underlining the superiority of biblical revelation.[13]

Eliot's key distinction in this section was between "the Religion of Nature," which was "the same it ever was," and Christianity, which encompassed it, but "with some wise and merciful additions, accommodated to the state of mankind as sinners." Whereas "the light of nature cannot assure us, that God will forgive a sinner upon his repentance," scriptural revelation unveiled a treasure trove of truths that directly addressed the most pressing needs of the human condition:

---

12. Bailyn, "Religion and Revolution," 92–93; Eliot, *Discourse on Natural Religion*, xxi, xxii, xxiv, xxv–xxvi, citing and somewhat paraphrasing Halyburton, *Natural Religion Insufficient*, 38.

13. Eliot, *Discourse on Natural Religion*, xxvii–xxviii, xxx, xxxii, xxviii, xxxii. Eliot purportedly cited, xxviii, a passage from Tindal, *Christianity*, which he actually seems to have quoted from a summary of Tindal's argument by Leland, *Advantage and Necessity*, 1:7.

> The revelation with which God hath favored us, teaches how He can be just and yet justify the sinner; it opens the mysteries of redeeming love and grace; it contains the most gracious declarations of God's readiness to pardon the penitent believer; it offers the most gracious assistance, and promises the most glorious rewards. By the help of this, we know many truths, which unassisted reason never would have taught us.

In the final analysis, Eliot argued, "The proper use and improvement of Natural Religion" that was the brief of all Dudleian lecturers, was to lead their hearers to "that which is Revealed" and, therefore, superior. Furthermore, in citing authorities as diverse as Locke, Tindal, and the Scottish Calvinist Riccaltoun in support of his view of the nature and imitations of natural religion, Eliot's clear implication was that his understanding of the superiority of biblical revelation was not the exclusive preserve of reformed theologians like himself. It was a rational conclusion for any thinking person. In that sense, he concluded, "We, in this favored land, are lift up to Heaven, with respect to our spiritual privileges; we have many and great advantages to know our Master's will."[14]

Judging from *Discourse on Natural Religion* and other works, Eliot can hardly, therefore, be termed a rationalist thinker, if the intended implication is that he prioritized reason over revelation in developing his ideas. His vision of Christianity was indeed that of a rational faith that would ideally be accepted and followed by any reasonable person. But such were his continuing Calvinist convictions of the gravity of human depravity and of the resulting separation between God and humankind, that he consistently stressed the necessity and primacy of divine grace and revelation both in conversion and spiritual growth.

Trinitarian Orthodoxy

Eliot's faith was thus biblicist and heartfelt, as well as reasonable. It involved a commitment to the rationality of Christianity, but not to reason as an independently decisive source of religious authority. Unlike the "rational biblicists" perceptively identified by Nathan Hatch (1982), who relied more heavily on "the right of private judgment in handling Scripture," Eliot's

---

14. Eliot, *Discourse on Natural Religion*, xxxviii–xxxix, xxxiv, xxxvi–xxxvii, xxxix, xli–xlii, xliv, citing Locke, *Reasonableness of Christianity*, 225–26; Riccaltoun, *Inquiry*, 95; Tindal, *Christianity*, 66.

biblicism also discouraged any significant departure from traditional New England doctrine. Inspired by such examples as Clarke and the contemporary English dissenter John Taylor, the "'free, impartial, and diligent' method of examining Scripture," which Eliot's contemporaries Chauncy and Mayhew had pursued since the 1750s, led to radical results. They included Chauncy's thorough redefinition of original sin and embrace of universalism, as well as Mayhew's "subordinationist" Christology and his open rejection of the Athanasian Creed. But Eliot's commitment to the Reformation principle of *sola scriptura* ("by Scripture alone") remained balanced by a traditional dedication to established theological and/or confessional orthodoxy. There is no evidence that he ever seriously considered universalism, and a fascinating document concealed within a manuscript booklet listing the weddings that he conducted between 1742 and 1778 clearly shows that while the New North minister considered critical questions about the full divinity of Christ, he ultimately upheld it.[15]

Trinitarianism had been a key assumption, if not a major preoccupation, for earlier generations of New England Puritans. Ordained ministers and those to whom they ministered were expected to affirm the basic tenets of the *Westminster Confession* (1646) and their distillation in the *Westminster Shorter Catechism* (1647). The reformed doctrines which those documents encapsulated were built on Nicene, Trinitarian foundations that had been central to ecumenical Christian orthodoxy since the fourth century. According to the *Shorter Catechism*, "there is but one [God] onely, the living and true God," and "there are three Persons in the Godhead, the Father, the Son, & the holy Ghost; and these three are one, true, eternal God, the same in substance, equall in power and glory." The more extensive affirmations of the *Larger Catechism* (1647) were also common knowledge, or at least intended to be. It was a standard Puritan conviction, however widely taught, that "the Scriptures manifest that the Son, and the Holy Ghost are God, equall with the Father, ascribing unto them such Names, attributes,

---

15. Hatch, "Sola Scriptura," esp. 61–63; Eliot, "List of Marriages by A. Eliot from 1742 to 1778," in Andrew Eliot Papers. For examples of Chauncy's doctrinal heterodoxy, see esp. *Five Dissertations* and *Mystery Hid*. Chauncy explicitly acknowledged his "obligations" to Taylor. It was the latter's "example and recommendation that put [him] upon the studying the scriptures in that free, impartial, and diligent manner," he wrote, "which led [him] into these sentiments" (*Mystery Hid*, xi–xii). See esp. Clarke, *Scripture-Doctrine of the Trinity*; Taylor, *Paraphrase* and *Scripture-Doctrine of Original Sin*. On the rise of anti-Trinitarianism, see further, Oakes, *Conservative Revolutionaries*, 75–82.

works, and worship, as are proper to God onely." Moreover, belief in the full divinity of Christ was an essential part of this theological heritage.[16]

Explicitly anti-Trinitarian teaching did not really emerge in New England until the 1730s, but it became increasingly evident through the 1750s—most notably, in a series of church councils amounting to heresy trials which targeted ministers of more heterodox views such as Benjamin Kent and Robert Breck. To varying degrees, the latter appear to have shared the problems with orthodox Trinitarianism and Christology which Mayhew voiced more forcefully in two of his works, *Sermons upon the Following Subjects* (1755) and *Christian Sobriety* (1763). Front and centre were the allegedly questionable scriptural foundations, as well as perceived irrationality of belief in one God and in the three persons of a triune divinity. Mayhew especially struggled with the idea that Jesus Christ could be fully God and fully human, preferring to attribute somewhat subordinate status to Christ as the "Logos," ultimately inferior to God the Father.[17]

Clarke was a major influence on such thinking, especially through his *Scripture-Doctrine of the Trinity*, which modeled a hermeneutical methodology drawn from Taylor. Clarke also features in Eliot's notes, but his main focus in "Texts brought to prove our Saviour's Divinity" was on biblical exposition. Eliot considered no fewer than twenty-seven Bible verses altogether, all but two from the New Testament. In some instances, as with Titus 2:13, Matthew 28:20, John 21:17, and 1 Corinthians 3:16, he simply cited key texts, ostensibly allowing them to testify in support of Christological orthodoxy for themselves. In others, he accompanied quotations from verses with brief words of explication. He argued, for example, that the prophecy in Micah 5:2 of one "to be ruler in Israel" was "spoken of our Saviour as is evident Matt 2:6," and that John 1:1 showed that Jesus "w[a]s [not] from, but in [th]e beginning, & [the]r[e]fore he existed w[he]n all [thi]ngs began to be & subsequently f[ro]m Eternity." He viewed Hebrews 1:10 as evidence that "Our Saviour is said to be unchangeable" and contended that in John

---

16. Westminster Assembly, *Shorter Catechism*, 6; *Larger and Shorter Catechisme*, 3. As McGrath has noted, "The Nicene creed—or, more accurately, the Niceno-Constantinopolitan creed—of 381 declared that Christ was 'of the same substance' with the Father. This affirmation has since come to be widely regarded as a benchmark of Christological orthodoxy within all the mainline Christian churches" (*Introduction*, 277; cf. Oakes, *Conservative Revolutionaries*, 75).

17. Mayhew, *Sermons upon the Following Subjects*, 403, 417–18n. See also 254, 269n; Mayhew, *Christian Sobriety*, 57–61. On the "heresy trials" of Benjamin Kent and Robert Breck, see Oakes, *Conservative Revolutionaries*, esp. 44–45.

3:13, "Omnipotence is ascribed to him." Eliot likewise saw Hebrews 9:14 as "Implying [tha]t [th]e Unction he received f[ro]m [th]e Holy G[host], w[a]s [th]e mea[ns] to preserve h[i]m f[ro]m all sinful defilem[en]t, upon s[u]ch acc[oun]t. [tha]t C[hri]st . . . was w[i]thout blemish."[18]

Eliot went beyond basic proof-texting or simple exposition when he engaged in more exegetical detail to counter those who denied the divinity of Christ, and "Socinians" or "anti-Trinitarians." He contended, for example, that "they w[h]o deny our Saviour's Divinity" misinterpreted Isaiah 9:6 because of their misunderstanding of the underlying Hebrew. Eliot also argued that "some of [th]e Socinians" misconstrued New Testament Greek grammar when they took the view that the words "My Lord and My God" in John 20:28, contained "an exclamation & [tha]t Thomas being surprised, cries out in a rapture . . . intending hereby [th]e Father," rather than the resurrected Christ. Elsewhere, particularly when addressing the readings of contentious verses by Clarke or "anti-Trinitarians," Eliot went into more detail. Clarke's interpretation of 1 John 5:20, and especially of the meaning of "This is the true God, and eternal life," was incompatible with "[th]e natural sense of the words," ungrammatical, and inconsistent with usage elsewhere. Clarke's understanding of Hebrews 13:8 ("Jesus Christ the same yesterday, and to day, and for ever"), which he applied to the "doctrine," rather than to the person of Christ "once taught by [th]e apostles" was similarly distorted, as were his readings of Revelation 1:8 and Acts 5:3–5. Eliot thought anti-Trinitarians equally ill-informed in their misreadings of Philippians 2:6 and of key verses from John 5 and 10. He also went out of his way to uphold the historical authenticity of 1 John 5:7—"For there are three that bear record in heaven, the Father, the Word, and the Holy Ghost: and these three are one"—against those who had argued that it was not quoted by fourth-century church fathers.[19]

When defending traditional interpretations of key verses apparently supporting the divinity of both Christ and the Holy Spirit—and thus of Nicene Trinitarianism as a whole—Eliot often relied on his own linguistic and exegetical education and expertise. But he also appealed to the authority of another source which offers further insight into the continuing orthodoxy of his doctrinal positions. Based on lectures on the *Westminster Larger Catechism*, *A Body of Divinity* (1731) by the English Congregationalist minister and tutor Thomas Ridgley was one of the most popular

---

18. Clarke, *Scripture-Doctrine*.

19. Eliot specifically countered Clarke's arguments in *Scripture-Doctrine of the Trinity*.

eighteenth-century presentations of reformed theology. Known as a "moderate Calvinist," Ridgley was also a vigorous upholder of traditional Christology, who "entered deeply into the Arian controversy" among dissenters and favoured subscription to confessional orthodoxy. He devoted no fewer than 103 of the 580 pages of the first volume of his *Body of Divinity* to an exposition and defence of the Trinity, including fifty-three pages upholding Christ's divine status. Eliot thought so highly of this work that he referred to it five times in the course of his four pages of notes on the scriptural foundations of Christ's divinity.[20]

Such evidence adds to the absence of obvious heterodoxy in Eliot's works to belie the contentions of Shipton and Clark that he was so influenced by the rationalist and moralist tendencies of his age that he presaged or even embraced Christological heresy. Shipton was right to note that Eliot "regarded himself as opposed to Arminianism," but his parallel argument that "in his openness to logic and Biblical cnticism," Eliot effectively was effectively a precursor of Harvard's later Unitarianism is misleading. In light of the available evidence, Clark's interpretation of Eliot as one whose Christological heterodoxy ultimately proved a revolutionary force among eighteenth-century New England Congregationalists is equally flawed. Eliot clearly raised critical questions of Trinitarianism, especially concerning the divinity of Christ, but his answers to them all were fully consistent with his moderate Calvinist orthodoxy.[21]

---

20. Gordon, "Ridgley, Thomas (1667–1734)"; Ridgley, *Body of Divinity*, esp. 1:100–203. Eliot specifically referred to *Body of Divinity*, 1:146, 152, 155.

21. See esp. Clark, *Language of Liberty*, 365–66; Shipton, *New England Life*, 408–9.

7

Man of the World

ELIOT SHOWED CLEAR INTEREST in wider political questions as early as his Harvard days. It has already been noted how when he was required to deliver an address at his MA Commencement of August 27, 1740, for example, his main thesis was that absolute and arbitrary monarchy was contrary to reason. Eliot's subsequent standing as one of Boston's leading pastors then gave him a very significant public voice and the New North minister took that position seriously. His cautious nature did not prevent him from speaking out or writing on key issues of the day, including the Stamp Act crisis, growing tensions with Britain, and the American Episcopacy Controversy, for example. Eliot also engaged in the kind of wider church, town and even colonial leadership that might have been expected, if not demanded, of the minister of one of Boston's largest churches. A major institution to which he devoted many hours of his time was his *alma mater* Harvard College.[1]

Active *Alumnus*

Having effectively remained in residence until his appointment at New North, Eliot began serving on the Board of Overseers of the college from 1742 to 1744. He resumed that service in 1749 and 1751, followed by a twenty-five-year stretch of unbroken service from 1753 to 1778, which ended only with his death. Together with the Corporation, the Overseers

---

1. Harvard University, Commencement Theses, 1740.

constituted one of Harvard's two main governing boards. Their primary responsibilities were conducting visitations and offering counsel. As evident from the pages of his neat handwriting in the minutes, Eliot was also Board Secretary from 1758 to 1778. In addition, as Shipton observed, he played a crucial role following a major fire of 1764, and he was a Fellow and thus member of the Corporation from 1765 to 1778. Eliot was appointed to fundraising and library committees. Then following his election to the Corporation, "he became more than ever, particularly because of [President] Holyoke's advancing years, the agent, secretary, and spokesman of the college." Eliot's position and influence at Harvard were certainly greater than ever in his later years. The Corporation, which was established by charter by the Massachusetts General Court in 1650, just fourteen years after the college's foundation, was its primary governing body. The Presidents and Fellows of Harvard, who were members, undertook all the basic management duties of the College, including appointing and removing faculty, staff and administrators, creating orders and by-laws, and managing finances, properties, and donations.[2]

Eliot's official positions at Harvard sometimes prompted him to engage with others there on more personal matters. Following what Clifford Kenyon described as "the student disorders of 1768," for example, he took the unusual step of writing to Professor John Winthrop on a Sunday to express his concern about the possible rustication of the scion of a very prominent Boston family, James Bowdoin. Eliot had learned of this development "in confidence" from his son Andrew, who was then teaching at the college, and he was so concerned about it that he had visited Samuel Cooper of Brattle Street, who had advised him to send Winthrop a letter. Suspecting that "such a child as Bowdoin . . . has been led on by others & th[at]t he was by no means a principal," the New North minister urged Winthrop also to consider "a parent's merits, connections etc." and not to alienate his father, who was a future Governor of Massachusetts and already a highly influential local merchant, politician and scientist. In the end, as Kenyon pointed out, Bowdoin was never sent down from Harvard for any period, but he did graduate *in absentia* in 1771 after James Bowdoin senior had obtained permission for him to go to England for his health.[3]

---

2. Harvard University, "Board of Overseers"; "Corporation"; *Historical Register*, 7-8, 15-16, 69, 194; Shipton, *New England Life*, 407-8.

3. Eliot to John Winthrop [1768], in Harvard College Papers, 1st series, 2:41; "James Bowdoin," in *SHG* 17, esp. 487-88. On Bowdoin's father, see *SHG* 11:514-50.

Eliot's correspondence with the English Whig Hollis further reflects his Harvard interests and activities, especially with regard to Hollis's generous donations of books to the college library. "It will give you pleasure to know that the generous addition you have made to your benefactions to the College, is safely arrived in Capt. Bruce," Eliot informed his English friend on January 7, 1767. "As a friend to Harvard College, I sincerely thank you for your liberality to that society. The books you have sent are vastly curious and valuable, and the binding elegant. I hope their external appearance will invite our young gentlemen to peruse them, which I am persuaded was your principal design in sending them." "I received by the same conveyance, a box of prints and a parcel of valuable pamphlets," he reported on April 28 of that year. "Such of the prints as you ordered for the College, I delivered to the President. Be pleased to accept my acknowledgments for those with which you have favored me; and for the Tracts."[4]

On November 13, 1767, Eliot commented on his own work in connection with Hollis's donations: "I have been this week at the College, to assist in the disposing your last generous donation. The books you send are all admirably chosen, and must have cost you much pains to collect. They make a fine appearance, and I am persuaded will be the most useful part of the library." Just a month later, Eliot wrote with similar sentiments. "I conveyed the book which came to me for the College, in Capt. Scott, and the eight books I found directed to Harvard College, among those with which you have been pleased to enrich me. You have laid me, Sir, under greater obligations than ever, by this generous present of some of the most valuable books in the English language." "I have sent the parcel to Cambridge, which you put under my care for Harvard College," Eliot wrote again on January 29, 1769. "All your generous donations to that society, mentioned in yours of Nov. 1, 1768, have been received, and acknowledgments made by the corporation." Eliot also conveyed more general Harvard news to Hollis. Following the appointment of Samuel Locke, he shared that

> the corporation have at length chose a President. His name is LOCKE—a truly venerable name! This gentleman is minister of a small parish, about twenty miles from Cambridge. He has fine talents, is a close thinker, had at College the character of a first rate scholar; he is possessed of an excellent spirit, has generous,

---

4. Eliot to Hollis, in "Letters from Eliot to Hollis," January 7, April 28, 1767, 402, 406.

catholic sentiments, is a friend to liberty, and is universally acceptable, at least so far as I have heard.[5]

Providentialist Political Thinker

The Whiggish elements of Eliot's political thought clearly reflected the influence of men like Hollis and the authors that he was so keen to introduce to the Harvard library. But while he drew liberally upon and was clearly inspired by the ideas of both English Whigs and continental European theorists, Eliot also developed his conclusions within the overarching framework of a biblicist, providentialist worldview that had much in common with that of his Puritan forebears. Like many of his age, including Mayhew and Chauncy, Eliot embraced a filiopietistic vision of New England's founders as pilgrims of grace and pillars of virtue. Thus in *An Evil and Adulterous Generation* (1753), he compared the tarnished evidence of declension that he saw all around him with the shining example of virtuous predecessors:

> Like the Jews, we descend from pious ancestors; the first settlers of New England were men of exalted goodness . . . What ardent zeal! What disinterested affection to God and his cause possess'd their souls, when they left a good and pleasant land, where some of them had large possessions, and sought in this New World, a covert from the storm of persecution, which was raised against them . . . A man might live seven years among them, and not hear a profane oath, or see a man drunk in the street: such was the honourable testimony which was once given of this land. But *how is the gold become dim! How is the most fine gold changed!* Oh New-England, how art thou fallen![6]

Eliot returned to this theme in *Sermon Preached October 25th, 1759*, where he praised the founders for having chosen "to venture their lives among salvages [*sic*], rather than to give up their religious liberty, and the rights of conscience." In his other major political sermon, *Sermon Preached before His Excellency Francis Bernard* (1765), Eliot reiterated the example of the first settlers' sacrifice. It was "our fathers," he wrote, who "dearly bought

---

5. Eliot to Hollis, November 13, 1767; December 10, 1767; January 29, 1769; December 25, 1769, in "Letters from Eliot to Hollis," 409, 412, 441, 447–48.

6. Eliot, *Evil and Adulterous Generation*, 8, citing Lam 4:1. On Mayhew's and Chauncy's filiopietism, see, for example, Oakes, *Conservative Revolutionaries,* 149–50, 234–35.

the privileges we enjoy. It is evident, when they left their native land, they thought the rights of Englishmen would follow them wherever they sat down, and be transmitted to their posterity; and we hope their posterity have done nothing to forfeit them." Finally, in *Twenty Sermons* 1774), Eliot saw the founders as continuing exemplars of Christian virtue despite their obvious human mortality:

> If we look back to the first settlement of New-England, not one is to be found who was then alive. Of those who laid the foundation of these rising colonies it would be hard to find even the dust. There are none now on the stage who have seen or known them. What was once visible of them is forgotten—the memory of these excellent men still remains—their names, their love to God, his truths and ways, will, we trust, be had in everlasting remembrance, and be an incitement to their posterity to imitate their virtues.[7]

If Eliot's moral and ethical analysis of contemporary New England society was grounded in this pristine vision of ancestral virtue, it was also, as Bailyn and others have argued, strongly influenced by the writings of seventeenth- and eighteenth-century political philosophers and by the network of Whig correspondents, in which he participated so enthusiastically during the final twelve years of his life. Among Eliot's published works, such influences are most apparent, in the 1765 Election Sermon that Bailyn has described as "a ritualistic statement of the duties and characteristics of the just magistrate." Eliot delivered the sermon on May 29, 1765, just two months after enactment by the British Parliament of the Stamp Act that was due to go into effect November 1. Under the terms of the new legislation, which was fiercely resisted in Massachusetts and other colonies, the colonists would be "taxed without consent for purposes of revenue, their rights to common-law trial abridged, the authority of one prerogative court (admiralty) enlarged, and the establishment of another (ecclesiastical) hinted at." Eliot thus found himself called upon to preach the year's major, formal political sermon in Massachusetts at a time of impending, if not actual political crisis. He was also working within the context of more than 130 years of homiletic tradition, with standard expectations that he would address topics like God's covenantal relationship with New England, church-state relations, and the duties and responsibilities of both rulers and ruled. Bailyn has pointed to the sermon's "rigid embodiment of inherited formulas"

---

7. Eliot, *Sermon Preached October 25th, 1759*, 19; *Sermon Preached before Bernard*, 52; *Twenty Sermons*, 441–42.

in its structure and its "fine articulation of a tradition of thought familiar to every New Englander." But he has also described "Eliot's thought" in the sermon as "platitudinous throughout," resting on "the solid bedrock of the contract theory of government, and the concepts of the innate corruption of man and of the Hobbesian consequences of unlimited freedom."[8]

The form of *Sermon Preached before His Excellency Francis Bernard* is indeed conventional in the sense that Eliot systematically structured it, more or less explicitly, within the established framework of "exposition"-"doctrine"-"application" that was the standard pattern of Massachusetts Election Sermons. He also addressed two of the major themes expected on such occasions, namely "the character of a good ruler" and "the duty of subjects to their rulers." In so doing, Eliot stayed, for the most part, on familiar ground, and he drew on what would have been, for many in his congregation, familiar sources. But he also, as Bailyn conceded, included "more personal and provocative elements," which have tended to ensure the sermon's place as a staple item in the literature of American pre-revolutionary sentiment and ideology. Eliot took as his text for the occasion 1 Chronicles 12:32, which he expounded as "the model of a happy state ... where rulers are wise and good, and the people are quiet and submissive!" Moreover, he plainly stated a Lockean, social contract understanding of government authority right from the start. "All power has its foundation in compact and mutual consent," he argued:

> If men could subsist as well in a state of independency and absolute liberty, there is nothing in reason or conscience to oblige them to subjection. The necessity of government arises wholly from the disadvantages, which, in the present imperfect state of human nature, would be the natural consequence of unlimited freedom.[9]

Above and beyond any human institution, however, it was crucial to recognize that "all power is from God, as that constitution, which makes government necessary, originates with him who is the author of nature." It was thus, "the design of heaven that there should be civil government," Eliot

---

8. Bailyn, "Religion and Revolution," 95, 96–97; Morgan and Morgan, *Stamp Act Crisis*, 74. On Massachusetts election sermons and their history and content, see esp., Plumstead, *Wall and the Garden*, 3–37; Counts, "Political Views."

9. Eliot, *Sermon Preached before Bernard*, 8, 17, 7, expounding 1 Chr 12:32: "And of the children of Issachar, which were men that had understanding of the times, to know what Israel ought to do, the heads of them were two hundred; and all their brethren were at their commandment"; Bailyn, "Religion and Revolution," 96; cf. Locke, *Two Treatises of Government*, 365–71.

stated, and he justified this claim from a traditional text, Romans 13:4. He praised the peculiar virtues of the British system, which he described as "a happy mixture of monarchy, aristocracy, and democracy" and "perhaps the most perfect form of civil government." Yet Eliot freely admitted that, while "reason dictates that there should be government; and the voice of reason is the voice of God," people had to make their own choice as to "what form . . . they will be under," because "God has never determin'd this." He thus appealed directly to the writings of the Swiss legal scholar Burlamaqui and the French political philosopher Montesquieu in support of the British model. Both these authors had also warned of the inherently temporal and passing nature of any type of government, however well constituted, and such considerations made the choice of good rulers all the more important.[10]

Eliot's list of qualifications for strong leadership was fairly standard, including awareness of "the public interest," "a good degree of wisdom and knowledge," acquaintance with the constitution, "prudence," and last but not least, "religion and virtue." He stressed this final point repeatedly, inasmuch as "whatever qualities a man has, it can by no means be safe, to entrust our lives, our estates, our liberty, everything that is dear and valuable, to one who evidences by his conversation, that he has no regard to God, and is destitute of virtue and goodness." In general terms, Eliot saw "the duty of subjects" to be submissive to such rulers and he cited a series of traditional biblical teachings to support that view. But it is significant to note that he also argued for the right of civil disobedience and resistance from precisely the same text that he used to justify submission. Thus in the following passage, Eliot actually contended for both from Romans 13:4:

> St. Paul very plainly teaches us how far subjection is due to a civil magistrate, when he gives it as a reason for this subjection, "for he is the minister of God to thee for good." The end for which God has placed men in authority is, that they may promote the public happiness: when they improve their power to contrary purposes, when they endeavour to subvert the constitution, and to enslave a free people, they are no longer the ministers of God; they do not act by his authority; if we are obliged to be subject, it is only

---

10. Eliot, *Sermon Preached before Bernard*, 9, 18, 17, 18–19, 22, citing Montesquieu, *Spirit of Laws*, 1:198; Burlamaqui, *Principles of Natural and Politic Law*, 2:95, 92. The full text of Rom 13:4, of which Eliot only cited from the first sentence, is: "For he is the minister of God to thee for good. But if thou do that which is evil, be afraid; for he beareth not the sword in vain: for he is the minister of God, a revenger to execute wrath upon him that doeth evil."

for wrath and not for conscience sake and they who support such rulers betray their country, and deserve the misery they bring on themselves. Happy would it be if it was confined to them![11]

It is clear from later statements in *Sermon Preached before His Excellency Francis Bernard,* that Eliot struggled with the whole issue of civil disobedience and that his general inclination was to err on the side of caution rather than outright rebellion. But Bailyn has rightly highlighted Eliot's "fierce insistence that when rulers 'pervert their power to tyrannical purposes, submission ... is a crime ... an offense against the state ... an offense against mankind ... an offense against God.'" In a 1956 dissertation on Massachusetts Election Sermons, Martha Counts showed how Eliot was not unique in advocating such views. He was representative of a growing trend among clergy, beginning with Mayhew in 1754 and continuing through Eliot to Samuel Cooke in 1770, John Tucker in 1771, Charles Turner in 1773 and Samuel West in 1776, to urge the right of resistance. Mayhew's Election Day comments were relatively restrained compared with the sentiments expressed in his earlier work *Discourse Concerning Unlimited Submission* (1750). But he still made the point that "it is not to be forgotten that as in all free constitutions of government, law, and not will, is the measure of the executive magistrate's power, so *it is the measure of the subject's obedience and submission."* Counts suggested that the people's "right to resist tyranny and oppression stemmed from the theory" that ministers had expounded in sermons of the first half of the eighteenth century. However, "By 1776," she contended,

> several premises had been accepted: The people had a right to judge for themselves whether or not they were being oppressed; it was their duty to complain of these oppressions; if they received

---

11. Eliot, *Sermon Preached before Bernard*, 9–10, 14, 23, 23, 30, 40–43, citing, more or less fully, Matt 22:21: "They say unto him, Caesar's. Then saith he unto them, Render therefore unto Caesar the things which are Caesar's; and unto God the things that are God's"; Rom 13:1–2, 4: "Let every soul be subject unto the higher powers. For there is no power but of God: the powers that be are ordained of God. . . . Whosoever therefore resisteth the power, resisteth the ordinance of God: and they that resist shall receive to themselves damnation . . . For he is the minister of God to thee for good. But if thou do that which is evil, be afraid; for he beareth not the sword in vain: for he is the minister of God, a revenger to execute wrath upon him that doeth evil"; 1 Pet 2:13–15: "Submit yourselves to every ordinance of man for the Lord's sake: whether it be to the king, as supreme; Or unto governors, as unto them that are sent by him for the punishment of evildoers, and for the praise of them that do well. . . . For so is the will of God, that with well doing ye may put to silence the ignorance of foolish men."

no relief, then they were obliged to stand up and fight. Both the law of self-preservation and their commitment to pursue the common good required the people to do this. If they were to obey the magistrate to further the happiness of society, they had to resist when the magistrate invaded their rights and liberties and perverted the ends of government.

Within a New England context, Eliot's 1765 sermon was thus somewhat pioneering in the boldness with which he advocated a general right to civil disobedience. But to the extent that he and other ministers "were not developing a new political theory" and "much of what they said might well have come from Locke's *Second Treatise on Government*," his ideas were not original.[12]

Having defined "the character of a good ruler" and defended the right of resistance, as well as the duty of submission among Christian subjects, Eliot closed *Sermon Preached before His Excellency Francis Bernard* by offering a few applications of its principles to the contemporary situation of the Stamp Act crisis. But while he characterized the "present" as "a critical season" and reminded the assembled worthies of their responsibility to rectify any "mistakes" made by the British, Eliot's general tone remained protective of colonial authority. "I am far from impeaching the justice of the British Parliament," he said and he expressed his trust that "our King and his Parliament will yet hear us and confirm our liberties and immunities to us." Such tensions between Eliot's sometimes forthright political convictions in principle and his generally cautious attitudes towards British rule in practice were to prove a persistent feature of his life and ministry. It is also clear from other sources that Eliot was strongly influenced not only by the writings of Locke and other political philosophers, but by the

---

12. Eliot, *Sermon Preached before Bernard*, 43: "I am sensible, it is difficult to state this point with precision; to determine where submission ends and resistance may lawfully take place, so as not to leave room for men of bad minds unreasonably to oppose government, and to destroy the peace of society. Most certainly people ought to bear much, before they engage in any attempts against those who are in authority." Making passing reference to the New North minister, Breen, *American Insurgents*, 254, cited this passage in support of his view that "ministers such as Eliot laid out for insurgents a practical justification for resistance." See further Bailyn, "Religion and Revolution," 97, citing Eliot, *Sermon Preached before Bernard*, 47–48; Counts, "Political Views," 123–27 citing, in addition to Mayhew and Eliot: Cooke, *Sermon Preached at Cambridge*; Tucker, *Sermon Preached at Cambridge*; *Sermon Preached before Hutchinson*; West, *Sermon Preached before the Honorable Council*. See also Mayhew, *Sermon Preach'd*, in Plumstead, *Wall and the Garden*, 288–319, esp. 300; Mayhew, *Discourse Concerning Unlimited Submission*; cf. Locke, "Two Treatises," 424–46.

connections that he established and by the worldview that he came to share with like-minded correspondents in England. Eliot's thought cannot be understood *in toto*, however, without prior recognition of its foundational providentialist, as well as biblicist assumptions.[13]

Eliot's providentialism is apparent throughout his published works. He clearly saw God's sovereign and guiding hand superintending every aspect of human and natural history. It was part of the very purpose of his 1750 memorial sermon delivered the Sunday after Pastor John Webb's funeral to "inquire into the reasons of this part of the divine conduct." Although Eliot was not afraid to offer possible grounds why divine providence might extinguish such "a burning and shining light," he prefaced his conjectures with the bleak recognition that "it is indeed enough effectually to silence us, that God is a sovereign agent." Moreover, in applying his message more directly to his own congregation of New North, Eliot described Webb's death as a great "frown of heaven." The demise of such ministers was, he observed, "a providence of a very dark aspect upon all whom their light and influence reached." If God could remove a prominent minister like Webb, God could also uproot whole churches. Eliot saw no inconsistency in warning representatives of the "evil and adulterous generation" of his age, gathered to hear his 1753 fast sermon, of the harsh realities of historical precedent. "There have been Christian churches," he noted, "who have left their first love, sunk into lukewarmness and indifference, and proceeded from one iniquity to another, 'till God has removed their candlestick out of its place.'" Even while Eliot praised God that "we have magistrates, who discountenance vice, and with some laudable zeal, endeavour to suppress it" and "ministers, who preach the pure doctrines and precepts of the Gospel," he still described New England's position as "dishonourable," "dangerous" and cause for humiliation. His understanding of the accountability of peoples before God was thus closely linked to Eliot's vision of a sovereign deity who could punish and reward whole nations according to their just deserts.[14]

---

13. Eliot, *Sermon Preached before Bernard*, 51–52, 54.

14. Eliot, *Burning and Shining Light*, 6, 21, 24–25; *Evil and Adulterous Generation*, 7, 21–22. Eliot's providentialism is not being represented here as in any sense exceptional in the context of eighteenth-century New England. See, for example, Guyatt, *Providence and the Invention of the United States*, 6. But it is highlighted as a significant element in Eliot's moderate Calvinist worldview and thus of the personal and political tensions with which he eventually struggled. "Providentialism" is here defined as "the belief that God controls everything that happens on earth" (Guyatt, *Providence*, 5).

In his 1759 Thanksgiving Sermon "for the success of the British arms . . . in the reduction of Quebec," Eliot argued that God's blessings in the temporal and political realm should be cause "to rejoice and be glad," whereas "afflictions are design'd to awaken and alarm us; to convince us of the evil of sin; to humble us for what has been amiss; to produce holy watchfulness and circumspection." Eliot had no reservations about attributing direct government over all things to Christ himself:

> Every new instance of divine goodness, every mercy in providence, every blessing of grace should lead our tho'ts to Christ who is the fountain from whence all our mercies flow, and we should take occasion from thence to bless God for redeeming love. Christ has purchased all the good we receive, and he is the immediate dispenser of it. All power is given to him, he rules in the Kingdom of providence, as well as in the Kingdom of grace.[15]

Eliot was also prepared to list many events in biblical and post-biblical history that he saw as examples of God's providence. These included not only the people of Israel's victories over Ai and Jericho, portrayed in the Old Testament, but their escape from Egypt, survival in the desert, and eventual entry into the land of Canaan. Since "no event comes to pass without the concurrence of his [God's] providence," the Protestant Reformation could be clearly traced to divine initiative, as could the defeat of the Spanish Armada in 1588 and of the Gunpowder Plot of Guy Fawkes and his co-conspirators in 1605. The Glorious Revolution of 1688 and the Duke of Marlborough's defeat of the French forces of Louis XIV in the early 1700s were both ultimately the work of God, as was the settlement of New England by the first Puritans. In that sense, the conquest of Quebec by General Wolfe and his forces in 1759 was simply part of a divine plan, in which God had consistently prospered the Protestant cause of truth, justice, and religious freedom over the forces of oppression and corruption associated with "popish superstition and error." It was, therefore, no exaggeration to see "in every step of the [Quebec] expedition . . . the providence of God," for "it was God, the great ruler of the universe, that gave Quebec into our hands."[16]

Although he did not dwell on the prospect, Eliot clearly nurtured a millennial vision of "a time, when the religion of Jesus will prevail throughout the world." In the meantime, he did not hesitate to interpret the history of Britain and New England, together with their governing structures

---

15. Eliot, *Sermon Preached October 25th, 1759*, 8, 11.
16. Eliot, *Sermon Preached October 25th, 1759*, 12–38, esp. 14–15, 42, 38.

and religious institutions, in openly providentialist terms. He was so convinced of "the dominion of an omnipotent deity" that he included a whole sermon on the topic in his last published work, where he reasserted his view that "the providence of God extends as far as the creation." Such a thought would be "full of terror" for "enemies to God by wicked works," Eliot argued, but should be a source of consolation and thanksgiving for Christians with "reason to rejoice in the divine government." It was partly Eliot's providentialism and, in particular, his providential understanding of the vital role of British Protestant ideals and institutions which made it so difficult for him to support any break from imperial rule until the late 1770s. But they were counterbalanced and eventually outweighed by the Whig, even radical Whig, ideas that he also espoused, by religious as well as political concerns for the growth and protection of what he understood to be fundamental, British liberties wherever and whenever they were threatened, and by the personal and practical realities of living and ministering in time of war.[17]

---

17. Eliot, *Sermon Preached October 25th, 1759*, 42; *Twenty Sermons*, 79, 87, 103, 97.

8

Anti-Slavery Libertarian

The Indian Question

IN HIS BRIEF HISTORY of New North Church, which includes an account of his father's life and ministry, Ephraim Eliot made a point of noting that "Mr. Eliot was always a zealous opposer of African slavery." He then told a colourful and revealing story to illustrate his point. Many in Boston had slaves as family servants, he observed, but not Eliot. In fact,

> Soon after his marriage, a sum of money was subscribed by his friends, sufficient to buy a black boy for him; but he declined the present, unless he might be permitted to put him as an apprentice to some business, when he should be of a suitable age; and at the termination of his apprenticeship, that he should be a free man. These conditions not suiting the gentlemen, the matter was dropt [sic]. He did not live to witness the abolition of slavery in this commonwealth.

In making this bold decision, Eliot may well have been influenced by his reading of the prominent anti-slavery work of Paul Dudley, *Essay on the Merchandize of Slaves & Souls of Men*, which was published in Boston in 1731.[1]

Eliot was inevitably a man of his time and place. His position as pastor of New North thus involved ministering in a society that was structurally

---

1. Ephraim Eliot, *Historical Notices*, 30. A copy of Dudley, *Essay*, in the Massachusetts Historical Society library is clearly listed as inscribed as "Andw Eliot['s] Book 1736."

racist by definition and to a congregation which included slave-owners. Slavery had been a dark reality in Massachusetts since the 1630s and 1640s. According to the City of Boston itself,

> By 1720, there were more than 1,500 enslaved people living in Boston, or about 12 percent of the town's population at the time. Enslaved people would make up between 10–12 percent of Boston's population throughout the early and mid-1700s. Boston was the center of New England slavery and more than 30 percent of the region's enslaved population lived in the town.[2]

Eliot kept his own account of the Boston population, based on figures collated by the town overseers and recorded 1,541 "blacks" out of a total of 15,731 people in July 1752. He paid further attention to the number (693) infected during the smallpox epidemic of the same year which struck over 50 percent of the population. Eliot's approach to African slavery and to African Americans generally also seems to have been relatively enlightened for his age. The New North records show that Eliot's church was somewhat inclusive of black people right from the start, but in small numbers. There were ten "negro" or "malatto" [sic] admissions before 1789, three identified as slaves and the remainder as "free" or uncategorized. Between 1719 and 1781, some forty-six African Americans were baptized, twenty-four of whom were listed as slaves or "servants" or members of their households. The church records note sixteen formal African American weddings between 1744 and 1783, when slavery was finally abolished in Massachusetts. But on Eliot's recommendation, at a meeting of June 10, 1767, the church took a significant move in a more liberal direction, when it voted to extend the right to be baptized to the children of black slave women who had not been able to get legally married, but were part of common law partnerships approved by their owners.[3]

Eliot's approach to the first nations in Massachusetts and elsewhere was apparently less progressive. In fact, as Shipton noted, he engaged enthusiastically in efforts to "civilize," as well as to evangelize indigenous communities and was active in no fewer than three missionary societies, including the London Society for Promoting the Gospel in New England and Parts Adjacent, the Edinburgh Society for Propagating Christian Knowledge among the Indians, of which he was a Boston commissioner, and the Massachusetts Society for Propagating Christian Knowledge among the Indians

2. Hardesty et al., "Boston Slavery Exhibit."
3. AED 1752; Wells and Fanning, *New North Church*, 80–85; NNR 1:260–61.

of North America and Others in North America [SPCKINA]. In an extended letter to Samuel Chandler, who was then minister of the First Congregationalist Church in Gloucester, MA, which is undated, but was probably sent in about 1762, Eliot noted that "it has often been objected against the people of New England that they have neglected [th]e Heathen upon their borders." He also conceded that "not so much as ought to have been done" had been, "considering that the evangelizing the Indians was one professed design of our Fathers in coming into America" Now, he thought, with the British firmly in control of Canada, "the good people among us seem more convinc'd than ever of their obligations to attempt the recovery of the Indians from [thei]r present state of barbarity & ignorance by bringing [the]m to an acquaintance with theG[ospel] of J[esus] C[hris]t." With that in mind, Eliot wrote, more than £2,000 sterling plus a further £200 a year had been subscribed to fund a new missionary society [SPCKINA]. An Act for incorporating this new society had already been passed by the authorities in New England and was awaiting official approval in London.[4]

At this stage, Eliot actively sought Chandler's help with the initiative. But things did not proceed as he hoped. By June 1, 1763, he regretfully wrote to Jasper Mauduit in London that he had already heard that

> the Act incorporating a Number of Persons into a Society for propagating the Gospel among the Indians is not like to have the Royal Approbation. We have a grateful Sense of your Care in managing that Affair, but it gives us the greatest Concern that the Act has met with such Opposition. It is strange that Gentlemen who profess Christianity will not send the Gospel to the Heathen themselves nor permit it to be sent by others. We hope the Design will not fail. The Commissioners from London and Scotland are hearty in the Cause and we doubt not will receive considerable Assistance from well-disposed Persons among ourselves.[5]

Eliot remained concerned to proselytize indigenous peoples, but his enthusiasm for training first nations leaders to educate and share the Christian gospel with their own people waned significantly following the failure of Moor's Indian Charity School in Lebanon, Connecticut. Founded by Eleazar Wheelock in 1754, Moor's was established, according to Dartmouth College library, "on the premise Indians would make better missionaries

---

4. Shipton, *New England Life*, 406–7; Eliot to Samuel Chandler, c. 1762, in Andrew Eliot Letters.

5. Eliot, "Letter to Jasper Mauduit, June 1, 1763," 119.

than their Anglo counterparts in part because Indian missionaries could be supported for half the cost of English missionaries; they spoke the Indian languages; and they were accustomed to Indian lifestyles." Students there were given a classical education that included, in addition to biblical studies, Latin and Greek and by 1768 about fifty students had attended, with fifteen returning to their homes as "missionaries, schoolmasters, or assistants to non-Indian Ministers." But Wheelock soon realized that his "plan of sending missionaries to Indian homelands to educate and convert Indians was not working as he desired." So he began "to move in new directions," receiving a charter for a new school, which would be named for the second Earl of Dartmouth, eventually Dartmouth College, in 1769. Eliot clearly shared Wheelock's disillusionment. In a letter to Hollis of December 10, 1767, he expressed himself freely on the matter:

> The Commissioners for Indian Affairs, appointed by a corporation in London, (... of which Board I have ... the honor to be a member,) at first encouraged this school which Mr. Wheelock set up; not because we had any great opinion of him, but because we were willing to try every method to serve the poor Indians. We soon found that he had great, and as we feared, romantic designs; and besides, he was, as we thought, very unreasonable in his charges. We therefore withdrew ourselves.

A much more detailed account of Wheelock's school from August 1767, which remains in Eliot's papers, expands on these and other critiques, Eliot also took a dim view of the English fundraising efforts by Samson Occom who was a Wheelock protégé and "employed for many years to preach, and keep a school, in some Indian settlements in Connecticut and on Long Island," although he enjoyed no obvious success among the "six nations." Occom had no backing from Boston ministers, Eliot informed Hollis. "We are ignorant of the plan, we have no great opinion of the projectors, nor of the methods that are taken to procure money—for what purpose is Mr. Occum [sic] sent to England, &c." Eliot clearly regarded the missionary as among the "frauds of every kind, especially in religion," whom he detested.[6]

Shipton took the view that by 1769, "Eliot's zeal for the missions had completely evaporated because of their miserable failure" and there seems some justification for that interpretation. "I begin to be of your mind as to the impracticability of converting the Indians," he wrote to his

---

6. Rauner Library, "'A Matter of Absolute Necessity'"; Eliot to Thomas Hollis, in "Letters from Eliot to Hollis," December 10, 1767, 415–17.

correspondent William Harris on July 3, 1769, for example. Yet the evidence would suggest that Shipton was also right to observe that "the degree of Eliot's withdrawal from the mission work has been exaggerated." After the death of Andrew Oliver in 1774, he took over much of the correspondence of the Commissioners and a significant collection of letters at the Massachusetts Historical Society clearly indicate that missionaries regularly reported to him. "He was most active in this work on the very eve of the Revolution," Shipton noted, despite his many other responsibilities. But "this was typical of the good work with which Eliot busied himself." Other duties that he freely took on over the years included serving as secretary of the Massachusetts Convention of Ministers from 1758 to 1761, preaching the Convention Sermon of 1767, and representing the interests of Congregationalist churches in Nova Scotia.[7]

"The Sacred Cause of Liberty"

In all his efforts, even at proselytization of indigenous peoples, Eliot's ultimate goal, as he would have seen it, was spiritual. His primary concern was people's human salvation and thus liberation from the penalty and power of sin. Moreover, "liberty" in this and other senses was a consistent concern that permeated his political as well as religious worldview. Unlike Mayhew,

7. Eliot to William Harris, July 3, 1769, in Andrew Eliot Correspondence Transcripts, 156–58. "The Sacred Cause of Liberty" is a direct quotation from Nathan Hatch's book of the same title. The reports of the missionaries to Eliot are in MHS Miscellaneous Manuscripts Collection, 1773–75. See especially Eliot's correspondence with Sam Brown, Samuel Kirkland, and Stephen West, for example. See further the following remarks from "Mr. Wheelock's Indian School," Andrew Eliot Correspondence Transcripts, 169–77, an eight-page account of the school's history and problems from August 1767, to which Eliot almost certainly contributed, if he did not write the whole document: "I wish well to the Indians, and would not for the world do any thing to prevent the enlargement of the Redeemer's Kingdom. If Christ is preached, & his cause advanced, I shall rejoice, let who will be the instruments. But I have no great expectations from Mr. Wheelock. I look upon him & Mr. Whitefield, who are the chief projectors, as not proper persons to conduct such an affair, & I fear it will turn out as Mr. Whitefield's orphan house did, on which amazing sums were thrown away. However, the event must determine who is right. I am much pleased that the money collected is to be kept in England, & put into the hands of trustees there. I have sometimes been ready to think the Indians are not to be Christianized, but that Providence designs their extirpation. A dark cloud seems to hang over that unhappy people. When the Europeans get among them the Indians gradually dwindle to nothing. The most probable attempts to bring them to the knowledge of the truth have failed of success. The Commissioners do every thing in their powers. I wish I could say we saw any remarkable, visible good effects."

Eliot presented no systematic *schema*, in which he expounded different definitions of "liberty." But he did follow the example of his ministerial colleague in using the word in a variety of different senses, ranging from "gracious" to "philosophical" through to "religious" and "civil" liberty. There is also evidence that he developed, in the process, a libertarian discourse that is of considerable significance in understanding his thought.[8]

Eliot's only extended treatment of "philosophical" liberty is found in his *Discourse on Natural Religion* (1771), in which he devoted some four pages to the topic of freedom and necessity. The context of Eliot's discussion is his previous argument that once the existence of an "all-perfect" God is allowed, "it is reasonable to conclude that he will evidence his approbation and dislike, by rewarding those who do his will, and punishing those who do it not" in an afterlife. Such conclusions would, however, be meaningless, Eliot argued, unless humankind was assumed to have genuine freedom of choice, as well as moral responsibility. Indeed,

> The whole of this reasoning is founded on the supposition that man acts freely; and upon any other supposition, it is idle to talk of moral government, of rewards and punishments, or indeed of religion or virtue. "That," says Mr. [William] Wollaston, "which hath not the opportunity or liberty of chusing for itself, and acting

---

8. See Mayhew, "Memorandum," in Bailyn, "Religion and Revolution," 140–43, esp. 141–42, for no fewer than six "ac[c]eptations of the word" liberty, including: "1. Philosophical liberty, or freedom of choice & action. 2. Gracious liberty, given in regeneration, and consisting in a will or disposition to do good, in opposition to the slavery of [sin]. 3. What is commonly called religious liberty; or that natural right which every man has to worship God as he pleases, provided his principles & practices are [not] prejudicial to others. 4. Liberty, or freedom from the ceremonial law, which law is considered in scripture as a yoke & burthen to those who were under it. 5. That liberty which every man has, in what is commonly called a state of nature, or antecedent to the consideration of his being a member of civil society; consisting in a right to act as he pleases, in opposition to being bound by any human laws; always provided that he violates no law of God, nature or right reason; which no man is at liberty to do. 6. Civil liberty . . . supposes men to be united together in civil society, or a body politic: since they who continue in that, which is usually termed a state of nature, can with no propriety be said to enjoy civil liberty . . . This also supposeth, that men, for the sake of common good, and mutual security, give up some part of their natural liberty, or the right which they have in a state of nature, to act as they please, each individual for himself . . . It supposeth the restraint of laws, some persons to govern, and some to be governed . . . Civil liberty also supposeth, that those laws, by which a nation is governed, are made by common consent & choice; that all have some hand in framing them, at least by their representatives, chosen to act for them, if not in their own persons."

accordingly, from an internal principle, acts, if it acts at all, under a necessity incumbent *ab extra*."

Supporting his argument with a citation from James Beattie, Eliot maintained that the view that "all our volitions, determinations and actions proceed from God, as infrustrable effects from their proper cause, hath hitherto been embraced by a very few." Moreover, such a doctrine entailed, Eliot thought, in the words of Henry Home, "a black conception of God, that he should be supposed irresistibly to determine the will of man to the hatred of his own most blessed self, and then to exact the severest punishments for the offence done."[9]

It was, therefore, partly to protect his understanding of divine justice that Eliot defended human freedom of choice. But he was also swayed by the common sense, empirical observation that people thought themselves free to act as they saw fit:

> It is a conclusive argument against such a fatal necessity as some men plead for, that it is contrary to the perceptions of the human mind—we have a consciousness of liberty, we perceive no external influence, we have a moral sense, we pass a judgment on our own actions, approve or disapprove our selves and others.

The Calvinist Eliot thus defended "philosophical" liberty, in that he allowed for freedom of the will on similar grounds to Mayhew. But unlike the Arminian Mayhew, who felt free to dismiss Calvinist solutions to "some of the difficulties respecting fore-knowledge, predestination, and . . . conversion," Eliot's basic theology still required him to uphold the absolute sovereignty of God. So Eliot ended his consideration of this thorny philosophical question with a citation from Locke that Bailyn has rightly portrayed as providing no real solution to the dilemma:

---

9. Eliot, *Discourse on Natural Religion*, xviii–xxii, xv, xvii, xviii, citing Wollaston, *Religion of Nature Delineated*, 5, xix, citing Beattie, *Essay on the Nature and Immutability*, 367–68, xx, citing Howe, *Works*, 2:502. Eliot made a similar argument in the seventh of his *Twenty Sermons*, "Practical Observations on the History of Judas and his Tragical End," where he cited (and somewhat paraphrased), 405–6, a commentary on Matt 26:23–24: "I say, without any necessitating agency, because I apprehend that this text, among many others, must entirely overthrow the scheme, which some laboriously endeavour to establish, that where God foresees an event, he always determines to render it necessary, and so, to suspend the moral agency and accountableness of the creature concerned in it. Were this the case, nothing could be more unjust, than to foretell punishments to be inflicted for such actions; which is plainly the case here, and indeed in other places where evil actions are foretold" (Doddridge, *Family Expositor*, 2:434–35n).

> I freely own the weakness of my understanding, that though it be unquestionable, that there is omnipotence and omniscience in God our Maker, and I cannot have a clearer perception of any thing, than that I am free; yet I cannot make freedom in man consistent with omnipotence and omniscience in God, though I am as fully persuaded of both, as of any truths I most firmly assent to.

In the final analysis, therefore, Eliot defended the "philosophical" liberty of humankind, even though he could not completely reconcile it with his doctrine of God. At the same time, his assumption of total human "depravity" entailed that he saw what Mayhew described as "gracious" liberty, "consisting in a will and a disposition to do good," as entirely dependent on the intervention of God's grace.[10]

In view of the demonstrable Calvinism of Eliot's overall theological position, there can be little doubt that he saw spiritual liberty as the central and most important form of human freedom. Thus Eliot portrayed the attitude of the "faithful minister" as involving "such an affecting sense upon his mind, of the inestimable value of precious and immortal souls, that he is in earnest to free them from that condemned state, in which we all naturally are, and to bring them into 'the glorious liberty of the children of God.'" In his memorial sermon for Webb, Eliot likewise commended the "unwearied pains he took to 'set at liberty them that were bruised.'" Elsewhere in his writings, he also drew on biblical texts to urge masters to instruct their slaves "in the principles of religion, and to make them partakers of 'the glorious liberty of the sons of God,'" and in exegeting one of the most obscure passages in the New Testament epistles, 1 Peter 3:19, he referred to "that Spirit of Christ, the Spirit of liberty." Although it is noteworthy that Eliot nowhere addressed the apparent inconsistency between his understanding of "gracious" liberty as resulting solely from spiritual regeneration and "philosophical" liberty as freely available to all, in his various references to "religious" and "civil" liberty, there is similar evidence of the power of biblical language in shaping his libertarian discourse.[11]

---

10. Eliot, *Discourse on Natural Religion*, xx; Mayhew, *On Hearing the Word*, 163; Eliot, *Discourse on Natural Religion*, xxi, citing Locke, *Works*, 9:305; Mayhew, "Memorandum," in Bailyn, "Religion and Revolution," 140–43, esp. 141. See also Eliot, *Twenty Sermons*, 39: "It is not easy to conceive how God could have done more than he hath done to make us happy, unless he had taken away the freedom of our wills, and compelled us to that, which he designed should be our own choice." Cf. Bailyn, "Religion and Revolution," 93.

11. Eliot, *Faithful Steward*, 14–15 (citing Rom 8:21); *Burning and Shining Light*, 33 (citing Luke 4:18); *Twenty Sermons*, 320 (citing Rom 8:21), 184 (citing Isa 61:1): "The

Eliot's ideas of religious freedom, in Barry Shain's "prescriptive" sense of a right to which English citizens were inherently entitled, emerge most clearly in his "Remarks on the Bishop of Oxford's Sermon" (1766/1767). Here Eliot not only offered a vigorous response to factual allegations about the state of religion in the American colonies; he also made a strong case for the retention of American religious liberties. "The glorious errand" of New England's first settlers was ultimately a quest for freedom. Their descendants must, therefore, "stand fast in the liberty, wherewith Christ hath made them free." What such steadfastness primarily involved for Eliot, as noted earlier, was maintaining freedom from the establishment of religion and from what he saw as a conscious British design "to episcopize the colonies." His view of the "fathers of New England" was not totally uncritical, as has been noted. Elsewhere, when stating his shared opposition with them to religious "subscriptions" of any kind, he also criticized their understanding of religious liberty. But because he thought that "the principles of liberty and Christian candour have gradually obtained in New-England, as in other places," Eliot showed some optimism about longer-term prospects, and he repeatedly warned his contemporaries to guard their freedoms with care.[12]

Like Mayhew, Eliot often linked religious and "civil" or political liberty as key elements in a package of prescriptive freedoms that was not only desirable in the present but definitive of what was most laudable in his English and New England heritage. He may have taken the view that "the necessity of government" was primarily a matter of practical expediency

---

Spirit of the Lord God is upon me; because the Lord hath anointed me to preach good tidings unto the meek; he hath sent me to bind up the brokenhearted, to proclaim liberty to the captives, and the opening of the prison to them that are bound." First Peter 3:18–20 reads as follows: "For Christ also hath once suffered for sins, the just for the unjust, that he might bring us to God, being put to death in the flesh, but quickened by the Spirit: By which also he went and preached unto the spirits in prison; Which sometime were disobedient, when once the longsuffering of God waited in the days of Noah, while the ark was a preparing, wherein few, that is, eight souls were saved by water."

12. Eliot, "Remarks on the Bishop of Oxford's Sermon," 190–216; Secker, *Sermon Preached*; Eliot, *Remarks on the Bishop of Oxford's Sermon*, 197, 209, 197 (citing Gal 5:1), 196, 204; Andrew Eliot to Francis Blackburne, May 13, 1767, cited in Shipton, *New England Life*, 416. See also, 413–14; cf. Shain, *Myth of American Individualism*, 171–72. Shain identified no fewer than eight concepts of liberty in eighteenth-century colonial America (168). He defined "prescriptive" liberty in a plural sense as "an inherited set of rights that were applicable to members of a particular class or a local corporation (often a town or village)—rights to which, as English subjects, Americans believed themselves duly entitled" (171).

"in the present imperfect state of human nature." But he saw England, once free of "the papal yoke," as "the bulwark of the Protestant cause" and he bemoaned "how often . . . its religious, as well as civil liberties [had] been bro't into the most imminent hazard." England's "popish adversaries" had long been "forming plots and conspiracies to overthrow our religion and liberties." Yet thankfully, in events like the 1588 defeat of the Spanish Armada or more recently, military success in Quebec, such devilish schemes had been thwarted. In particular, it was the "Glorious Revolution in Britain, to which noble exertion of national virtue, we owe the preservation of our liberty, and the present happy establishment of the House of Hanover." As a result, Britain remained "a happy mixture of monarchy, aristocracy and democracy," which was "the glory of Britons and the envy of foreigners." Moreover, liberty was central to this. "In free governments people are apt to feel much quicker," he argued. "To touch their liberties is to touch the apple of their eye." In 1765, Eliot could still proclaim the happiness of "Great-Britain in a Prince, who accounts it his glory to reign over a free people, and who, we trust, will always make the laws of the land the rule of his administration."[13]

It was the duty of rulers "to know very well what it is to act right, where power ends and liberty begins" and constitutional change could endanger the latter. Those in authority also had a responsibility to "promote the public happiness" and if they failed to preserve civil liberty, they deserved to forfeit the biblical title of "ministers of God." Eliot was deeply conscious of the sacrifices that New England's founders had made for "the privileges we enjoy," including "the rights of Englishmen." So even in the midst of the Stamp Act crisis, he expressed his trust that "our King and his Parliament will yet hear us and confirm our liberties and immunities to us." He also prayed for New England that

> that kind providence, which has so often appeared for our nation [may] still watch over it for good; disappoint every attempt to subvert their liberties, and preserve them from those internal vices and corruptions, which they have more reason to fear than any foreign enemy, or open violence![14]

Eliot echoed similar themes in his correspondence. He frequently wrote of liberty, both civil and religious, together with its "cause," its "spirit"

---

13. Eliot, *Sermon Preached before Bernard*, 8, 39, 18, 20, 48; *Sermon Preached October 25th, 1759*, 16–17.

14. Eliot, *Sermon Preached before Bernard*, 21, 43, 54, 52, 54, 49.

and its "friends," in very general terms as a kind of ultimate good. In one of his earliest letters to Hollis, for example, he told how he rejoiced "to find the cause of liberty undertaken by one [Francis Blackburne] so every way able to defend it," and how he saw Mayhew's recent death as a "loss" to "the cause of learning, of liberty, and of religion." He also argued that "the spirit of liberty would soon be lost" without a vigilant press and that "syndics" deserved "to lose their liberty, who [could] so tamely resign it." Eliot repeated his concerns for the "liberty of the press" in subsequent letters and drew attention to a number of other "friends" to the cause, including Milton, the legendary fourteenth-century Swiss hero William Tell, the eighteenth-century English dissenter Caleb Fleming, Harvard President Samuel Locke, and another contemporary, the Bostonian Baptist pastor, Jeremiah Condy. When Eliot wrote of the lack of New England concern for independence in 1767, he proudly observed that "the people ... glory in the name of Englishmen, and only desire to enjoy the liberties of Englishmen." He described "liberty of the press" as "the *palladium* of English liberty" in the same letter.[15]

Significant to Eliot's internal struggles, as conflict with Great Britain escalated from the late 1760s onwards, were his competing concerns to maintain allegiance to his British libertarian heritage, as well as to see liberty in action closer to home. In January 1769, he wrote to Hollis, addressing him as "you who have such just sentiments of liberty," but he also justified Bostonians' possible lack of prudence by asking "what could be expected from a people struggling for liberty and made almost desperate by the measures taken with them?" Later that year, he not only praised Blackburne and echoed condemnations of William Pitt, but he warned that Thomas Hutchinson "must not attempt any thing against our liberties," and described the "declamations and forensic disputes" of Harvard students as breathing "the spirit of liberty." In 1771, when discussing religious matters with Hollis, including the now diminished threat of an American

---

15. Eliot, *Sermon Preached before Bernard*, 21, 43 (citing Rom 13:4), 52, 54, 49; Eliot to Thomas Hollis, November 14, 1766; May 13, 1767, in "Letters from Eliot to Hollis," 399, 401, 400, 404, 405. On Blackburne's contributions to the cause of liberty, see further: Eliot to Hollis, May 13, 1767; November 11, 1767, in "Letters from Eliot to Hollis," 406, 408: "The fugitive pieces that worthy man writes in the papers, are admirably calculated to promote the cause of truth and liberty." On "liberty of the press," see Eliot to Hollis, May 13, 1767; April 18, 1768; December 25, 1769, in "Letters from Eliot to Hollis," 405, 425, 445. On the various "friends" of liberty, see Eliot to Hollis, December 10, 1767; October 17, 1768; December 25, 1769, in "Letters from Eliot to Hollis," 413, 429, 431, 447–48.

episcopate, Eliot suggested that "there is nothing in the present complexion of this country, that looks like persecution. Both magistrates and ministers are as free from it as they ever were in any age or country." Nevertheless, Eliot noted internal tensions that had given rise to reports in the Philadelphia papers that the Massachusetts Charter was under threat and "this," he reported, "hath raised a spirit against them [local Baptists] among our sons of liberty."[16]

Eliot's last use of the word "liberty" in any general political sense in his published correspondence was in a 1775 letter to Thomas Brand Hollis, where he expressed his "design" that "the friends of liberty" might join other supporters of the colonial cause. But two months later, he was still expressing his fears and forebodings about the possible outcome of colonial victory in the Anglo-American conflict. In the meantime, he continued to appeal to Scripture in his letters, as well as his sermons and other works. One of the "ends" of those pleading for an American bishop in 1767, for example, was "to tyrannize over those who yet 'stand fast in the liberty wherewith Christ hath made them free.'" So Eliot gave thanks, three years later, following the obvious delay of such a scheme, and argued that "the future friends of the cause of liberty will be under great advantages for its defence against any future attempts on it of the like nature."[17]

Liberty was thus a major theme in both his religious and political thinking. His various writings also show that Eliot, like Mayhew, prioritized notions of spiritual liberty and quite often deployed a libertarian discourse shaped by biblical texts, which served to inject scriptural content and to evoke spiritual allusions even in overtly political contexts. Such a conflation of what we might now consider sacred and secular themes is not surprising in light of Eliot's thought as a whole. For he was primarily a religious thinker, motivated by theological concerns.[18]

---

16. Eliot to Hollis, January 29, 1769; December 25, 1769; January 26, 1771, in "Letters from Eliot to Hollis," 439, 440, 445-48, 454-59, esp. 447, 456.

17. Eliot to Thomas Brand Hollis, April 25, 1775, in "Letters," 282; Eliot to Isaac Smith Jr., June 19, 1775, in "Letters," 287-89; Eliot to Hollis, November 13, 1766; June 28, 1770, in "Letters from Eliot to Hollis," 411 (citing Gal 5:1), 449-50.

18. Key texts were Isa 61:1; Luke 4:18; Rom 8:21; Gal 5:1.

9

Political and Pastoral Pragmatist

On June 19, 1775, two days after the Battle of Bunker Hill, which was a tactical victory for the British, but very costly for both sides, Eliot wrote a vivid account of the aftermath in a letter to his friend Isaac Smith Jr., who had fled England the previous month. Although he had sent the rest of his family out of town, Eliot was staying behind personally, he told Smith, "purely out of regard to the inhabitants who were left, that they might not be without ordinances and worship in the way which they choose." He thus became one of the few remaining ministers to witness the results of the battle in which half the British forces were casualties and up to a third of the 1,500 Americans were killed, wounded, or captured. Eliot's graphic description of the scene in Boston did not conceal his horror at recent events:

> It was a new and awful spectacle to us to have men carried through the streets groaning, bleeding, and dying . . . Amidst the carnage of Saturday, the town of Charlestown was set on fire, and I suppose every dwelling-house and every public building is consumed till you have passed the passage to the mills, and are come to the houses where Woods the baker dwelt.[1]

But rather than lambasting the British occupiers, or lauding the heroism of American patriots, Eliot wrote of his distress at seeing and hearing "Englishmen destroying one another, and a town with which we have been so intimately connected all in flames. We are left in anxious expectation

---

1. Eliot to Isaac Smith Jr., June 19, 1775, in Eliot, "Letters," 288.

of the event," he continued. "God grant the blood already spilt may suffice." Even with his beloved Boston aflame, Eliot worried that a meeting of Harvard dignitaries might come to "sudden resolutions" and thus "give offence." Three days later, he added a postscript to Smith, in which he doubted any positive outcome of Anglo-American hostilities, whichever side should ultimately prevail.²

The concerns expressed in his June 1775 letter were typical of Eliot's anxious, often vacillating approach to political issues in the revolutionary era. Historians have periodically debated the significance of the Boston minister's attitudes to the advent of the American Revolution and they have been divided over whether he was the convinced patriot characterized by Baldwin, the prudent "Liberal" sketched by Heimert, the cautious mediator described by Shipton, or the Whig with a temperamental "reluctance to declare for independence" portrayed by Bailyn. The picture that emerges from a thorough exploration of Eliot's views on Anglo-American relations in the decade before, as well as in the earliest years of the War for Independence, is more complex.³

Chapter 8 showed how his political thought was significantly influenced by seventeenth- and eighteenth-century Whigs and how he defended similar ideas to those of more progressive-minded contemporaries, not least his friend and ministerial colleague, Mayhew. But Eliot's politics also remained firmly grounded in the thoroughly biblicist doctrine of his moderate Calvinism and the ambivalence of his libertarian discourse reflected its deep religious grounding. His intellectual worldview was still shaped by the distinctive contours of the dissenting Protestant traditions of New England Congregationalism. Eliot's writings from the revolutionary period not only reflect dramatic personal and pastoral challenges; they continue to reveal a more traditionalist thinker, politically as well as theologically, than has often been portrayed. Eliot's continuing commitment to English national identity, authority and ideals were especially instrumental in preventing him from becoming an outspoken advocate of the American Revolution, despite his Whig sympathies and the pressures of his position

---

2. Eliot, "Letters," 288-89. Recent books on the Battle of Bunker Hill include Nelson, *With Fire and Sword*, and, more popularly, Philbrick, *Bunker Hill*.

3. Baldwin, *New England Clergy*, esp. 111, 111–12n18, 90, citing Eliot, *Sermon Preached before Bernard*; Heimert, *Religion and the American Mind*, e.g., 260, 291, 261; Shipton, *New England Life*, esp. 409–25; Bailyn, "Religion and Revolution," esp. 88. See further, Clark, *Language of Liberty*, 365–66, citing Bailyn, "Religion and Revolution," esp. 88, 95, 97.

as minister of one of Boston's leading churches, until open hostilities were well under way.

Radical Whiggery and Colonial Ambivalence

As tensions between Great Britain and the American colonies escalated from the 1760s onwards, one of Eliot's major problems was how to reconcile his continuing loyalty to a providentialist vision of the progressive force of Protestant British ideals and influence in post-Reformation history with the obviously increasing practical difficulties associated with British rule in action. As the letters of his later years clearly show, the growth of Anglo-American hostilities left Eliot deeply perplexed, irrespective of his stated views on the right to civil disobedience and rebellion. Moreover, Eliot's ambivalence reflected more than a simple "temperamental" reluctance to declare for one side over the other, as Bailyn has suggested. It embodied quite a profound intellectual conflict.[4]

Eliot's 1766–1775 correspondence with the English Whig leaders, Hollis, Francis Blackburne, and Thomas Brand Hollis is especially revealing in this regard. Bailyn has arguably overstated the extent to which Eliot shared their darkly pessimistic interpretation of events in Britain and their causes. But there is little question that Eliot endorsed much of his correspondents' radical Whig outlook on major events and issues of his day. Eliot began writing to Hollis in 1766 after Hollis approached him following the death of his previous correspondent Mayhew. His first letter, which was written in the immediate aftermath of the repeal of Stamp Act, can hardly have left his English benefactor in any doubt as to where Eliot's sympathies lay, either religiously or politically. He praised Blackburne's *Confessional* (1766), which Hollis had sent to him, as "one of the most valuable performances of the age." The "imposition of subscriptions" to confessions of faith in churches was, Eliot thought "a yoke . . . not to be borne. It can answer no end but to promote bigotry and hypocrisy, and has occasioned more perjury and prevarication, than perhaps any one thing in the world." He sounded a strongly anti-Catholic note when he expressed surprise that "we have attended so little to the settling a Popish bishop in Canada" and he voiced his support for Mayhew in his controversies with English clerics over the role in America of the SPG. In view of various newspaper articles sent by Hollis, Eliot also expressed forthright opinions about British politics

4. Bailyn, "Religion and Revolution."

in general. "In the present state of things," he wrote, "we must expect to find syndics, men of contracted minds and mean tools of power." Eliot particularly lamented the apparent defection of former Prime Minister William Pitt the Elder (1708–1778), "the great patriot," following his 1766 elevation to the House of Lords as Earl of Chatham.[5]

Such evidence of aggressive religious non-conformity, anti-Catholicism, and radical Whig political views is as consistent throughout Eliot's 1766–1775 correspondence as his determination to resist what he saw as unjustifiable British encroachments on colonial prerogatives. In response to Hollis's continuous supply of relevant literature, Eliot was unstinting in his praise of such luminaries as Philip Sidney, James Harrington, Locke, and John Milton. He defended liberty of the press. He described John Trenchard's *Short History of Standing Armies* (1698) as "excellent." "To have a standing army! Good God!" he wrote Hollis in September 1768, "What can be worse to a people who have tasted the sweets of liberty." In religious terms, Eliot revealed himself to his correspondents as anti-establishmentarian, as well as anti-Catholic. "I wish our fathers had contrived some other way for the maintenance of ministers, than by a tax," he told Hollis in 1771. "Thank God, we have none in Boston. I do not like anything that looks like an establishment." Moreover, Eliot's anti-Catholicism extended well beyond the particular local concern of the establishment of a Canadian bishopric "to encourage the inhabitants of this newly conquered country in their fatal superstitions." He wrote, for example, of "the papists . . . not ashamed, neither do they blush, to fly in the face of all history, and to assert the most infamous falsehoods." In a letter of December 12, 1767, Eliot was even more direct. "I have observed," he wrote, "with pleasure, the care taken by Parliament, one branch at least, to have a list taken of the papists. I wish success to every attempt to curb the violence of those enemies of truth, of liberty, of mankind."[6]

5. Bailyn, "Religion and Revolution," 98; Eliot to Thomas Hollis, November 14, 1766, in "Letters from Eliot to Hollis," 399–400, citing Blackburne, *Confessional*, 400–401.

6. See, for example, Eliot to Thomas Hollis, May 13, 1767; December 10, 1767; June 28, 1770; September 27, 1768; January 26, 1771; November 13, 1767 in "Letters from Eliot to Hollis," 403–6, 410, 412–21, esp. 414–15, 428, 452 (citing Trenchard, *Short History of Standing Armies*), 432, 455. Jean-Olivier Briand, who became Bishop of Quebec in 1766, was the first Catholic bishop whose position was formally recognized by the British Government following the conquest of Canada. See Vachon, "Briand, Jean-Olivier." In the context of Eliot's opposition to church "establishment," it is worth noting, however, that it was not until 1833 that Massachusetts actually became the last to end state support for churches. Moreover, it was only nine years earlier that a measure was adopted to allow

Eliot's attitudes towards the attempts of various British institutions to control events in New England were sometimes similarly negative, although they were generally more ambivalent. In May 1767, Eliot was quite unequivocal in his positive assessment that "the people here have no notion of aiming at independence. They highly value their connection with their mother country." As the colonial power's interference in American affairs became stronger and more oppressive, Eliot's concern for the very liberties that he thought so integral to English national identity and ideals prompted him to adopt a more independent and critical stance. Eliot never produced a systematic defence of New England polity, although there is no reason to doubt his Congregationalist ecclesiological orthodoxy. In correspondence with Hollis, he opposed the possible establishment of a Church of England bishopric in North America on similar grounds to those expressed in his critique of the activities of the SPG in his "Remarks on the Bishop of Oxford's Sermon" (1766/1767). He opposed all forms of church establishment and took the view that history taught that the consequences of Anglican influence would be costly both financially and politically.[7]

In the political arena, Eliot's letters to Hollis provide something of a running commentary on his opposition to various British measures, but continuing, albeit somewhat equivocating allegiance to British authority in face of the series of legislative Acts passed by the British Parliament. These actions were ostensibly taken in attempts to raise revenues to pay down a national debt approaching £133 million after defeating France in the Seven Years' War, but they also served to increase economic and eventually military control over British colonies, including Massachusetts. Major measures included the Sugar and Currency Acts of 1764, which negatively impacted New England production and trade in rum, wine, coffee, and textiles, outlawed the direct shipment of several important commodities such as lumber to Europe, and banned colonial paper currency, requiring the taxes levied by the Sugar Act to be paid in gold and silver. The Stamp Act, which was in effect from November 1765 until news of its repeal reached North America about six months later, then raised further

---

other officially recognized religious societies, not only Congregationalists, to assess taxes on all church members.

7. Eliot to Thomas Hollis, May 13, 1767, in "Letters from Eliot to Hollis," 404; Eliot, "Remarks," 196, 209, 202, 210; Eliot to Thomas Hollis, November 13, 1767, in "Letters from Eliot to Hollis," 398–461, esp. 411; cf. Eliot to Thomas Hollis, October 17, 1768, in "Letters from Eliot to Hollis," 431, where Eliot states, "I dread a bishop of the Church of England, in any shape."

taxes by requiring many printed materials to be produced on paper from London carrying an embossed revenue stamp. Eliot scarcely commented on it in his extant correspondence, but in a letter to Hollis dated August 27, 1767, he recommended Mayhew's "sermon on the Stamp Act," *Snare Broken*, which was written in thanksgiving for its appeal, as "by far the best that was published."[8]

On December 12, 1767, Eliot wrote much more negatively to Hollis, among other things, about the Townshend Acts. This British legislation, which was sponsored by Chancellor of the Exchequer Charles Townshend, and formally enacted on July 2, 1767, was intended to raise revenues and improve customs enforcement. Asserting British taxation authority, the main statute levied duties on china, tea, glass, paper, lead, and paint. The stated purpose of the import tariffs was "for making a more certain and adequate provision for the charge of the administration of justice, and the support of the civil government, and defraying the expense of defending, protecting and securing the said colonies." But the new duties were much resented in the American colonies and gave rise to retaliatory non-importation measures. "The people in this town are not pleased with the late regulations of Parliament," observed Eliot, "—the new burthens laid upon them . . . The people are sullen, and think themselves ill-treated. They cannot be persuaded that the Parliament hath a right to impose taxes upon them." Just seven months earlier, Eliot could write of a relatively contented populace, happy to remain under British rule, but now he was more doubtful:

> Unreasonable impositions tend to alienate the hearts of the Colonists. We are not ripe for a disunion, but our growth is so great, that in a few years Great B---n will not be able to compel our submission . . . The colonies, if disunited from Great Britain, must undergo great convulsions before they would be settled on a firm basis . . . I hope not to live to see the American British colonies disconnected from Great Britain.

Less than a month later, Eliot informed Hollis that "our assembly is greatly warmed with the late Acts of Parliament" and he expressed the conviction that "the dispute between Great Britain and her colonies will never be amicably settled."[9]

---

8. Eloranta and Land, "Hollow Victory?" 110; Eliot to Thomas Hollis, August 27, 1767, in "Letters from Eliot to Hollis," 407, citing Mayhew, *Snare Broken*.

9. Chaffin, "Townsend Acts Crisis," esp. 138–39, citing *London Magazine* 37 (1768) 1777; Eliot to Thomas Hollis, December 10, 1767, in "Letters from Eliot to Hollis,"

Of course, Eliot was not only an interested observer, but an engaged participant in the events of his day. In September 1768, for example, he observed that "things are far from being in that happy state in which you, and all friends to Great Britain and her colonies, wish them to be." On Christmas Day of 1769, he offered Hollis the following reportage:

> The Colonies wait with patience to hear the result of Parliament. Lord Hillsboro' has written a letter to soothe them, wherein he promises a repeal of the duties on glass, paper and painters' colors, but leaves out tea. The Colonies will never be happy without a repeal of the whole ... The Americans are determined to hold out. I wish in some things they were more temperate—but certainly it is best for Great Britain to repeal the obnoxious Acts. The non-importation [of British goods] takes place throughout almost all the Colonies.[10]

The Tea Act of May 1773 effectively granted the British East India Company a monopoly on tea sales in the American colonies, leading to the dramatic events of the Boston Tea Party on the night of December 16, 1773, when a group of radical "Sons of Liberty," disguised as Mohawk Indians, boarded three ships moored in Boston Harbor and destroyed over 92,000 pounds of tea. But tea taxation had remained in place since the imposition of the Townshend Acts and it and other taxes prompted Eliot with others to complain bitterly about such examples of so-called "taxation without representation." "What can we do!?" he asked Hollis rhetorically when contemplating the situation in September 1768. He had no doubt that "tamely to give up our rights, and to suffer ourselves to be taxed at the will of persons at such a distance" was a servile and unwarranted concession.[11]

418–421; Eliot to Thomas Hollis, January 5, 1768, in "Letters from Eliot to Hollis," 422. In addition to the imposition of duties, the Townshend Acts included measures to establish an American Board of Customs Commissioners headquartered in Boston, and to suspend the New York Assembly under the provisions of the New York Restraining Act.

10. Eliot to Thomas Hollis, September 27, 1768; December 25, 1769, in "Letters from Eliot to Hollis," 427, 446. Lord Hillsborough was Secretary of State for the Colonies in the British Government. In April 1768, he had ordered colonial governors to stop their own assemblies from endorsing Samuel Adams's circular letter protesting the Townshend Acts. Hillsborough also instructed Governor Barnard of Massachusetts to dissolve the General Court if the Massachusetts assembly did not revoke the letter, which he did.

11. Boston Tea Party, "Tea Act"; Eliot to Thomas Hollis, September 27, 1768, in "Letters from Eliot to Hollis," 428. Hutchinson had already briefly acted as Governor in 1760 and was again Acting Governor from August 1769 until his appointment became official in March 1771.

The quartering of British troops in Boston also provoked Eliot's consternation. Following protests against the Townshend Acts, Francis Bernard, Governor of Massachusetts from 1759 to 1769, who was soon to be replaced by Hutchinson, successfully lobbied for military forces to protect those in government service. Two regiments, numbering up to four thousand men, were eventually dispatched to a town with a population of no more than sixteen thousand, and at the end of September 1768, troop ships, accompanied by British men of war, arrived in Boston Harbor. The troops disembarked and initially encamped on the Boston Commons, as well as in the Court House, and Faneuil Hall. But the colonists resisted the provisions of the 1765 Quartering Act, which required colonial authorities to provide food, accommodation, and transportation to British troops stationed in their towns or villages. As a result, British troops ended up billeted at Wheelwright's Wharf, Castle Island and wherever proved possible elsewhere in Boston. That led to considerable everyday tensions with the local population, as well as to principled resistance of the kind expressed by Eliot in a letter to Hollis of September 27, 1768. "To be under military government, is to consent to be slaves, and to bring upon us the curses of all posterity; and yet how unable to cope with Great Britain!"[12]

Just four months later, on January 29, 1769, Eliot expressed a more sanguine view. "The situation of my country, and the present aspect of things, lies near my heart," he wrote, and despite recent provocations, he sought to exculpate his fellow colonists of charges of disloyalty:

> We have just had the King's speech, and the echo of the Lords and Commons. They are exceeding high against this Town and Province. What can the ministry propose further? We have troops. We do not resist them. The duties, unreasonable as we think them, are paid without opposition. Perhaps the Town has not in every thing acted with that prudence that might be wished; . . . I will not say we have none among us of malevolent dispositions, but, in general, I believe the King has not more loyal subjects in any part of his dominions.

As time progressed, however, Eliot's assessment of the prospects of reconciliation grew more pessimistic. Even as he proclaimed Bostonian loyalty, he went on to express nostalgia for the status quo before "the unhappy Stamp Act," together with the opinion that "the colonies will never be so easily managed as they were before that fateful aera." Just six months later,

---

12. Eliot to Thomas Hollis, September 27, 1768, in "Letters from Eliot to Hollis," 428.

in July 1769, Eliot conceded that he had begun to doubt his previous opposition to some measures of local resistance. But although he continued to voice his personal opposition to "independency," he was also of the view that "things will not be settled till we have an American bill of rights."[13]

Eliot's resistance to open advocacy of independence continued for some time, but that did not prevent him from distinguishing his own, often rather cautious, response to events from that of others who took a more radical position, or from plainly stating political realities, as he perceived them. In September 1768, Eliot wrote that "our increase is so great, that time will be, when we shall be free," but he still thought it "impolitic to precipitate a disunion." About a year later, noting growing opposition to the British military presence in Boston, Eliot predicted that "things cannot long remain in the state they are now in; they are hastening to a crisis," and he repeated the prediction in another letter dated three months afterwards. Following the Boston Massacre of March 5, 1770, when a group of nine British soldiers killed five people among a crowd of three or four hundred, who were harassing them verbally and throwing various projectiles, Eliot's view was understandably more pessimistic. In June of that year, after decrying "the impossibility of our living in peace with a standing army," Eliot opined that "unless there is some great alteration in the state of things, the aera of the independence of the Colonies is much nearer than I once thought it." Even then, however, by adding the phrase, "or now wish it" to this last sentence, he again took pains to separate what he expected from what he actually wanted to see happen. It remained "for the interest of both countries to be united," he thought, "if it can be on equitable terms." Finally, in one of his last letters to Hollis, Eliot declared his continuing doubts about the desirability of war with Britain. "We daily look for war," he wrote. "We are at a loss which is best—peace or war. Peace is in itself desirable—but war hath sometimes happy effects."[14]

---

13. Eliot to Thomas Hollis, January 29, 1769; July 10, 1769, in "Letters from Eliot to Hollis," 440, 439, 442.

14. Eliot to Thomas Hollis, September 27, 1768; September 7, 1769; January 26, 1771, in "Letters from Eliot to Hollis," 428, 444, 452, 458–59; cf. Eliot to Thomas Hollis, December 25, 1769, in "Letters from Eliot to Hollis," 447: "Things must come to some crisis—and if the [Townshend] Acts are not repealed, I am very fearful of the consequences."

Pastor Under Siege

Against such a background, the grim but still hesitant and ambivalent tone of Eliot's later published letters to family and friends from war-torn Boston is less surprising than it might have been. By April 1775, the situation had indeed deteriorated dramatically. In response to colonial non-importation measures, the British had passed the so-called "Intolerable" or "Coercive Acts" of 1774, including the Boston Port Act (March 31), the Administration of Justice Act (May 20), the Massachusetts Government Act (May 20), a second Quartering Act (June 2) and the Quebec Act (June 22), which effectively stripped Massachusetts of self-government and judicial independence following the Boston Tea Party. Colonial resistance then increased in a much more organized way with a general boycott of British goods and the gathering of delegates from twelve colonies at the First Continental Congress, which issued a Declaration of Rights (October 14), formed the Continental Association (October 20), and made a formal Petition to the King (October 26).[15]

By September 14, 1774, Eliot expressed pessimism about the current state of affairs in Boston, but longer-term optimism for the future. "At present it's [sic] situation is melancholy," he wrote an unnamed southern correspondent, "guarded by troops and ships—an asylum for those who dare not appear elsewhere—it's [sic] trade destroyed—and not knowing from whence Deliverance is to come." Yet Eliot had "no doubt but that great things are designed in Providence for America, and that Boston will emerge from it's [sic] present unhappy situation." In his view, "there never will be a submission to the late unrighteous ['Intolerable'] acts—our people in the Country towns are universally armed." As the First Continental Congress convened in Carpenters' Hall in Philadelphia, Pennsylvania, between September 5 and October 26, 1774, delegates from twelve of Britain's thirteen American colonies met to discuss America's future under growing British aggression. In the meantime, Eliot reported, "all [were] in anxious expectation of the Result of the Congress," because what was "determined there will be Law to America."[16]

On April 19, 1775, overt military hostilities then began with the Battles of Lexington and Concord. From the same day, with thousands of British

---

15. For helpful summaries of such events, see, for example, British Library, "Timeline of the American Revolution"; Wallenfeldt, "Timeline of the American Revolution."

16. Eliot to "My Dear Sir," September 14, 1774, in Papers of Andrew Eliot, box 1, folder 2.

troops occupying the town within and colonial militiamen blockading it from without, in protest against British measures, Boston was effectively under siege, and it remained so for nearly a year until March 17, 1776. Eliot described his hometown as "now almost depopulated" by "the late cruel and oppressive measures gone into by the British Parliament" and his own situation as highly precarious. His sole intent was that "the friends of America, the friends of liberty, the friends of humanity, may unite their efforts for our deliverance."[17]

Eliot's description of Boston's trials and travails to his son John a few days later is not only dramatic, but highly revealing of his personal predicament:

> Poor Boston! May God sanctify our distresses, which are greater than you can conceive. Such a Sabbath of melancholy and darkness I never knew. Most of the meeting-houses shut up, the ministers gone, our congregation crowded with strangers. A town meeting in the forenoon agreed to give up their arms, in order to get leave to depart. A provincial army in Rochester, Dorchester and Cambridge. College dispersed, &c. This town a garrison; every face gathering paleness; all hurry and confusion; one going this way, and another that; others not knowing where to go. What to do with our poor maid I cannot tell. In short, after the melancholy exercises of the day, I am unable to write anything with propriety or connection.

Even so, Eliot refused to leave Boston when he had the opportunity, for fear that his "going would hurt religion," and he continued to express the hope, in another letter to John less than two months later, that present hostilities might "terminate in a lasting harmony between Great Britain and the colonies."[18]

Bound by Duty

In many ways, Eliot's correspondence with family members in 1775 reads like a catalogue of woes, as it documents his effective captivity in Boston and some of the horrors of pastoral ministry in time of war. "It is inconceivably

---

17. Eliot to Thomas Brand Hollis, April 25, 1775, in "Letters," 281–82.

18. Eliot to John Eliot, April 28, 1775, in "Letters," 182; Eliot to John Eliot, June 5, 1775, in "Letters," 286. On contemporary military operations in Boston, see, for example, Conway, *War of American Independence*, 73–79.

difficult," he told his son Samuel in August 1775, when the town remained under siege after the failed attempt to liberate it at the Battle of Bunker Hill. "I have hardly time to think of it, being perpetually in sick and dying rooms . . . I want supports myself, but am continually called to give them to others." Just weeks later, he wrote again about his embarrassment at the thought of leaving and then about the hardships of his personal circumstances. "I have no fuel, and very little provision," he informed Samuel. "To tarry here through winter will be dreadful." By October Eliot came to regret his decision to stay in Boston and he was very frank in his observation that "I have gone through the most trying scenes that I ever did through my whole life." But despite his sufferings, in a letter to Isaac Smith Jr. written just two days after Bunker Hill, Eliot could still express the doubts about the wisdom of the colonial struggle. "Can no way be found to accommodate these unhappy differences?" he asked Smith.

> If Great Britain should finally subjugate us, I fear for the College, I fear for the churches. There is great wrath against the President [of Harvard], and indeed against the Presbyterian ministers in general. If the Americans prevail . . . The God of heaven preserve us![19]

Eliot's diaries and letters for the period of the siege show the major changes in his life and work which resulted from the developing war. In 1774, he was able to continue his regular family life. Through a round of pulpit exchanges, he preached only four or five times out of the eight to ten morning and evening services a month at New North, and he gave fewer than fifteen evening lectures or midweek sermons all year. He also maintained attendance at Harvard meetings and did quite a lot of local travel, especially in the summer. But from April 1775 onwards, Eliot's circumstances changed dramatically. His family departed Boston, his children sailing for Salem on April 30, 1775, "Dear Mrs Eliot set[ting] out for Fairfield," Connecticut, on May 2, 1775, and his unmarried daughter "Betsey" leaving for Dartmouth on May 9, 1775. Eliot's workload meanwhile increased significantly. From April 16, 1775, until April 14, 1776, he preached morning and evening at all New North services. His extracurricular activities were curtailed, including attendance at Harvard meetings, following the dismissal of students on May 1, 1775, the resumption of classes in Concord on October 5, and the occupation of Harvard's Cambridge buildings by British troops. Thousands had fled Boston, but with only three Congregationalist

19. Eliot to Samuel Eliot, August 19, 1775; September 6, 1775; undated; October 20, 1775, in "Letters," 295, 298, 300; Eliot to Isaac Smith Jr., June 19, 1775, in "Letters," 289.

ministers remaining in town, Eliot's pastoral duties caring for the sick and dying must have grown exponentially.[20]

In the absence of others, it was left to Samuel Mather of Bennet Street Church and him alone to sustain Boston's Thursday Lecture, which they continued between them from April 27 to November 30, 1775, with just five weeks cancelled during that seven-month period. Eliot preached at thirteen lectures and at one Thursday Fast Day sermon in 1775 alone. He and Mather only ended the Thursday Lecture altogether on November 30, when an unusually emotional and poignant note in Eliot's diary indicated that they had reached a sad decision about one of Boston's longest-standing church traditions:

> Preached T[hursday] L[ecture]—*Laetus vere parvo*—The attendance of this lecture being exceed[ingly] small—& our work greatly increased in other Respects—Dr. Mather and I who since the departure of the other Brethren had preached it alternately tho't proper to lay it down for the present. I preached the last sermon from those words in Rev[elation] 2 *Remember how thou hast recd & heard & hold fast & repent*—an affecting occasion the laying down a Lecture which had subsisted more than 140 years—The small congregation was much moved at the consid[eratio]n.[21]

In a letter of April 25, 1775, Eliot commented on his personal change in circumstances with some feeling:

> Filled with the troops of Britain, and surrounded by a Provincial army, all communication with the country is cut off, and we wholly deprived of the necessaries of life, and this principal mart of America is become a poor garrison town . . . The last week I thought myself in comfortable circumstances, had a convenient dwelling, well furnished; a fine library, made so very much by the

---

20. *AED* 1774-1775; Corydon, "Harvard's Year of Exile." Harvard did not reoccupy its Cambridge buildings until June 11, 1776. Major repairs were subsequently needed, for which the Massachusetts House of Representatives awarded £417 in 1778. Ephraim Eliot summarized the pastoral situation in Boston as follows: "Dr. Samuel Mather and Dr. Eliot were the only Congregational ministers left in the town, excepting at the southern extremity, where Dr. Mather Byles officiated, who, being in the tory interest, was neglected by most of the inhabitants, although he performed service for some time in one of the central meeting-houses. The New North was opened every Lord's day during the blockade, and was decently filled with hearers. A small congregation assembled at Dr. Mather's, and another at the Second Baptist meeting-house, then under the care of the Rev. Isaac Skil[l]man" (*Historical Notices*, 26).

21. *AED* 1775. "*Laetus vere parvo*" can be translated "with truly little joy."

munificence of our late most worthy friend; attended by a large, affectionate, and generous congregation; happy in a consort, one of the best of women; and surrounded by a large number of desirable children. Now, I am by a cruel necessity turned out of my house; must leave my books and all I possess, perhaps to be destroyed by a licentious soldiery; my beloved congregation dispersed, my dear wife retreating to a distant part of the country, my children wandering, not knowing whither to go, perhaps left to perish for want; myself soon to leave this devoted capital, happy if I can find some obscure corner which will afford me a bare subsistence.

In his letters, Eliot several times noted his desire to leave Boston and return to family, but he felt duty-bound to remain. "Nothing keeps me from leaving the town but the obligation I am laid under not to leave so many people without any ordinances," Eliot wrote to his son John on May 4, 1775. Five days later, his thoughts were similar. "What Providence designs concerning me, I know not. At present, it seems to be my duty to tarry here, though much against my inclination, but I submit to the will of Heaven."[22]

Eliot repeated such sentiments many times in a remarkable series of some fifteen letters to his sons John or Samuel dating from almost the entirety of the Boston siege. "You left us shut up," he wrote to Isaac Smith Jr. on June 19,

and the people removing from the town as fast as they were permitted. I am told that more than nine thousand are removed. Many more were preparing to follow, but passes have been stopped for some time. So that thousands are detained who desire to go, among whom I am one. I tarried purely out of regard to the inhabitants who were left, that they might not be without ordinances and worship in the way which they choose. It is now perhaps too late to think of removing, as all communication is at present stopped.

Eliot sounded consistent themes once he realized that there was no escaping his predicament: lamenting it, expressing his desire to leave, but also insisting on his sense of duty that he must remain and vowing to entrust the whole situation into divine, providential care. "How long I may stay in the town I know not," he told his son John on May 12, "I am in a lonely and melancholy state, but the will of the Lord be done" "My situation is unpleasant, but know not how to leave it," he wrote a week later. " What God designs I know not. I desire to leave all with him." "When I shall see you

22. Eliot, Letters to John Eliot, April 25, May 4 and 9, 1775, in "Letters" 281–83.

God only knows," he informed John on June 5. "I thought to leave the town soon, but so many remain here that I fear my going would hurt religion. I stay much against my inclination, and yet dare not go. May I have direction from above."[23]

Among Eliot's particular challenges were the lack and poor quality of food, and sickness in the besieged town. "The difficulty of food is the least concern I have, though I very seldom meet with ·anything fresh," he wrote to friend and congregation member, Daniel Parker, in Salem, on July 31. "But to live amid scenes of blood and slaughter, and other trials I do not care to mention, is hard; and yet, on the whole, I cannot say I am sorry I tarried. I hope God has made me in some measure useful in my labors both in public and private. I visit the sick in all parts of the town, but alas! I do but little in comparison with what I ought to do for so good a Master. This is my greatest distress." "I remain still in town, much beyond my expectation and desire," he explained to John, on August 1,

> I intended at first to continue only a few weeks; but the numbers who still· remained, and the solicitations of many that I would not leave them, prevailed. I thought it my duty to give up my inclination to what I esteemed a call of Providence. I have been called to scenes of difficulty and distress, but have been carried through them. When I shall be able to go out, I know not. I wish it might be soon; and yet why should I wish for this, if I can be more useful here? I have not yet learned the great lesson of self-denial as I ought and as I desire. Amidst all the fears, dangers, and anxieties with which I am surrounded, I commit myself to my heavenly Father.

A special challenge was "a dysentery," he continued, "which carries off many of the inhabitants" and the resulting deaths "greatly increase . . . my labors." Just under three weeks later, he described the situation as "inconceivably difficult . . . The sickness doth not increase; but the aged die for want of strength of nature to grapple with it, the poor for want of necessary comforts."[24]

Eliot's keen conscience and painful self-awareness compounded his predicament. On the one hand, he informed his son Samuel on August 27, "I am tired of writing about coming out." On the other, he was "more tired

23. Eliot to Isaac Smith Jr., June 19, and to John Eliot, May 12, May 19, June 5, 1775, in "Letters," 287, 283, 285, 286.

24. Eliot to Daniel Parker, July 1, 1775, to John Eliot, August 1, 19, 1775, in "Letters" 292, 294, 295.

of being here, and yet . . . greatly afflicted at the thought of leaving such numbers." As a result, "I never was so embarrassed in my life. May God direct and support me!" "I have great difficulties to go through," he wrote John just a day later, "but I submit because I know God doeth all things well." On September 6, Eliot gave Samuel a particularly detailed account of his efforts to leave Boston, and of the British authorities' resistance:

> What I greatly feared is come upon me. I had prepared my things for a speedy departure from this devoted town, but heard yesterday that it was determined in a conclave of our newfangled councillors that I should not have a pass. However, I was determined to apply. This day I waited on the Town Major, who peremptorily refused to give me a pass. I endeavored to expostulate the matter with him, but could have no reason assigned but that he was to allow only women and children. I argued that men had been allowed to go. He said they had made particular interest, but that there were some who would not be allowed to go. When I found that all I could say availed nothing, I left him. I shall soon wait on the General, but fear it is already determined that I should not go. It is very hard treatment. I have no fuel, and very little provision. Some of those gentlemen who have inserted themselves in this affair insinuated that I made money by tarrying. So far from this, I do not receive one-half of what I received from my people, and, if I must tarry, should be willing to preach only for my wood, which would cost more than I am like to receive, if it is to be got at all. If I cannot go, I must submit; but what will be the event with me and a great number of others, God knows. To tarry here through winter will be dreadful; but I hope Providence will find out a way for our relief. I am at present in health, but great numbers die, chiefly children and old persons. I commit myself to my heavenly Father . . . I am at length allowed again to visit the prisoners. They were overjoyed to see me. Except poor Delaune, the butcher, they seemed all in a good way, most of them very hearty and well. There are but eleven living out of thirty.[25]

On September 18, he warned Samuel to be "cautious" when writing to him, "as your letters will be opened, unless you take particular care." By October 20, he saw "no prospect of my having liberty to leave the town," and was "preparing as well as I can to lay in for the winter." He was concerned that his wife would "be distressed at this long separation" and remained in a state of personal turmoil. "I have gone through the most trying scenes

25. Eliot to Samuel Eliot, August 27 and 28, 1775, in "Letters," 296–98.

that I ever did through my whole life," he told Samuel. "God knows what I am yet to endure." "I desire to commit myself to Providence," he told his son in a later undated letter. But Eliot could not help second-guessing his decision to remain in town. "Had I known what I was to endure, I should have been among the first that left the town, though I had lost all. Since that time, I have not been able to go. Had laid in provision for the winter; sold it again. Shall be miserably provided. If I had thought of tarrying, might have done well enough. But little is to be procured at this day." By January 18, 1776, his outlook was still uncertain, but more positive. "What awaits me God knows. If I leave Boston, I should be glad to come to Braintree, but should he obliged to make the best of my way to Fairfield." Above all, he missed his wife and family. "My heart aches for your dear mother, my faithful companion, whose absence is my daily distress." "My situation is full of cares and anxieties," he informed Samuel on February 16, 1776, "and yet I bless God I have many mercies. I hope you and yours are in health. Remember me to your dear wife, and kiss the pretty babes for me." Just over a month later, things were clearly moving in a positive direction and Eliot was thankful. In a letter to Jeremy Belknap of March 26, 1776, he told his friend: "The British troops are not all gone from Nantasket. Some departed today. I never expect to see them or any other British soldiers in Boston. God hath done great things for us whereof we are glad. God grant we may never forget his works."[26]

---

26. Eliot to Samuel Eliot, September 18 and October 20, 1775, undated, January 18, 1776; February 16, 1776, in "Letters," 299, 300, 301, 303, 305; Eliot to Jeremy Belknap, March 26, 1776, in Belknap et al., "Belknap Papers," 96.

10

Reluctant Revolutionary

Interested Observer to Active Partisan

ON APRIL 9, 1776, following the evacuation of British troops from Boston, Eliot was finally able to express his full relief in another letter to Isaac Smith, a wealthy Boston merchant still in London. "When I wrote you last I did not dare to write with any kind of freedom," he told Smith, "lest what I wrote should fall into the hands of our then Masters, which would have exposed me to their resentment, which I greatly feared, for their wrath was cruel." He was now able to take a more measured view of his decision to remain. "I cannot repent my having tarried in town"; he continued, "it seemed necessary to preserve the very face of religion. But nothing would induce me again to spend eleven months in a garrison town." Eliot was also quite clear about the restrictions under which he had been operating:

> We have been afraid to speak, to write, almost to think. We are now relieved—wonderfully delivered! The town hath been evacuated by the British troops so suddenly that they have left amazing stores behind them . . . Great numbers of the friends to Government, as they are called, are gone to Halifax, crowded in vessels which will scarce contain them. What will become of them there, God knows! The place is full already.

The net effect of the British withdrawal had meanwhile been to raise "the spirits of the colonists to the highest pitch. They look upon it as a compleat victory." That prompted Eliot himself to write with much more boldness, even to a transatlantic correspondent. "I dare now to say what I did not dare to say before this,—I have long thought it,—that G[reat] B[ritain] cannot subjugate the colonies. Independence, a year ago, could not have been publickly mentioned with impunity. Nothing else is now talked of, and I know not what can be done by G[reat] B[ritain] to prevent it."[1]

For Eliot personally, the lifting of British occupation enabled his life to resume more familiar patterns. On April 15, he was able to leave on a five-day trip to Fairfield, where he stayed with his wife and family until May 2, preaching at his son Andrew's church and at an important funeral. This journey became his first month away from New North since ordination, but the industrious Eliot typically undertook a full array of ministerial commitments. On his twelve-day return to Boston, he preached two Sundays at Wethersfield, Connecticut, and Worcester, Massachusetts, as well as at two lectures at Wallingford and Suffield, Connecticut [for James Dana and Ebenezer Gay], before he reported his return "with my dear wife & family, who had been absent more than a year" to Boston on May 14. Eliot's son Ephraim came back from Fairfield on June 1. Although he continued to minister more than usual at his own church on Sundays, as other ministers became available, pulpit exchanges became more regular over the course of 1776. Major milestones were meanwhile marked with the return of the Thursday Lecture, which Chauncy of First Church "opened" again on June 20, and an evening lecture, which Eliot preached on July 19, "the first since [th]e Town hath been open." For the first time since April 10, 1775, Eliot was also able to return in early April 1776 to Harvard Corporation and Overseers meetings now in Watertown, as well as Cambridge, as the college's leadership embarked on the process of returning students from Concord to the original campus on June 11, and working and fundraising to repair facilities damaged and pillaged by British troops.[2]

Eliot clearly hated war. After reporting "Battle at Charlestown—Town consumed" on June 17, 1775, he was moved to exclaim in Latin, "*oh Diem horrendum!*" ["Oh, dreadful day!"] followed by a quotation from Book 6 of Virgil's Aeneid, "*Bella, horrida bella*" ["wars, horrible wars!"]. Following the British evacuation, although his tone remained that of a very interested observer, rather than a passionate partisan, his support for some of the consequences of the independence movement was clearer in deed as well as word. "I attended last week a meeting of the Overseers and Corporation

---

1. Eliot to Isaac Smith, April 9, 1776; Annotated Almanacs 1776.
2. Eliot, Andrew Eliot Diaries, 1776; Ireland, "Harvard's Year of Exile."

[of Harvard College] at Watertown, for the first time since our enlargement," he told Smith in his April 9 letter. "We voted Gen[eral] Washington a degree of LLD. He is a fine Gentleman, and hath charmed everybody since he hath had the command." By this time, Eliot could also speak from personal experience about the Patriot commander-in-chief. He had dined with the Continental Army's Quartermaster General and Washington's former *aide-de-camp*, Colonel Thomas Mifflin, on March 23. Then, just ten days following the British evacuation of Boston, he reported in his 1776 diary, "Cambridge dined with Gen[e]r[al] Washington" on March 27 and "Preached before Gen[e]r[al] Washington" the next day. Even so, he informed Smith that he remained anxious about the appointment of "a committee of the Overseers . . . at the motion of the General Court, to examine the political principles of those who govern the College" and hoped "no evil w[ould] come to several worthy men there." Then commenting on a speech urging "an intire disconnection with G[reat] B[ritain]," Eliot described this position somewhat dispassionately as "the fashionable doctrine," but was even more definitive in his observation that "I do not see that G[reat] B[ritain] can prevent it. When she rejected the last petition of the Congress it was all over with her."[3]

Eliot made a similar prediction in a letter to Thomas Brand Hollis just a few weeks later:

> Great Britain may ruin the Colonies, but she will never subjugate them. They will hold out to the last gasp. They make it a common cause, and they will continue to do so. In this confusion, the College is broken up: nothing is talked of but war. Where these scenes will end, God only knows; but, if I may venture to predict, they will terminate in a total separation of the Colonies from the parent country.

Eliot's later extant letters from the revolutionary period reflect similar views, but in correspondence with local friends and family, his support for the cause of independence emerges more strongly.[4]

In August 1776, he drafted a letter to John Hancock, then President of the Continental Congress, in response to a request that he had received through a third party to send "a copy of the sermon [he] preached at the Funeral of [Hancock's] late excellent Relative," his aunt Lydia, who been

---

3. Eliot to Isaac Smith, April 9, 1776; Andrew Eliot Diaries, 1776; Virgil, *Aeneid*, 6:86, in *Opera*, 229.

4. Eliot to Thomas Brand Hollis, April 26, 1776, in "Letters," 282.

laid to rest on April 30, 1776, in Fairfield. Lydia Henchman Hancock and her husband Thomas, who had died twelve years earlier, had been very important figures in Hancock's life. Soon after the death of his father and namesake, who had been minister of Braintree Congregationalist Church, his childless aunt and uncle had effectively become his adoptive parents in 1745. As a result, Hancock had been able to enjoy the privileged upbringing and education that his wealthy uncle provided, eventually becoming his chief heir and head of his prospering merchant business, Thomas Hancock and Company. Despite Hancock's wealth and rank, Eliot's tone was very pastoral. He praised Lydia Henchman as universally "beloved and admired," a compassionate woman with such "goodness of heart [tha]t every one's sufferings were her own," and a godly person "who had thro' her whole life been preparing for the last solemn scene." He also saw her "sudden departure" as providential. In his sermon, Eliot wrote, he had "endeavored to draw a just Character of the deceased" and "no one," he believed, "tho't [he] exceeded." He excused himself from publishing the work, since he had had so little time to prepare "at so great a distance from those papers which [he] should have chose on such occasion" in Boston. Instead, he offered to send a copy, although he was "very certain it would fall short of your expectation both for matter or manner, as it does her real merit."[5]

Eliot was most pastoral in inviting Hancock to heed God's call "by this affecting stroke, amidst the great & very important public cares you are engaged in, to consider the instability of earthly comforts, & to contemplate on mortality." He "hope[d] & believe[d]" that the Continental Congress leader had "been humbled to those serious reflections which are proper on [th]e occasion" and he prayed that he might "feel the power & enjoy the comforts of Religion." Eliot then complimented Hancock on his recent marriage, before concluding with strong, though not uncritical words of support for the patriot cause and its leaders:

> I rejoice with you on [th]e happy views these Colonies have with respect to our public affairs & for which we are greatly indebted to [th]e wisdom of ... [the] Cont[inen]t[a]l board. I wish there was more of a religious sense of his goodness at [th]e board at w[hi]ch you preside. God hath done great things for us ... Please to present my particular regards to your hon[ora]ble Colleagues [and fellow

---

5. Eliot to John Hancock, August 1776, in Andrew Eliot Letters; "Hancock, John," in *ANB*. An unfinished draft of Eliot's sermon remains in the form of Sermon on the Death, Eliot Family Papers, box 4.

patriot leaders] Mr Sam[u]el & Mr John Adams. I have often seen the Lady of [th]e latter & heartily congratulate him.⁶

A couple of months later, on October 5, 1777, Eliot wrote from Boston to his son John in Fairfield, combining family with general news and comment, primarily about military issues. "The Northern Army is numerous," he told John, "and we expect every hour to hear of an action. God is the Sovereign arbiter of events. Things look very promising in that Quarter. But every confederate mind must feel great anxiety at this important Crisis." Eliot reported dealings with a group of would-be volunteers to join colonial forces to the north, but he did not hesitate to align himself with the "confederate" cause. Writing to Alexander Hill of Newbury in November 1777, he later expressed his wish that the report that "Gen[era]l Howe and his army are ... taken Prisoners" should prove correct, because "it would go a great way towards settling this unhappy dispute." He described "the affair of Gen[era]l Burgoyne"—clearly the British general's defeat on October 17, 1777, when he was forced to surrender his entire army, numbering 5,800—as "wonderful" and as giving "a mighty turn to our military reputation." Eliot also noted the achievement of the New England commander, General John Stark, in leading "the way to this great Event which will give us an éclat thro' all Europe" and offered brief commentary on other developments. His overall perspective remained providential. "We can see but a little way into the designs of Providence," he wrote, but he remained confident that "if we have chosen God for our portion all will end with respect to us."⁷

A series of letters from Eliot's namesake son Andrew dating from the last eighteen months of his life between January 29, 1777, and August 21, 1778, just three weeks before his death, continued to reveal his engagement and interest in the war for independence, as well as the close family relations which Eliot had long enjoyed with his children. Eliot had personally had a hand in settling his son as pastor in Fairfield, Connecticut in 1774, and he offered ongoing pastoral and paternal support. In addition to providing an extended running commentary on wartime news, Andrew Jr. wrote of the demands of his ministry and his needs and requests from Boston. In a postscript to his letter to his father of February 2, 1777, for example, Andrew Jr. described the details of the kind of busy week in ministry, with which Eliot himself would have been personally familiar:

6. Eliot to John Hancock, August 1776, in Andrew Eliot Letters.

7. Eliot to John Eliot, October 5, 1777, in Fawcett, *Missing Links*, 264–65; Eliot to Alexander Hill, November 1777, in Andrew Eliot Letters.

> Sabbath Evening. I visited sick after service. Truly I have had a busy week. Preached all day last Sabbath. Visited the sick on Tuesday by day and in the Night. Preached all day on Wednesday being fast. Thursday attended a funeral. Friday went four miles & preached a Lecture in a private house. Saturday the sick & prisoners from York to visit & a funeral to attend. Today preached a.m. & p.m. and administered sacrament. What with external services and preparing therefor I am tired & can write but this tonight. Sweet Lassitude! I would not be engaged in any other business for the World.

But he combined this kind of report with updates on events and feelings in town as well as family news.[8]

On March 14, 1777, Andrew Jr. shared news about British military failures, but he clearly shared his father's providential perspective on events. "From all accounts compared," he wrote, "I can't but think that providence has appeared in our Behalf. The design of the enemy was to have landed . . . Providentially the storm hindered them from landing that night and prevented dreadful consequences." Andrew Jr. offered similar updates in twenty letters sent to his father between March and December 1777 and a further twenty-one between January and August 1778. Two excerpts from Andrew Jr.'s final letter to his father on August 21, 1778, amply display the consistent and contrasting themes of their correspondence. On the one hand, he offered this military briefing:

> We are exceeding anxious about Rhode Island. The light infantry of Washington's Army are formed into a Brigade, and are advanced near King's Bridge. A scouting party were caught by a fog and fell into the Enemies hands. Boats are collecting at Norwalk for some purpose or other. Gen. Tryon is on his return from the East End of Long Island with 1,000 head of cattle and provisions in proportion. A party has gone over from Norwalk . . . We see but few of the Enemies ships and are very quiet and easy. The good women of Greens farms are collecting a present of the best of their Butter for Gen. Washington.

On the other, he concluded with this intimate family picture:

> Thus much for public news. I come to that of a domestic kind. Polly has a daughter born twenty minutes after five o'clock on Sabbath morning which weighed nine pounds and two ounces.

8. Andrew Eliot Jr. to Eliot, February 2, 1777, postscript to letter of January 29, 1777, in Fawcett, *Missing Links*, 7–9, esp. 8.

The child was baptised the same day. Little poll and Betsey are in fine health. Your new Granddaughter Eunice Burr Eliot put in for her share in the affections of her Grandpa and Grandma. Polly & Peggy join in dutiful and loving regards and I am your dutiful son. Andrew Eliot.[9]

All in all, there is thus clear evidence that, especially once hostilities had been engaged, Eliot was a very interested and quite committed supporter of the cause of independence. But he remained cautious and said or did nothing to make his pastoral ministry in a divided Boston or his leadership at Harvard or elsewhere more challenging than it needed to be. As always, while Eliot was careful and moderate in his stance, he did not refuse to take any at all. At the same time, he remained deeply conflicted, as did many, by past allegiances to Britain and present commitments to the best of the values for which he thought it stood. In that sense, however far he travelled, he was perhaps always going to be a somewhat reluctant revolutionary, especially since he died in 1778 well before full American independence had been achieved.[10]

---

9. Andrew Eliot Jr. to Eliot, January 29, 1777; August 21, 1778, in Fawcett, *Missing Links*, 11, 80–81. Andrew Jr.'s other letters to his father are in *Missing Links*, 9–81, dated as follows: 1777—March 14, March 21, May 14, June 23, June 26, July 4, July 11, July 18, July 25, August 1, August 8, August 22, August 29, October 24, October 30, November ??, November 13, November 21, December 4, December 11; 1778—January 2, January 18, January 16, January 22, February 18, February 24, March 7, April 3, April 17, April 29, May 21, May 29, June 11, June 26, July 10, July 10, July 21, July 31, August 7, August 14, and August 21. *Missing Links*, 237–44, 252–57, contains two letter, dated January 12, 1774, and April 7, 1774, from James Dana to his friend Eliot, which refer to Andrew Jr.'s appointment at Fairfield and Dana's involvement in and approval of it. *Missing Links*, 243–45, 258–61, 249–51, also includes letters of April 2, 1774, April 10, and September 26, 1774 from Ebenezer Silliman to Eliot, praising his son.

10. Bernadine Fawcett brings to light some helpful source materials in her book, *Missing Links*. But her suggestion that Eliot and his son were part of the revolutionary Culper Spy Ring, which passed information from New York and elsewhere via Fairfield to George Washington's headquarters in New Jersey, is highly conjectural and is based on little evidence beyond the understandable concern with military matters which Andrew Eliot Jr. showed in his correspondence with his father and the personal connections which were predictable for men in their positions. See Rose, *Washington's Spies*, for a strong historical account of the Culper Spy Ring.

Reluctant Revolutionary

Eliot's political positions were puzzling even for his contemporaries. Following his death in 1778, former Governor Thomas Hutchinson noted some of the conflicting views and impressions in his diary for November 18:

> Dr Eliot was long my friend. One of my last letters from Dr Pemberton, said his sentiments were the same they used to be [presumably loyalist]. After [General] Howe left the town, he wrote two letters to England which were intercepted, and carried to Halifax, and copies given. They were very strong in favour of American proceedings [i.e., pro-independence]. Some thought he expected they would be intercepted, and that he desired to have it known at Boston that he publickly owned the cause. He said to my son at Boston he was afraid, or had reason to think his continuing in Boston [during the siege] had made him obnoxious to the people without the town.

At the same time, while Hutchinson thought that "great allowance must be made for the difficulty of his circumstances," no "man is without infirmity," and "his might be a disposition to temporize, always, I trust, having satisfied himself he was to be justified:—but this must be left. Some of the Americans speak lightly upon the news of his death. I heard the news with grief, and wished to see him again in this world. Dr Pemberton and he, for many years, were the best neighbours I had."[11]

As a committed loyalist, Hutchinson's own position had become untenable after General Thomas Gage replaced him as Governor on May 17, 1774, and he was effectively forced into long-term exile back in Britain. But his friendship with Eliot had been strong, whatever their political differences. Eliot also shared his historical interests. Following an attack on Hutchinson's house in August 1765, after a mob scattered the latter's manuscripts through the streets of Boston, Eliot posted a notice asking that they, and any of the rest of his stolen goods, be returned to him personally. More generally, as Shipton noted, the New North pastor "preserved and copied documents for his friend . . . who used them in his History." In his *Biographical Dictionary* of 1809, Eliot's son noted that "several trunks of

---

11. Shipton, *New England Life*, 411; Hutchinson, *Diary and Letters*, 2:223–24.

mss. among them the second volume of the history of Massachusetts, were preserved by his care and attention."[12]

The strength of Eliot's relationship with Hutchinson undoubtedly caused him problems with those who espoused a more aggressive stance towards Britain. A big part of his labeling as "Andrew Sly" was clearly linked to the populist observation that he "oft draws nigh to Tommy Skin and Bones." Any such association was enough to make Eliot unpopular with those like John Adams who once contemptuously observed that Eliot "was Hutchinson's parish priest, and his devoted idolater."[13]

In light of Eliot's stated political views and deeply personal observations over time, as well as their inherent ambiguities, Bailyn's dismissal of his "reluctance to declare for [American] independence" as mainly "temperamental" would seem misguided. The Harvard historian seemed closer to the mark in his later observation that Eliot was "deeply sympathetic with the American cause, yet equally convinced that . . . independence would be a catastrophe for America as well as for England." At the same time, despite his earlier defences of the subject's right of civil resistance and even rebellion against unjust rule, Eliot clearly remained long attached to an overarching sense of English national identity which included ideals of personal and political liberty that inspired him throughout his public life. It was only once open hostilities directly threatened American freedoms that he decisively came to espouse the American cause against the British.[14]

When faced with the challenges arising from growing hostilities with Britain from the mid-1760s onwards, Eliot found himself in a quandary. On the one hand, he proudly adhered to libertarian ideals and to a vigorous sense of national identity that he shared with his English correspondents. His continuing respect for British authority also led him to resist calls for American independence. On the other hand, Eliot was highly critical of what he saw as British abuses of power. and his political philosophy provided for legitimate rebellion in similar circumstances. In a sense, therefore, as Bailyn has perceptively suggested, Eliot's political wavering between the causes of independence and loyalism long mirrored his theological and philosophical uncertainties over the issue of free will and divine necessity. In the final analysis, he was unhappy yielding submission to British

---

12. John Eliot, *Biographical Dictionary*, 191; Hutchinson, *History of the Colony/Province*, 2.

13. Stiles, *Literary Diary*, 1:491; Adams, *Works*, 10:243.

14. Bailyn, "Religion and Revolution," 88, 107.

sovereignty, but could only make a decisive break from it once war was well in progress and he could attribute the sequence of events to God. He also continued to prioritize his pastoral calling to such an extent that he remained in Boston under siege, despite the personal sacrifice involved, and he maintained good relations with all sides as long as he could.[15]

---

15. Bailyn, "Religion and Revolution," 105.

11

Finishing the Course

Persistent Principles

ON OCTOBER 5, 1778, Eliot's fourth son, John (1754–1813), who became his successor at New North just over a year later, replied to a letter from their family friend, Dover minister Jeremy Belknap, at one of the most difficult points in his life. Less than a month earlier, on September 13, John's father, Andrew, had died after a relatively short illness. He had done a full day of preaching at New Brick and New North churches as recently as August 23, but was laid up the following two Sundays. When Belknap's "late epistle" arrived, John was "indulging" his "grief," he informed Belknap, "for the loss of my dear and venerable father, whose death you so earnestly wished might not be near, but who was called to associate with the Father of Spirits a few days before." Yet John's sense of loss was also mixed with other emotions. "Tho' the recollection of the last scene of his life fills me with the most melancholy ideas, and every fibre of my bosom is in agitation," he wrote, "yet I must say that there is a pleasure mingled with my affliction, and I never oppose its coming fresh upon my mind." So, what explained this challenging "mingling"? John derived satisfaction, despite his bereavement, from one of the most traditional sources of Christian consolation following the loss of a loved one. Eliot's "death was fully adequate," his grieving son reported, "to the expectations which could be formed by the most partial of his friends who beheld his deportment and those amiable virtues which were ever exhibited in his character." John could, therefore, recall that "he died, as he lived, a Christian. To this his ambition led him, to this height he arrived, and from this height he took his flight to the regions of bliss and glory, as if ardently desiring to receive his reward."[1]

Following a transitional year in 1776, when his life had gradually returned to a degree of normality, albeit in time of war, after the end of British occupation in March, 1777 and 1778 had been typically busy for Eliot. In 1777, he spent less than half his full Sundays [just twenty-two], ministering both morning and afternoon at New North. In addition to regular exchange arrangements with John Lathrop of Old North and Samuel Cooper of Brattle Street Church, he did full exchange Sundays with ministers in Concord, Dedham, and Milton. On Sundays, when he exchanged for half a day elsewhere, he generally ministered morning or afternoon at New North, but such was his range of collegial relationships that he was able to invite nearly twenty others to preach at his church over the course of a year. His congregation thus enjoyed a rich variety of speakers, as well as the stability of a permanent minister who had been there for thirty-five years. Eliot traveled for short mid-week trips a little more than previously in 1777, especially in the warmer months. But his workload was boosted by attendance at more than fifteen Harvard Corporation or Overseers' meetings and preaching at six evening lectures, five Thursday Lectures and ministering at four fast or Thanksgiving days. There are few indications in Eliot's diary of the ongoing conflict with Britain, but he did go out of his way to note how on July 4, 1777, William Gordon, an English-born minister now settled in Jamaica Plain with whom Eliot recorded spending some time during his later years, "preached a Sermon in commemoration of the declaration of Independence."[2]

During the last eight months of Eliot's life, as he approached a sixtieth birthday which he never lived to celebrate, his activities remained undiminished. He ministered at New North both morning and afternoon for thirteen full Sundays of the thirty-four before the advent of his final illness. He also noted his ministry elsewhere, generally through exchange arrangements, on every other Sunday but three. Eliot preached at five Thursday Lectures and one Friday evening lecture in 1778, he continued to attend Harvard meetings, and he participated fully in other ministerial events.

1. John Eliot to Jeremy Belknap, October 5, 1778, in Belknap et al., "Belknap Papers," *CMHS* 6.4 130–34, esp. 130; Eliot, Andrew Eliot Diaries, 1778. According to *NNR* 1:279, John Eliot was ordained as his father's successor at New North on November 3, 1779. On John Eliot, see *SHG* 18:55–68.

2. Eliot, Andrew Eliot Annotated Almanacs, 1776.

On May 28, Eliot moderated a meeting of the Massachusetts Convention of Ministers and, having previously served this body as treasurer, he was elected to a committee "to audit the Treasurers Accompts [sic] and make Report to the next Convention." There is little evidence in his records of any physical decline before August 30. His "particular friend," Samuel Dexter (1726–1810), a merchant who served in high Massachusetts political office at different points between 1764 and 1785, wrote in a brief biographical account of Eliot for his son John's 1809 *Biographical Dictionary,* that while Eliot generally enjoyed "a good degree of health," he was "subject to bodily complaints" and "in the summer of 1778, he complained more than usual." On August 14, he was still so concerned about Harvard that he wrote to President Samuel Langdon reporting rumors of deism at the college. The last diary entry in Eliot's own hand records a visit to Gordon on August 25, after which Caleb Gannett is mentioned as the preacher on August 30 and September 6. There was no afternoon service at New North on the last Sunday in August, when Eliot took seriously ill.[3]

John Eliot's account of his father's final illness and closing days is arguably, and understandably, somewhat hagiographical. He informed Belknap that Eliot had such an uncanny sense of his own physical condition following what seems to have been some form of stroke that "he deliberated against a recovery" and predicted more than a week before he died that he would never leave his sickbed. When his friend Samuel Stillman visited him two days before his death, Eliot reportedly told the minister of Boston's First Baptist Church that "he was then rejoicing in the sight of God's countenance." "I have finished my course with joy," he later apprized his doctors, citing from 2 Timothy 4:7, when they warned that they could do nothing further, and on Saturday, September 12, he predicted to John that "he should begin an everlasting Sabbath the next morning." Just before he breathed his last, Eliot was said to have "cried out, 'Come, Lord Jesus, come quickly, lest I fail of that faith and patience by which I expect to inherit the promises.'" Then he had some special words for John: "It is a question with me whether I o[ug]t to wish to die, or to wait quietly till it is the will of my Father to call me hence. His will be done." Such Christlike fortitude in adversity clearly made a profound impression on Eliot's son, especially on "the

---

3. Eliot, Andrew Eliot Diaries, 1778, and Eliot to Langdon, August 14, 1778; MCCM, "Records 1749–1789," 133; John Eliot, *Biographical Dictionary,* 189–93, esp. 192, 193n. See MCCM, "Records 1749–1789," for Eliot's service with the Massachusetts Convention. See esp. 125, recording a vote of thanks to him on May 29, 1776, for his "faithful service as Treasurer."

most gloomy day I ever knew." But what may have been most striking—also to others to whom Eliot sought to communicate them—were the messages that he delivered first to Stillman and then through John to Peter Thacher of Malden, who was the preacher at New North on the day of his death. "The doctrines," he assured the Baptist pastor, "which I have preached to others are now my consolation. With much imperfection I have preached Jesus Christ and Him crucified; and in His name I now triumph over death." He accordingly asked John to request Thacher "to acquaint the people," which the minister did, "that in his dying moments he was enjoying the comfort of that religion and those principles which he had ever preached to them." It was finally at six thirty a.m. on Sunday, September 13, according to the New North records, that "departed this Life the Reverend Andrew Eliot DD pastor of this Church in the 60th year of his Age."[4]

The grieving John saw Eliot's faith as an "illustration . . . of the truth, the excellency, & the unspeakable advantages of our holy religion." Even allowing for filial embellishment, his account of Eliot's theological affirmations around the time of his death is also consistent with the record of his life. However much he had been influenced by the intellectual currents of his age, Eliot was a faithful steward of the moderate Calvinist theological heritage which he had inherited and consistently sought to share with others over the course of thirty-six years of public ministry in Boston. Notwithstanding the undoubted influence of radical Whig ideas and discourse, especially as tensions with Britain escalated from the mid-1760s onwards, Eliot's political thought also remained consistently grounded in the antiestablishmentarian, libertarian Protestant traditions of his New England heritage.[5]

Eliot was loyal to his friends, reliable in his commitments and remarkably industrious. He pursued his pastoral vocation with unwavering dedication, enduring the hardships of military occupation, as well as resisting repeated invitations to the highest academic office. He was highly regarded as a pastor of one of the largest congregations in Boston and proved able to meet the many demands of his ministry, even though he combined it with extensive commitments to service at Harvard, with various missionary societies, and elsewhere. He introduced significant change at New North but did so incrementally over more than three decades at the church. He

---

4. Eliot to Belknap, October 5, 1778, in Belknap et al., "Belknap Papers," *CMHS* 6.4 130–34, esp. 130–31; *NNR* 1:273.

5. Belknap et al., "Belknap Papers," 132.

enjoyed fruitful and cordial relationships with other Boston ministers, as well as with his colleague Webb during the earliest years of his pastorate.

Despite his prominent position in Boston society, Eliot was not one to draw attention to himself or to his own achievements and he was quite happy for others, like Chauncy, to take the lead when he thought them better qualified. He had a remarkable ability to support ministries, like that of Whitefield, of which he did not fully approve, and to engage with theologians, like Chauncy or Mayhew, whose ideas he did not fully share. Eliot avoided conflict wherever possible, preferring to focus on what he regarded as gospel essentials. He was also an inherently cautious and irenic man, who showed a remarkable attention to detail and nuance in his personal, as well as professional life.

Such characteristics were clearly reflected in his moderate positions on contentious issues, both theological and political, but he was not afraid to speak out, whenever he found it necessary. They also help explain why Eliot has so often been misunderstood and why this important figure has not received the attention that he clearly deserves. Eliot's late shift in favor of independence during the very last years of his life is an especially noteworthy omission from previous scholarship. It may also reflect how a tendency to focus on early and outspoken patriots or entrenched loyalists may have led to a distorted understanding of how American independence actually came to be. For Eliot, espousing freedom from colonial rule was arguably as much a pragmatic reaction to the realities of the War for Independence, as a reflection of previously held ideals of liberty. In that, he may have been more representative of many of his contemporaries than his elevated social background, advanced education, and pastoral vocation would lead one to expect.[6]

---

6. For a helpful and wide-ranging discussion of recent scholarship of the American Revolution, see Burnard, *Writing Early America*, 173–93.

Postscript
Eliot's Legacy

> In my beginning is my end. In succession
> Houses rise and fall, crumble, are extended,
> Are removed, destroyed, restored . . .
> Home is where one starts from. As we grow older
> The world becomes stranger, the pattern more complicated
> Of dead and living.
>
> T. S. Eliot, *Four Quartets*

WHEN T. S. ELIOT wrote these timeless words in the second of his *Four Quartets*, first published in 1944, its title was undoubtedly intended to refer to the English ancestral home of his branch of the American Eliots in East Coker, Somerset. That was where Andrew Eliot's great-grandfather and namesake had been born in 1627 before emigrating to Beverly, Massachusetts in 1670. The same man was sixth great-grandfather to the famous poet, who was directly descended from the subject of this biographical study, his third great-grandfather. Moreover, Christian ministry and literature have not been the only fields in which the Eliots have excelled.[1]

Eliot's pastoral success and financial acumen enabled him to educate three of his sons at Harvard, two of whom went on to strong careers in ministry and one as a pioneering pharmacist. His other two sons both became merchants and his married daughters all had partners of social standing in eighteenth-century Boston. Over time, the Eliots clearly established themselves among those elite families later defined by author and physician Oliver Wendell Holmes (1809–1894) as members of "the Brahmin Caste" or class of New England, with prominent figures in many areas, including

---

1. T. S. Eliot, "East Coker," 1:1–3; 5:190–92, in *Four Quartets*.

banking, politics, academia, and the arts. Among the most famous names in later generations were, for example, Charles William Eliot (1834–1926), President of Harvard for forty years, who was a direct descendant of Eliot's brother, Samuel. Those descended from Eliot himself include William Greenleaf Eliot (1811–1887), Unitarian minister and co-founder and third Chancellor of Washington University, St. Louis, Samuel Eliot Morison (1887–1976), Harvard historian and navy rear admiral, and Martha May Eliot (1891–1978), prominent pediatrician and public health official.[2]

But if Eliot's strong family legacy continues to this day, the influence of his church was much shorter lived. During his final years, he had introduced his sons Andrew and John to the New North pulpit. Between June 1776 and Eliot's death in September 1778, they ministered on ten Sundays altogether, and since Andrew became minister of Fairfield, Connecticut, in 1774 and John was still seeking a permanent pulpit, it is likely that the latter was in his father's church more often. Following Eliot's death, when John or Andrew ministered on October 4, 1778, the salary was specifically designated as a gift to his widow. John quite quickly succeeded his father. Exactly eight months after Eliot's passing, at a New North church meeting on May 13, 1779, he was chosen as one of four candidates to preach "on probation" for four Sundays. By August 23, he was elected to serve as pastor by written vote. On November 3, he subsequently began an ordained ministry that was to last until his own death twenty-four years later.[3]

John's brother Ephraim described his core convictions as follows:

> As a theologian, Dr. John Eliot took the Bible as his guide, in the light it was presented to his own mind. Good men he loved and associated with, although they differed from him in sentiment, and excluded none from his pulpit on that account . . . He was indeed a liberal Christian in the true sense of the word . . . He was a Trinitarian.

---

2. Wendell Holmes, *Elsie Venner*, 1–6. On the Eliot family, see chapter 4 above; Walter Eliot, *Sketch of the Eliot Family*; William Eliot, *Genealogy of the Eliot Family*. On individual family members, a good place to start is with relevant articles in the *ANB*.

3. Eliot, Andrew Eliot Diaries Copies, 1777 and *Annotated Almanacs*, 1776, 1778; *NNR* 174–79. On four of the Sundays, when Eliot listed one of his sons as preaching, he did not identify Andrew or John. According to Ephraim Eliot, the church went to "considerable expense in putting the female part of the doctor's large family, and the youngest son, who was a lad, into very handsome mourning [dress]. But this was done by a vote of the society at large, who were always devoted to the family. They also continued his salary to the widow (deducting the expense of supplying the pulpit) for a considerable time" (*Historical Notices*, 32).

In his brief biography of Eliot for *Sibley's Harvard Graduates*, Conrad E. Wright portrayed a more complex, even calculating figure, who "felt at ease with the liberals' rational doctrines," although "his theological journey probably resulted as much from convenience as from conviction." In support of this view, Wright cited, among other things, letters written in 1783 and 1804 from John to his good friend and mentor Jeremy Belknap, including the memorable comment that "I never drop a word about religion" in certain company for fear of offending others. Wright's conclusion? "So successful was he in masking his beliefs that after his death his closest acquaintances reached conflicting judgments about his theology." Yet there is also clear evidence of John's more liberal views in his active participation in a circle of friends surrounding First Church minister Charles Chauncy, for example, as the latter worked on a series of manuscripts promoting the universal salvation of humanity. John's political maneuvering surrounding the 1805 appointment of liberal Unitarian, Henry Ware, as Hollis Professor of Divinity at Harvard raises further questions about his Trinitarianism.[4]

Judging from Ephraim's predictably favorable account of his father's and brother's ministries, both were popular leaders, who enjoyed strong and harmonious relations with the people whom they served, not least because they lived in the same neighborhood and often frequented socially with those who attended New North. Yet writing in 1822, Ephraim was also well aware of the pressures under which New North came, especially during his brother's pastorate. Attendance suffered from the growth of other neighboring congregations and from the move of the popular minister Peter Thacher from Malden to nearby Brattle Street church in the same year. However, the opening of a new building for New North on May 2, 1804, which could seat one thousand people and was designed by prominent architect, Charles Bullfinch, in "the Early Republic style" evidently helped the seats to be "soon filled again," as Ephraim noted, and the church to remain "a very large congregation until his death."[5]

---

4. Ephraim Eliot, *Historical Notices*, 42–43; Wells and Fanning, *New North Church*, 25; Wright in *SHG* 18:55–68, esp. 59, citing John Eliot to Jeremy Belknap, April 2, 1782, and October 22, 1785, in *CMHS*, 6:4:227, 264, esp. the latter. See further on John Eliot, McKean, "Memoir"; Mace, "Eliot, John (1754–1813)," Harvard Square Library. He published only six sermons. On John Eliot and Chauncy's universalism, see Oakes, *Conservative Revolutionaries*, 72–74. On Hollis's appointment, see *SHG* 18:65–66; Harvard Square Library, "Ware, Henry, Sr. (1764–1845)."

5. Ephraim Eliot, *Historical Notices*, 41–42.

Given what Ephraim called "the local situation of the meetinghouse," a bigger threat to New North's continued strength was the sheer force of shifting demographics. As Alexander Keim has argued in a helpful summary,

> After the American Revolution, intentional destruction by British troops, along with neglect stemming from a massive exodus of Bostonians to the countryside for the duration of the war, resulted in a post-war North End typified by high residential and commercial rents, broken-down wharves, and degraded and obsolescent infrastructure. Moreover, over 1,000 residents of the North End remained loyal to the British and left Boston, never to return, including some of the neighborhood's wealthiest and most influential families. Even as Boston itself was fated to return to its former glory and prestige, the North End never would.[6]

Over time, New North lost many of its likely attenders. Writing in 1822, Ephraim Eliot expressed the challenge in rather quaint terms, suggesting that "the young gentlemen, who have married wives in other parts of the town, have found it difficult to persuade them to become so ungenteel as to attend worship at the north end." The reality was that wealthier residents steadily relocated to more fashionable neighborhoods in the West End, South End, and Beacon Hill. Ministers themselves also moved, leaving only one from the six large congregations in the area still resident there.

As the population of Boston increased dramatically, from 16,000 in 1780 to 136,881 in 1850, the changing North End became "increasingly distinct—economically, culturally, and socially—from the rest of the city," according to Keim, especially in the second quarter of the nineteenth century. Moreover, "at the same time that the neighborhood became more and more working class, migration into Boston increased, raising the demand for inexpensive housing." As a result, between 1800 and 1850, the North End became "Boston's first primarily working-class neighborhood."[7]

---

6. Keim, "Boston Inside Out," 114; Ephraim Eliot, *Historical Notices*, 42.

7. Kennedy, "Population Trends"; Keim, "Boston Inside Out," 114. On population trends, see Bushee, "Growth of the Population," 245–46: "The north end of the town, divided from the rest by Mill Creek (now Blackstone Street) was the most populous district. At the first enumeration of the population in 1722, this small district contained 4,549 persons, which was not quite one-half of the total population. In 1789 it was estimated to contain 5,848 inhabitants, about one-third of the whole. It now [1899] contains between eighteen and twenty thousand."

After the arrival of Francis Parkman (1788–1852), who served the church from 1818 to 1852, New North also underwent significant theological change, adopting a Unitarian form of worship and church covenant by 1827. With the latter, a congregation which had embraced a Trinitarian and much more traditional statement of faith under the Eliots thus shifted to a significantly vaguer set of convictions. The new covenant simply required members to "give up yourself . . . to the true God in Jesus Christ, promising to walk with God, and with this church of his, in all his holy ordinances, and to yield obedience to every truth of his, which has been, or shall be made known to you, as your duty, the Lord assisting you by His spirit and grace." Parkman was one of the most prominent Unitarian leaders of his age, becoming President of the Convention of Unitarian Ministers just before he died and founding a Professorship of Pulpit Eloquence and Pastoral Care at Harvard in 1829. Charles Wells and Steven Fanning have also suggested that at New North itself, he "was remembered not for being a great churchman and outstanding theologian, but for being a captivating preacher, a caring pastor and congenial person." Notwithstanding his efforts, New North steadily declined and during their combined tenure between 1749 and 1759, neither Joshua Young (1823–1904) nor Arthur Buckminster Fuller (1822–1862), who succeeded Parkman, saw any significant reversal of this trend.[8]

The major influx into the North End of Irish Roman Catholics fleeing the potato famine in the late 1840s meanwhile compounded the local demographic challenges. When Fuller began his ministry in 1853, he discovered only twenty-six church members still living in Boston, of whom twelve lived and worshiped in other parts of the town. Following his departure, New North settled no pastor at all, and in April 1863, the building was sold to the Catholic Archdiocese of Boston, becoming home to St. Stephen's Church, which still worships there. New North then merged with Bullfinch St. Congregationalist Church in the same year, accepting William Alger as pastor until he left in 1768 and the congregation held its final meeting on April 10, 1870.[9]

Such an outcome less than one hundred years after his own ministry ended would no doubt have disappointed Andrew Eliot, but he would have

---

8. On Parkman's ministry and what ensued, see Wells and Fanning, *New North Church*, 38–41, esp. 39, which quotes the brief "Covenant of 1827" in full. See further, Frothingham, *Francis Parkman*, 5–6; Sprague, *Annals*, 8:449–56, which lists ten published works by Parkman.

9. See Wells and Fanning, *New North Church*, 41–46.

been proud of his family legacy, especially of descendants who remained true to his faith. Typically Calvinist, he would have attributed the considerable achievements that were his major personal legacy to one source only, giving the glory to God. In his final published work, he gave full expression to his essentially providentialist understanding of history:

> The providence of God extends as far as the creation. Whatever he hath brought into being, depends upon him for its continuance in being; its having existence one moment, doth not make its existence necessary the next; its former existence is not the cause of its existing afterwards; it continues in being, not because it hath existed, but because this is the will of the Creator . . . There can be no accident with respect to him, no change or alteration unknown to, or unforeseen by him; because he always hath, in one grand view, all events, past, present and to come. Nothing comes to pass without his influence and appointment.[10]

In *Four Quartets*, Eliot's deeply religious, Anglophile, and high Anglican great-great-great-grandson, T. S. Eliot, expressed a much more poetic vision:

> Time present and time past
> Are both perhaps present in time future,
> And time future contained in time past.
> If all time is eternally present
> All time is unredeemable.
> What might have been is an abstraction
> Remaining a perpetual possibility
> Only in a world of speculation.
> What might have been and what has been
> Point to one end, which is always present.[11]

---

10. Eliot, *Twenty Sermons*, 87.
11. T. S. Eliot, "Burnt Norton," 1:1–10, in *Four Quartets*, 13.

Bibliography

Abbreviations

AED	Eliot, Andrew. *Diaries in Almanacs, 1740–1774*, in "Pre-Revolutionary Diaries at the Massachusetts Historical Society, 1635–1790." Reel 3, Microfilm. 9 Reels. Boston, MA: Massachusetts Historical Society, 1977.
ANB Online	*American National Biography*. New York: Oxford University Press, 2000. http://www.anb.org.
CMHS	*Collections of the Massachusetts Historical Society*. Boston, MA: Massachusetts Historical Society, 1792–.
EBO	*Encyclopaedia Britannica Online*. Encyclopædia Britannica, 2023. https://www.britannica.com.
NNR	*Records of the New North Church in North St., Boston, 1714–1870*. 2 vols. Boston, MA: Rare Books Department, Boston Public Library.
ODNB Online	*Oxford Dictionary of National Biography*. Oxford: Oxford University Press, 2004. Online ed., 2004–2015. http://www.oxforddnb.com.
OED Online	*Oxford English Dictionary*. Oxford: Oxford University Press, 1989. Online ed., 2015. http://www.oed.com.
PMHS	*Proceedings of the Massachusetts Historical Society*. Boston, MA: Massachusetts Historical Society, 1897–1998.
SHG	Sibley, John, and Clifford K. Shipton. *Biographical Sketches of Those Who Attended Harvard College*. Boston, MA: Massachusetts Historical Society, 1873–1999.

Bibliography

Primary Sources

Eliot, Andrew

Short titles are also listed for works by Andrew Eliot.

Eliot, Andrew. Andrew Eliot Correspondence Transcripts, Undated. Copied by John F. Eliot. Houghton Library, Harvard University, Cambridge, MA [Andrew Eliot Correspondence Transcripts].

———. Andrew Eliot Letters, 1767–1776 and Undated. Houghton Library, Harvard University, Cambridge, MA [Andrew Eliot Letters].

———. Andrew Eliot Papers, 1742–1778. 1 box. Massachusetts Historical Society, Boston, MA [Andrew Eliot Papers].

———. Annotated Almanacs, 1740–1784. Massachusetts Historical Society, Boston, MA. [Annotated Almanacs].

———. *A Burning and Shining Light Extinguished. A Sermon Preached the Lord's-Day after the Funeral of the Late Reverend Mr. John Webb, Pastor of the New-North Church in Boston; Who Died April 16, 1750. Aetat. 63.* Boston: Joshua Winter, 1750. [*Burning and Shining Light*].

———. *Christ's Promise to the Penitent Thief. A Sermon Preached the Lord's-Day Before the Execution of Levi Ames, Who Suffered Death for Burglary, Oct. 21, 1773. Aet. 22.* Boston: John Boyle, 1773. [*Christ's Promise*].

———. Copies from Andrew Eliot's Interleaved Almanacs 1740–1778. Copied by John F. Eliot. Andrew Eliot Diaries 1740–1778. 1 box. Massachusetts Historical Society, Boston, MA [Andrew Eliot Diaries Copies].

———. Deposition of Andrew Eliot against Nathan Prince, Nov. 26, 1741, Records Related to the Charges Against and Defense Made by Nathan Prince. University Archives, Harvard University, Cambridge, MA. [Deposition].

———. Diaries, 1740–1777. 2 boxes. Massachusetts Historical Society, Boston, MA [Andrew Eliot Diaries].

———. Diary, 1734, in Papers of Andrew Eliot. Box 1, vol. 1. University Archives, Harvard University, Cambridge, MA.

———. Diary, 1739, in Papers of Andrew Eliot. Box 1, vol. 2. University Archives, Harvard University, Cambridge, MA.

———. *A Discourse on Natural Religion Delivered in the Chapel of Harvard College in Cambridge, New-England May 8. 1771 at the Lecture Founded by The Hon. Paul Dudley, Esq.* Boston: Nicholas Bowes, 1771. [*Discourse on Natural Religion*].

———. Essay, Papers of Andrew Eliot. Box 1, folder 4. University Archives, Harvard University, Cambridge, MA. [Essay].

———. *An Evil and Adulterous Generation. A Sermon Preached on the Publick Fast, April 19, 1753.* Boston: Nicholas Bowes, 1753. [*Evil and Adulterous Generation*].

———. "Extracts from a Letter of Thomas Hollis, Esquire, to Rev. Andrew Eliot, DD, and from the Answer." *CMHS* 2.2 (1814) 276–80. ["Extracts from a Letter"].

———. *The Faithful Steward. A Sermon Delivered by Andrew Eliot, MA, at his Ordination to the Pastoral Charge of the New North Church in Boston, in Conjunction with The Rev. Mr. Webb. On April 14, 1742.* Boston: Samuel Eliot, 1742. [*Faithful Steward*].

Bibliography

———. *An Inordinate Love of the World Inconsistent with the Love of God. A Sermon Preached at the Thursday Lecture in Boston, August 2, 1744.* Boston: Rogers and Fowle, for S. Eliot, 1744. [*Inordinate Love*].

———. Letter from Andrew Eliot, Boston, to Samuel Langdon, August 14, 1778. Harvard College Papers, 1st series. Vol. 2.120. University Archives, Harvard University, Cambridge, MA. [Eliot to Langdon, August 14, 1778].

———. Letter to Isaac Smith, April 9, 1776. Smith-Carter Family Papers, 1669–1880, I. Loose Manuscripts, 1669–1880. Box 2, folder 16. April–October 1776. Massachusetts Historical Society, Boston, MA. [Eliot to Isaac Smith, April 9, 1776].

———. "Letter to Jasper Mauduit, June 1, 1763." *CMHS* 74 (1763) 119–20.

———. "Letters from Andrew Eliot to Thomas Hollis." *CMHS* 4.4 (1858) 398–461. ["Letters from Eliot to Hollis"].

———. "Letters of Andrew Eliot." *PMHS* 16 (1878) 182–83, 280–306. ["Letters"].

———. Papers of Andrew Eliot, 1734–1777. 3 vols., 4 folders. University Archives, Harvard University, Cambridge, MA. [Papers of Andrew Eliot].

———. "Profession of Faith of the Rev. Andrew Eliot." *Publications of the Colonial Society of Massachusetts* 13 (1912) 234–41. ["Profession of Faith"].

———. "Public Admonition of John Rowe at the New North Church by Rev. Andrew Eliot DD." Massachusetts Historical Society, Boston, MA ["Public Admonition"].

———. "Remarks on the Bishop of Oxford's Sermon Preached before the Incorporated Society for the Propagation of the Gospel in Foreign Parts, 1740." *CMHS* 2.2 (1814) 190–216. ["Remarks on the Bishop of Oxford's Sermon"].

———. *A Sermon Preached at the Ordination of Andrew Eliot, AM, to the Pastoral Care of the First Church in Fairfield: June 22, 1774.* Boston: John Boyle, 1774. [*Sermon Preached at the Ordination of Andrew Eliot*].

———. *A Sermon Preached at the Ordination of the Reverend Mr. Joseph Roberts, to the Pastoral Care of a Church in Leicester. October 23, 1754.* Boston: J. Winter, 1754. [*Sermon Preached at the Ordination of Joseph Roberts*].

———. *A Sermon Preached at the Ordination of the Reverend Mr. Joseph Willard, to the Pastoral Care of the First Church in Beverly, in Conjunction with The Reverend Mr. Joseph Champney, November XXV. MDCCLXXII.* Boston: Thomas and John Fleet, 1773. [*Sermon Preached at the Ordination of Joseph Willard*].

———. *A Sermon Preached before His Excellency Francis Bernard, Esq; Governor, The Honorable His Majesty's Council, and the Honorable House of Representatives, of the Province of the Massachusetts-Bay in New-England, May 29th, 1765. Being the Anniversary for the Election of His Majesty's Council for the Province.* Boston: Green and Russell, 1765. [*Sermon Preached before Bernard*].

———. *A Sermon Preached October 25th, 1759. Being a Day of Public Thanksgiving Appointed by Authority, for the Success of the British Arms This Year; Especially in the Reduction of Quebec, the Capital of Canada.* Boston: J. Winter, 1759. [*Sermon Preached October 25, 1759*].

———. *A Sermon Preached September 17, 1766. At the Ordination of The Reverend Mr. Ebenezer Thayer, to the Pastoral Care of the First Church in Hampton.* Boston: Thomas Leverett, 1766. [*Sermon Preached September 17, 1766*]

———. *Twenty Sermons on the Following Subjects, Viz. I. The Folly and Danger of Duplicity in Religion. II. The Excellency of the Human Soul. III. Jesus Christ the Only Source of Rest and Happiness. IV. The Dominion of an Omnipotent Deity a Reason for Joy and Praise. V. VI. VII. Charity More Excellent than Faith or Hope. VIII. Christ Preaching to the Spirits in Prison. IX. Redemption by the Blood of Christ. X. XI. The Connection between the Duties and Comforts of Religion. XII. The Obligations to Family-Religion. XIII. The Usefulness and Importance of Religious Education. XIV. XV. XVI. The Table of the Lord Rendered Contemptible. XVII. XVIII. Man Doomed to Return to the Dust from Whence He Was Taken. XX. The Blessedness of Those Who Have not Seen and yet Have Believed.* Boston, MA: John Boyle, 1774. [*Twenty Sermons*].

———. Unpublished Sermon on the Death of Eunice Hancock, Fairfield, 1774. Massachusetts Historical Society, Boston, MA [Sermon on the Death].

———. Unpublished Sermons on Ecclesiastes 1:4 and Luke 22:19. Massachusetts Historical Society, Boston, MA [Unpublished Sermons].

Eliot, Andrew, et al. Andrews, Eliot Correspondence, 1715–1814. 2 boxes. Massachusetts Historical Society, Boston, MA [Andrews-Eliot Correspondence].

———. Eliot Family Papers, 1688–1937. 4 boxes. Massachusetts Historical Society, Boston, MA [Eliot Family Papers].

Other Primary Sources

Ames, William. *Conscience with the Power and Cases thereof Devided* [sic] *into V. Bookes*. London: W. Christiaens et al., 1639.

———. *The Marrow of Sacred Divinity Drawne out of the Holy Scriptures, and the Interpreters Thereof, and Brought into Method*. London: Edward Griffin for Henry Overton, 1642.

Anders, Charlie Jane. "The Real-Life Letter of Apology Written by the Salem Witch Trial Jury." *Gizmodo*, September 30, 2014. https://gizmodo.com/the-real-life-letter-of-apology-written-by-the-salem-wi-1640827487.

Barnard, John. "Autobiography of the Rev. John Barnard [November 14, 1766]." *CMHS* 3.5 (1836) 177–243.

Barrow, Isaac. *Euclide's Elements: The Whole Fifteen Books Compendiously Translated*. London: William Nealand, 1760.

Beattie, James. *An Essay on the Nature and Immutability of Truth*. Edinburgh: Kincaid & Bell, 1770.

Belknap, Jeremy, et al. "Belknap Papers." *CMHS* 5.2–3 (1877).

———. "Belknap Papers." *CMHS* 6.4 (1891).

Bentley, William. *The Diary of William Bentley, DD, Pastor of the East Church, Salem, Massachusetts*. 4 vols. Salem, MA: Essex Institute, 1905–1914.

Blackburne, Francis. *The Confessional*. London: S. Bladon, 1766.

Boston Gazette, September 28, 1778. Supplement.

"The Boston Ministers: A Ballad, Advertisement—More Last Words." *New England Historical and Genealogical Register* 13.2 (1859) 131–33.

"The Boston Ministers: A Ballad—First and Second Parts." *New England Historical and Genealogical Register* 14.4 (1860) 369.

Bradford, William. *Bradford's History of the Plymouth Settlement, 1608–1650, Rendered into Modern English by Valerian Paget*. New York: John McBride, 1909.

Cambridge Synod. *The Cambridge and Saybrook Platforms with the Confession of Faith of the New England Churches, Adopted in 1680; And the Heads of Agreement Assented to by the Presbyterians and Congregationalists in England in 1690. Illustrated with Historical Prefaces and Notes*. Boston: T. R. Marvin, 1829.

Bibliography

Chauncy, Charles. *Five Dissertations on the Scripture Account of the Fall; and Its Consequences*. London: Charles Dilly, 1785.

———. *The Mystery Hid from Ages and Generations*. London: Charles Dilly, 1784.

Cicero, Marcus Tullius. *De Officiis: Libri Tres*. 4th ed. Cambridge: Cambridge University Press, 1881.

———. *Epistolae ad Diversos*. Leipzig: A. G. Weigel, 1822.

———. *Orationes*. Leipzig: B. G. Teubner, 1899–1908.

Clarke, John. *Corderii Colloquiorum Centuria Selecta: Or a Select Century of Corderius's Colloquies. With an English Translation as Literal as Possible; Designed for the Use of Beginners in the Latin Tongue*. Philadelphia: Joseph Crukshank, 1777.

Clarke, Samuel. *A Discourse Concerning the Being and Attributes of God*. 3rd ed. London: James Knapton, 1711.

———. *The Scripture-Doctrine of the Trinity*. London: James Knapton, 1712.

———. *The Works of Samuel Clarke, DD*. 4 vols. London: J. and P. Knapton, 1738.

Convention of Congregational Ministers of Massachusetts. *The Testimony of the Pastors of the Churches in the Province of the Massachusetts-Bay*. Boston, MA: S. Eliot, 1743.

Cordier, Mathurin. *Selecta Colloquiorum Maturini Corderii Centuria*. London: John Clarke, 1740.

Culman, Leonard. *Sententiae Pueriles, Anglo-Latinae. Quas E Diversis Authoribus Olim Collegerat, Leonard Culman; Et In Vernaculum Sermonem Nuperrime Transtulit, Carolus Hool: Pro Primis Latinae Linguae Tyronibus*. Boston: Buttolph et al., 1723.

Doddridge, Philip. *The Family Expositor*. 6 vols. London: Richard Hett, 1739–56.

Dudley, Paul. *An Essay on the Merchandize of Slaves & Souls of Men, Revel. XVIII. 13: With an Application Thereof to the Church of Rome: To Which Is Added, an Exercitation on Numb. XXXII. 10, 11, 12: With an Occasional Meditation on I. Sam. XXIII. 11, 12*. Boston: B. Green, 1731.

Eliot, Ephraim. *Historical Notices of the New North Religious Society in the Town of Boston, with Anecdotes of the Reverend Andrew and John Eliot*. Boston: Phelps & Farnham, 1822.

Eliot, John. *A Biographical Dictionary, Containing a Brief Account of the First Settlers, and Other Eminent Characters Among the Magistrates, Ministers, Literary and Worthy Men, in New-England*. Boston: Cushing and Appleton, Salem, and Edward Oliver, 1809.

———. *A Sermon, Delivered before the Members of the New-North Religious Society, Boston, May 2, 1804, upon the Completion of their House of Worship*. Boston: E. Lincoln, 1804.

———. *A Sermon, Delivered in the Chapel, Boston, before the Society of Antient and Honorable Free and Accepted Masons, On Monday, June 24, 1782*. Boston: N. Willis, 1782.

———. *A Sermon, Delivered on the Day of Annual Thanksgiving: November 20, 1794*. Boston: Samuel Hall, 1794.

———. *A Sermon, on the Propriety of Attending Public Worship, and an Attentive Serious Conduct, in the House of God*. Boston: John Russell, 1800.

———. *A Sermon, Preached in Milton, November 1, 1797: at the Ordination of the Rev. Mr. Joseph M'Kean*. Boston: Manning & Loring, 1797.

———. *A Sermon, Preached in Providence, at the Ordination of the Rev. Henry Edes, AM: July 17, AD 1805*. Providence, RI: J. Carter, 1805.

Eliot, T. S. *The Four Quartets*. London: Faber and Faber, 1974.

Bibliography

Erasmus. *Colloquia*. Edited by Cecilia Asso. Turin: Einaudi, 2002.

An Exact Table to Bring Old Tenor into Lawful Money: Also a Table to Know the Value of Pistoles, Guineas, Johannes, and Double Johannes, Moydores, English Crowns, Half Crowns, Shillings, and Copper Half-Pence, at the Rate of Dollars at Six Shillings a Piece, at Which Invariable Value They Are Fixed by a Late Act of This Government, the Act to Be in Force from and after the 31st of March 1750. Boston, MA: Rogers and Fowle, 1750.

First Church, Cambridge. *Records of the Church of Christ at Cambridge in New England, 1632-1830, Comprising the Ministerial Records of Baptisms, Marriages, Deaths, Admission to Covenant and Communion, Dismissals and Church Proceedings*. Edited by Stephen Paschall Sharples. Boston: E. Putnam, 1906.

Garretson, John. *English Exercises for School-Boys to Translate into Latin Comprising All the Rules of Grammar, and Other Necessary Observations: Ascending Gradually from the Meanest to Higher Capacities*. London: Thomas Cockerill, 1691.

Godwin, Thomas. *Romanæ Historiae Anthologia . . . An English Exposition of the Roman Antiquities . . . Newly Revised and Inlarged*. London: John Lichfield, 1631.

Green, Joseph. *Joseph Green Diary, 1700–1715*. Boston: Congregational Library and Archives. https://congregationallibrary.quartexcollections.com/manuscript-collections/browse-the-joseph-green-diary.

Halyburton, Thomas. *Natural Religion Insufficient*. Edinburgh: Heirs and Successors of Andrew Anderson, 1714.

Harvard University. *Commencement Theses, Quaestiones, and Orders of Exercises, 1642–1818*. Cambridge, MA: Harvard University Archives.

———. *Harvard Historical Register*. Cambridge MA: Harvard University Press, 1936.

Harvard University Corporation. Harvard College Papers, 1st series. Vol. 2. Cambridge, MA: Harvard University Archives, 1636–1831.

———. Minutes Extracted from the College Books. Vol. 2. Cambridge, MA: Harvard University Archives, 1643–1827.

Home, Henry. *Essays on the Principles of Morality and Natural Religion*. Edinburgh: Kincaid and Donaldson, 1751.

Howe, John. *The Works of the Late Reverend and Learned John Howe . . . in Two Volumes*. London: Clark et al., 1724.

Hume, David. *A Treatise of Human Nature*. Edited by David Fate Norton and Mary J. Norton. Oxford: Oxford University Press, 2000.

Hutchinson, Thomas. *The Diary and Letters of His Excellency Thomas Hutchinson: Captain-General and Governor-In-Chief of His Late Majesty's Province of Massachusetts Bay in North America . . . Compiled from the Original Documents Still Remaining in the Possession of his Descendants*. Boston: Houghton Mifflin, 1886.

———. *The History of the Colony/Province of Massachusetts-Bay*. 3 vols. Boston; London: Thomas & John Fleet/John Murray, 1767–1828.

Leland, John. *The Advantage and Necessity of the Christian Revelation*. 2 vols. London: R. and J. Dodsley, T. Longman, 1764.

Lily, William. *A Short Introduction of Grammar Generally to Be Used; Comp. And Set Forth for the Bringing Up of All Those That Intend to Attain to the Knowledge of the Latin Tongue. To Which Are Added Usefull Observations by Way of Comment out of Ancient And Late Grammarians*. Oxford: n.p., 1709.

Locke, John. *The Reasonableness of Christianity*. 1695. 7th ed. London: Millar et al., 1764.

———. *The Works of John Locke*. 11th ed. 10 vols. London: Otridge and Son, 1812.

Bibliography

Massachusetts Convention of Congregational Ministers (MCCM). "Records 1749-1789." Boston: Congregational Library & Archives, 1749-2019.

Massachusetts County, District and Probate Courts. "Massachusetts, US, Wills and Probate Records, 1635-1991." *Ancestry.com*, 2015. https://www.ancestry.ca/search/collections/9069.

Massachusetts Historical Society (MHS). Miscellaneous Manuscripts Collection. 51 boxes. Boston, MA: Massachusetts Historical Society Library, 1600-1993.

Mayhew, Jonathan. *Christian Sobriety: Being Eight Sermons on Titus II.6*. Boston: Richard and Samuel Draper, 1763.

———. *Sermons upon the Following Subjects, Viz. on Hearing the Word*. Boston: Richard Draper, 1755.

———. *The Snare Broken. A Thanksgiving-Discourse, Preached at the Desire of the West Church in Boston, NE, Friday, May 23, 1766. Occasioned by the Repeal of the Stamp Act*. Boston: R. & S. Draper, Edes & Gill, T. and J. Fleet, 1766.

New North Church. *The New North Church, Boston, 1714-1799*. Compiled by Thomas Bellows Wyman. Transcribed by Robert J. Dunkle. Edited by Ann S. Lainhart. Baltimore, MD: Clearfield, 1995.

Ovid. *Pub. Ovidii Nasonis De Tristibus: Libri V*. London: TM Pro Societate Stationariorum, 1691.

———. *Ovid's Metamorphoses in Latin and English*. Amsterdam: Wetsteins and Smith, 1732.

Parkman, Ebenezer. *The Diary of Ebenezer Parkman, 1703-1782*. Edited by Francis G. Walett. Worcester, MA: American Antiquarian Society, 1974.

———. *The Diary of Rev. Ebenezer Parkman, Part of The Ebenezer Parkman Project*. Westborough, MA: Westborough Center for History and Culture, n.d. https://diary.ebenezerparkman.org.

Pierce, Richard D., ed. *The Records of the First Church in Boston 1630-1868*. Boston: Colonial Society of Massachusetts, 1961.

Price, William, and John Bonner. "A New Plan of Ye Great Town of Boston in New England in America, with the Many Additionall [Sic] Buildings, & New Streets, to the Year, 1769." Norman B. Leventhal Map & Education Center, Boston Public Library. Boston, MA: Wm. Price, 1769.

Rexine, John E. "The 350th Anniversary of the Boston Latin School." *Classical Journal* 82.3 (1987) 236–41.

Riccaltoun, Robert. *An Inquiry into the Spirit and Tendency of Letters on Theron and Aspasio*. London: E. Dilly, 1762.

Ridgley, Thomas. *A Body of Divinity*. 2 vols. London: Midwinter et al., 1731-1733.

Secker, Thomas. *A Sermon Preached before the Incorporated Society for the Propagation of the Gospel in Foreign Parts*. London: J. and H. Pemberton, 1741.

Sewall, Samuel. "Samuel Sewall Jr.'s Memoranda in *Letter-Book of Samuel Sewall*." *CMHS* 6.2 (1981) 295–320.

Shepard, Thomas. "Thomas Shepard's *Confessions*." Edited by George Selement and Brice Woolley. *Publications of the Colonial Society of Massachusetts* 58 (1981) 1–28.

Stiles, Ezra. *Extracts from The Itineraries and Other Miscellanies of Ezra Stiles, DD, LLD, 1755-1794, With a Selection from His Correspondence*. Edited by Franklin Dexter. New Haven, CT: Yale University Press, 1916.

———. *The Literary Diary of Ezra Stiles, DD, LLD, President of Yale College*. Edited by Franklin Dexter. 3 vols. New York: Scribner's Sons, 1901.

Bibliography

Taylor, John. *A Paraphrase with Notes on the Epistle to the Romans*. London: J. Waugh, 1747.

———. *The Scripture-Doctrine of Original Sin*. London: J. Wilson, 1740.

Thacher, Peter. *The Rest Which Remaineth to the People of God, and the Character of Such as Shall Enjoy It, Shewn In A Sermon Preached At The New North Church In Boston, September 13, 1778*. Boston: Thomas and John Fleet, 1778.

Tindal, Matthew. *Christianity as Old as the Creation*. London: n.p., 1730.

Town and City Clerks of Massachusetts. "Massachusetts, US, Town and Vital Records, 1620–1988." *Ancestry.com*, 2011. https://www.ancestry.ca/search/collections/2495.

Trenchard, John. *A Short History of Standing Armies in England*. London: n.p., 1698.

Vergil. *P. Vergili Maronis Opera*. Edited by R. A. B. Mynors. Oxford: Oxford University Press, 1972.

Virkus, Frederick A. *Immigrant Ancestors: A List of 2,500 Immigrants to America before 1750*. 1964. Baltimore, MD: Genealogical, 1986.

Walker, William. *A Treatise of English Particles, Shewing Much of the Variety of Their Significations and Uses in English: And How to Render Them into Latin According to the Propriety and Elegancy of that Language. With a Praxis upon the Same*. London: John Baskett, 1720.

Wendell Holmes, Oliver. *Elsie Venner: A Romance of Destiny*. Complete Writings of Oliver Wendell Holmes 5. Boston: Houghton Mifflin, 1861.

Wolleb, Johannes. *The Abridgment of Christian Divinitie So Exactly and Methodically Compiled*. Translated by Alexander Ross. London: Joseph Nevill, 1660.

Webb, John. *A Brief Discourse at the Ordination of a Deacon*. Boston: D. Henchman and J. Phillips, 1731.

———. *The Believer's Redemption by the Precious Blood Of Christ. A Sermon Preach'd at Newport, on Rhode-Island: On Lord's Day, December 31. 1727. From I. Peter, I. 18, 19*. Newport, RI: J. Franklin and T. Fleet, 1728.

———. *Christ's Suit to the Sinner, While He Stands and Knocks at the Door. A Sermon Preach'd in a Time of Great Awakening, at the Tuesday-Evening Lecture in Brattle-Street, Boston, October 13. 1741*. Boston: S. Kneeland and T Green, 1741.

———. *The Duty of a Degenerate People to Pray for the Reviving of God's Work. A Sermon Preach'd June 18. 1734. Being a Day of Prayer with Fasting, Observed by the New North Church in Boston*. Boston: S. Kneeland and T. Green, 1734.

———. *The Duty of Ministers to Work the Works of Him That Sent Them, While It Is Day. A Sermon Occasion'd by The Much Lamented Death of The Reverend Mr. William Waldron, Late Faithful Pastor of a Church Of Christ in Boston, Who Departed This Life, Sept. 11. 1727*. Boston: S. Gerrish, et al., 1727.

———. *The Duty of Survivors [Sic] to Remember and to Follow the Faith of Their Godly Deceased Pastors. A Sermon Preach'd the Lord's-Day after the Death of The Reverend Mr. Peter Thacher. A Pastor of the New North Church in Boston. Who Deceased Feb. 26. 1738. Aetatis Suae 62*. Boston: D. Henchman and S. Eliot, 1739.

———. *The Government of Christ Considered and Applied. A Sermon Preached at Boston, In the Audience of His Excellency Jonathan Belcher, Esq; The Honourable His Majesty's Council; and The Honourable House of Representatives of the Province of the Massachusetts. May 31. 1738. Being the Anniversary for the Election of His Majesty's Council for the Province*. Boston: N. Procter and S. Eliot, 1738.

Bibliography

———. *The Great Concern of New-England. A Sermon Preached At The Thursday Lecture In Boston, February 11th. 1730,31. In The Time Of The Sessions Of The Great And General Court.* Boston: Thomas Fleet, 1730.

———. *The Greatness of Sin Improv'd by the Penitent as an Argument with God for A Pardon. A Sermon at The Thursday Lecture in Boston, October 17th. 1734. Preach'd in the Hearing of John Ormesby, and Matthew Cushing, Two Condemned Malefactors on the Day of Their Execution, the One for Murder, and the Other for Burglary . . . With an Appendix, Giving a Faithful Account of the Behaviour of Matthew Cushing, after his Condemnation, and at the Time of his Execution.* Boston: S. Kneeland & T. Green, 1734.

———. *Practical Discourses on Death, Judgment, Heaven & Hell. In Twenty-Four Sermons.* Boston: D. Henchman, 1726.

———. *A Seasonable Warning against Bad Company-Keeping: In a Discourse from Prov. XIII. 20.* Boston: Samuel Gerrish, 1726.

———. *A Sermon, Preached at the Thursday Lecture in Boston, Novemb. 15. 1722. At the Time of the Sessions of the Great and General Court. And Published at the Desire of The Honourable House of Representatives.* Boston: B. Green, 1722

———. *Some Plain and Necessary Directions to Obtain Eternal Salvation. In Six Sermons from Acts XVI.30.* Boston: Benj. Gray, 1729.

———. *Vows Made unto God in Trouble to Be Religiously Paid unto Him. A Sermon Preach'd on a Special Occasion: but Seasonable for All That Have Made Solemn Vows to God in Any Day of Trouble.* Boston: S. Gerrish, 1728.

———. *The Young-Mans Duty, Explained and Pressed upon Him. In a Sermon from Eccles. XII. 1. Preached to a Society of Young Men, on a Lords-Day Evening: And Now Published at Their Request.* Boston: D. Henchman, 1718.

West, Samuel, *A Sermon Preached before the Honorable Council.* Boston, MA: John Gill, 1776.

Westminster Assembly. *The Grounds and Principles of Religion, Contained in a Shorter Catechism.* London: Lords and Commons, 1647.

———. *The Humble Advice of the Assembly of Divines, Now by Authority of Parliament Sitting at Westminster, Concerning a Confession of Faith.* London: Company of Stationers, 1646.

———. *The Humble Advice of the Assembly of Divines, Sitting at Westminster, Concerning a Larger and a Shorter Catechisme.* Edinburgh: Evan Tyler, 1647.

Williams, Stephen. *Diary.* Longmeadow, MA: Richard Salter Storrs, n.p. https://www.longmeadowlibrary.org/stephen-williams-diary-online.

Wollaston, William. *The Religion of Nature Delineated.* London: n.p., 1722.

Secondary Sources

Akers, Charles W. *Called unto Liberty: A Life of Jonathan Mayhew, 1720–1766.* Cambridge, MA: Harvard University Press, 1964.

———. *The Divine Politician: Samuel Cooper and the American Revolution in Boston.* Boston, MA: Northeastern University Press, 1982.

Alexander, Kathy. "Procedures, Courts & Aftermath of the Salem Witch Trials." *Legends of America*, November 2022. https://www.legendsofamerica.com/ma-salemcourt/3.

Bibliography

Archer, Richard. *As If an Enemy's Country: The British Occupation of Boston and the Origins of Revolution.* Oxford: Oxford University Press, 2010.

Bailyn, Bernard. "Religion and Revolution: Three Biographical Studies." *Perspectives in American History* 4 (1970) 85–169.

Baldwin, Alice M. *The New England Clergy and the American Revolution.* 1928. Reprint, New York: F. Ungar, 1958.

Barbier, Brooke. *Boston in the American Revolution: A Town Versus an Empire.* Charleston, SC: History, 2017.

Basquin, Roberta A., and Robert A. Walsh. "Ephraim Eliot: First President of the Massachusetts College of Pharmacy." *Pharmacy in History* 21.1 (1979) 45–47.

Bercovitch, Sacvan. *The American Jeremiad.* 2nd ed. Madison: University of Wisconsin Press, 2012.

Boston Tea Party Ships & Museum. "The Tea Act." n.d. https://www.bostonteapartyship.com/the-tea-act.

Botein, Stephen. "Income and Ideology: Harvard-Trained Clergymen in the Eighteenth Century." *Eighteenth-Century Studies* 13.4 (1980) 496–513.

Breen, T. H. *American Insurgents, American Patriots: The Revolution of the People.* New York: Hill and Wang, 2010.

British Library. "A Timeline of the American Revolution from 1763–1787." *British Library*, June 17, 2016. https://web.archive.org/web/20170701001725/http://www.bl.uk/the-american-revolution/articles/american-revolution-timeline.

Bullock, Steven C. "'Often Concerned in Funerals': Ritual, Material Culture, and the Large Funeral in the Age of Samuel Sewall." In *New Views of New England: Studies in Material and Visual Culture to 1830*, edited by Martha McNamara and Georgia B. Barnhill, 181–211. Boston: Colonial Society of Massachusetts, 2012. https://www.colonialsociety.org/node/1416#.

Bullock, Steven C., and Sheila McIntyre. "The Handsome Tokens of a Funeral: Glove-Giving and the Large Funeral in Eighteenth-Century New England." *William and Mary Quarterly* 69.2 (2012) 305–46.

Burnard, Trevor. *Writing Early America: From Empire to Revolution.* Charlottesville: University of Virginia Press, 2023.

Burton, John. "Philanthropy and the Origins of Educational Cooperation: Harvard College, the Hopkins Trust, and the Cambridge Grammar School." *History of Education Quarterly* 37.2 (1997) 141–61.

Bushee, Frederick A. "The Growth of the Population of Boston." *Publications of the American Statistical Association* 6.46 (1899) 239–74.

Byrd, James P. *Sacred Scripture, Sacred War.* New York: Oxford University Press, 2013.

Chaffin, Robert. "The Townsend Acts Crisis, 1767–1770." In *A Companion to the American Revolution*, edited by Jack Greene and J. R. Pole, 134–50. Oxford: Blackwell, 2000.

Clark, Jonathan C. D. *The Language of Liberty, 1660–1832: Political Discourse and Social Dynamics in the Anglo-American World.* Cambridge: Cambridge University Press, 1994.

Conway, Stephen. *The War of American Independence 1775–1783.* London: St. Martin's, 1995.

Corrigan, John. *The Hidden Balance: Religion and the Social Theories of Charles Chauncy and Jonathan Mayhew.* Cambridge: Cambridge University Press, 1987.

Cutter, William Richard. *Genealogical and Personal Memoirs Relating to the Families of Boston and Eastern Massachusetts.* 3 vols. New York: Lewis Historical, 1908.

Bibliography

Drake, Samuel. *The History and Antiquities of Boston, the Capital of Massachusetts and Metropolis of New England, from Its Settlement in 1630, to the Year 1770. Also, An Introductory History of the Discovery and Settlement of New England. With Notes Critical and Illustrative*. Boston, MA: Luther Stevens, 1856.

Earle, Alice. *Customs and Fashions in Old New England*. New York: Scribner's Sons, 1906.

———. "Old-Time Marriage Customs in New England." *Journal of American Folklore* 6.21 (1893) 97–102.

———. *The Sabbath in Puritan New England*. New York: Scribner's Sons, 1891.

Eliot, Walter Graeme. *A Sketch of the Eliot Family*. New York: Livingston Middleditch, 1887.

Eliot, William H. *Genealogy of the Eliot Family*. New Haven, CT: Bassett & Co., 1854.

Ellis, Joseph J. *The Cause: The American Revolution and Its Discontents, 1773–1783*. New York: Norton, 2021.

Eloranta, Jan, and Jeremy Land. "Hollow Victory? Britain's Public Debt and the Seven Years' War." *Essays in Economic & Business History* 29 (2011) 101–18.

Fawcett, Bernadine. *Missing Links to the Culper Spy Ring*. West Conshohocken, PA: Infinity, 2005.

Fea, John. *Was America Founded as a Christian Nation?: A Historical Introduction*. Rev. ed. Louisville, KY: Westminster John Knox, 2016.

Fiering, Norman. *Jonathan Edwards's Moral Thought and its British context*. Chapel Hill: University of North Carolina Press, 1981

———. *Moral Philosophy at Seventeenth-Century Harvard: A Discipline in Transition*. Chapel Hill: University of North Carolina Press, 1981.

Fowle, William B., ed. "Schools of the Olden Time in Boston." *Common School Journal* 12.20 (1850) 311–15.

Frothingham, Octavius B. *Francis Parkman: A Sketch*. Boston: J. Wilson and Son, 1894.

Frothingham, Richard. *History of the Siege of Boston, and of the Battles of Lexington, Concord, and Bunker Hill. Also, an Account of the Bunker Hill Monument. With Illustrative Documents*. 6th ed. Boston, MA: Little, Brown, 1896.

Gordon, Alexander. "Ridgley, Thomas (1667–1734)." Revised by Alan Ruston. *ODNB Online*, September 23, 2004. https://doi.org/10.1093/ref:odnb/23625.

Griffin, Edward M. *Old Brick: Charles Chauncy of Boston, 1705–1787*. Minneapolis: University of Minnesota Press, 1980.

Griffith, Patrick. "Andrew Elliot (1627–1704)." *WikiTree*, April 25, 2013. https://www.wikitree.com/wiki/Elliot-564#R-845690148.

Guyatt, Nicholas, *Providence and the Invention of the United States, 1607–1876*. Cambridge: Cambridge University Press, 2007

Hall, David. *The Faithful Shepherd: A History of the New England Ministry in the Seventeenth Century*. Chapel Hill: University of North Carolina Press, 1972.

Hardesty, Jared Ross, et al. "Boston Slavery Exhibit." *City of Boston*, February 23, 2024. https://www.boston.gov/departments/archaeology/boston-slavery-exhibit.

Harper, George W. *A People So Favored of God: Boston's Congregational Churches and Their Pastors, 1710–1760*. 2nd ed. Eugene, OR: Wipf & Stock, 2007.

Harvard College. "Harvard's 1786 Graduating Class and Their Theses, Dedicated to Gov. James Bowdoin." Boston: Edmund Freeman, 1786. https://www.sethkaller.com/item/1712-23331-Harvard.

Harvard Square Library. "Ware, Henry, Sr. (1764–1845)." *Harvard Square Library*, n.d. https://www.harvardsquarelibrary.org/cambridge-harvard/henry-ware.

Bibliography

Harvard University. "Board of Overseers." *Social Networks and Archival Context*, n.d. https://snaccooperative.org/view/87699614.

———. "Corporation." *Social Networks and Archival Context*, n.d. https://snaccooperative.org/view/87699867.

Hasselgren, Per-Olof. "The Smallpox Epidemics in America in the 1700s and the Role of the Surgeons: Lessons to be Learned During the Global Outbreak of COVID-19." *World Journal of Surgery* 44.9 (2020) 2837–41. https://www.ncbi.nlm.nih.gov/pmc/articles/PMC7335227.

Hatch, Nathan. "Sola Scriptura and Novus Ordo Seclorum." In *The Bible in America: Essays in Cultural History*, edited by Nathan Hatch and Mark Noll, 59–78. New York: Oxford University Press, 1982.

Heimert, Alan. *Religion and the American Mind from the Great Awakening to the Revolution*. Cambridge, MA: Harvard University Press, 1966.

Holifield, E. Brooks. *Theology in America: Christian Thought from the Age of the Puritans to the Civil War*. New Haven, CT: Yale University Press, 2003.

Holmes, Pauline. *A Tercentenary History of the Boston Public Latin School, 1635–1935*. Harvard Studies in Education 25. Cambridge, MA: Harvard University Press, 1935.

Howe, Daniel Walker. "The Decline of Calvinism: An Approach to Its Study." *Comparative Studies in Society and History* 14.3 (1972) 306–27.

Humpage, Owen F. "Paper Money and Inflation in Colonial America." *Federal Reserve Bank of Cleveland*, May 13, 2015. https://doi.org/10.26509/frbc-ec-201506.

Hurd, Charles Edwin. *Representative Citizens of the Commonwealth of Massachusetts*. Boston: New England Historical, 1902.

Ireland, Corydon. "Harvard's Year of Exile." *Harvard Gazette*, October 13, 2011. https://news.harvard.edu/gazette/story/2011/10/harvards-year-of-exile.

Jedrey, Christopher M. *The World of John Cleaveland: Family and Community in Eighteenth-Century New England*. New York: Norton, 1979.

Jenks, Henry F. *Catalogue of the Boston Public Latin School, with an Historical Sketch*. Boston: n.p., 1886.

Jones, Alice Hanson, and Boris Simkovich. "The Wealth of Women, 1774." In *Strategic Factors in Nineteenth Century American Economic History: A Volume to Honor Robert W. Fogel*, edited by Claudia Goldin and Hugh Rockoff, 243–63. Chicago: University of Chicago Press, 1992.

Jordan, Louis. "Introduction to Early Massachusetts Currency: December 10, 1690–1750." *Colonial Currency*, February 1, 1998. https://coins.nd.edu/colcurrency/CurrencyText/MA-1690-1750.html.

Judd, Sylvester. *History of Hadley, Including the Early History of Hatfield, South Hadley, Amherst and Granby, Massachusetts*. Northampton, MA: Metcalf, 1863.

Kammen, Michael. *People of Paradox: An Inquiry concerning the Origins of American Civilization*. Ithaca, NY: Cornell University Press, 1972.

Keim, Alexander Donald. "Boston Inside Out: A Brothel, A Boardinghouse, and the Construction of the Nineteenth-Century North End's Urban Landscape through Embodied Practice." PhD diss., Boston University, 2015.

Kennedy, Lawrence W. "Population Trends in Boston 1640–1990." In *Planning the City Upon a Hill: Boston Since 1630*. Amherst: University of Massachusetts Press, 1992. http://www.iboston.org/mcp.php?pid=popFig.

Kidd, Thomas S. *The Protestant Interest: New England after Puritanism*. New Haven, CT: Yale University Press, 2004.

Bibliography

Kraus, Joe. "The Development of a Curriculum in the Early American Colleges." *History of Education Quarterly* 1.2 (1961) 64–76.

Kunitz, Stephen J. "Mortality Change in America, 1620–1920." *Human Biology* 56.3 (1984) 559–82.

Loring, James Spear. *The Hundred Boston Orators*. Boston: John P. Jewett, 1853.

Mace, Emily. "Eliot, John (1754–1813)." *Digital Library of Unitarian Universalism*, September 29, 2012. https://www.harvardsquarelibrary.org/biographies/john-eliot-1754-1813-2.

Marsden, George. *Jonathan Edwards: A Life*. New Haven, CT: Yale University Press, 2003.

Marshall, P. D. "Thomas Hollis (1720–74): The Bibliophile as Libertarian." *Bulletin of the John Rylands Library* 66.2 (1984) 246–63.

McCullough, David. *1776*. New York: Simon & Schuster, 2005.

McGrath, Alister. *Christian Theology: An Introduction*. 5th ed. Oxford: Wiley-Blackwell, 2011.

McKean, Joseph. "Memoir Towards a Character of Reverend John Eliot, STD." *CMHS* 2.1 (1814) 211–51.

McNeill, John T. *The History and Character of Calvinism* New York: Oxford University Press, 1954.

Middlekauff, Robert. "A Persistent Tradition: The Classical Curriculum in Eighteenth-Century New England." *William and Mary Quarterly* 18.1 (1961) 54–67.

Miller, Perry. *The New England Mind: From Colony to Province*. 1953. Boston: Beacon, 1961.

———. *The New England Mind: The Seventeenth Century*. 1939. Cambridge, MA: Harvard University Press, 1954.

Monroe, Paul. *A Cyclopedia of Education*. Vol. 2. New York: Macmillan, 1911.

Moore, Kathryn McDaniel. "Freedom and Constraint in Eighteenth Century Harvard." *Journal of Higher Education* 47.6 (1976) 649–59.

Morgan, Edmund S. *The Gentle Puritan: A Life of Ezra Stiles, 1727–1795*. New Haven, CT: Yale University Press, 1962.

Morison, Samuel Eliot. *Three Centuries of Harvard, 1636–1936*. Cambridge, MA: Harvard University Press, 1965.

Mullins, J. Patrick. *Father of Liberty: Jonathan Mayhew and the Principles of the American Revolution*. Lawrence: University Press of Kansas, 2017.

Murdock, Kenneth B. "The Teaching of Latin and Greek at the Boston Latin School in 1712." *Publications of the Colonial Society of Massachusetts* 27 (1927) 21–29.

Nelson, James L. *With Fire and Sword: The Battle of Bunker Hill and the Beginning of the American Revolution*. New York: Thomas Dunne/St. Martin's, 2011.

Noll, Mark. *America's God: From Jonathan Edwards to Abraham Lincoln*. Oxford: Oxford University Press, 2002.

———. *Christians in the American Revolution*. Washington, DC: Christian College Consortium, 1977.

Noll, Mark, et al. *The Search for Christian America*. Westchester, IL: Crossway, 1983.

Oakes, John S. "Beyond the 'Democrat'/'Conservative' Dichotomy: John Wise Reconsidered." *New England Quarterly* 88.3 (2015) 483–508.

———. "'Conservative Revolutionaries'—A Study of the Religious and Political Thought of John Wise, Jonathan Mayhew, Andrew Eliot, and Charles Chauncy." PhD diss., Simon Fraser University, 2008.

Bibliography

———. *Conservative Revolutionaries: Transformation and Tradition in the Religious and Political Thought of Charles Chauncy and Jonathan Mayhew*. Eugene, OR: Pickwick, 2016; Cambridge: James Clarke & Co., 2017.

Pettit, Norman. *The Heart Prepared: Grace and Conversion in Puritan Spiritual Life*. New Haven, CT: Yale University Press, 1966.

Philbrick, Nathaniel. *Bunker Hill: A City, A Siege, A Revolution*. New York: Viking, 2013.

Pirulis, Alecia. "What to Consider When Moving to a Small Town." *Apartments.com*, July 6, 2020. https://www.barringtonresidential.com/what-to-consider-when-moving-to-a-small-town.

Powell, Chilton. "Marriage in Early New England." *New England Quarterly* 1.3 (1928) 323–34.

Rauner Library, Dartmouth College, "'A Matter of Absolute Necessity': Eleazar Wheelock & Moor's Indian Charity School." Online: https://www.dartmouth.edu/library/rauner/exhibits/matter-absolute-necessity-moors-charity.html

Ray, Benjamin. "Salem Witch Trials Documentary Archive and Transcription Project." 2018. https://salem.lib.virginia.edu/home.html.

Robbins, Caroline. "The Strenuous Whig: Thomas Hollis of Lincoln's Inn." *William and Mary Quarterly* 7.3 (1950) 406–53.

Saunders, William. "Ordination Confers Indelible Stamp." *Catholic Education Resource Center (CERC)*, 2003. https://www.catholiceducation.org/en/culture/catholic-contributions/ordination-confers-indelible-stamp.html.

Schmotter, James W. "The Irony of Clerical Professionalism: New England's Congregational Ministers and the Great Awakening." *American Quarterly* 31.2 (1979) 148–68.

———. "Ministerial Careers in Eighteenth-Century New England: The Social Context, 1700–1760." *Journal of Social History* 9.2 (1975) 249–67.

Scott, Donald M. *From Office to Profession: The New England Ministry, 1750–1850*. Philadelphia: University of Pennsylvania Press, 1978.

Shain, Barry Alan. *The Myth of American Individualism: The Protestant Origins of American Political Thought*. Princeton: Princeton University Press, 1994.

Shipton, Clifford K. *New England Life in the Eighteenth Century: Representative Biographies from Sibley's Harvard Graduates*. Cambridge, MA: Harvard University Press, 1963.

Silverman, Kenneth. *The Life and Times of Cotton Mather*. New York: Welcome Rain, 2002.

Smith, Daniel Scott, and J. David Hacker. "Cultural Demography: New England Deaths and the Puritan Perception of Risk." *Journal of Interdisciplinary History* 36.3 (1996) 367–92.

Sprague, William B. *Annals of the American Pulpit*. 9 vols. New York: Robert Carter, 1859–69.

Stout, Harry S. *The New England Soul: Preaching and Religious Culture in Colonial New England*. New York: Oxford University Press, 1986.

Torry, Clarence A. *New England Marriages Prior to 1700*. Baltimore, MD: Genealogical, 2004.

Tracy, Joseph. *The Great Awakening: A History of the Revival of Religion in the Time of Edwards and Whitefield*. Boston: Tappan and Dennet; New York: Josiah Adams, 1844.

Tracy, Patricia J. *Jonathan Edwards Pastor: Religion and Society in Eighteenth-Century Northampton*. New York: Hill & Wang, 1980.

Bibliography

Vachon, André. "Briand, Jean-Olivier." In vol. 4 of *Dictionary of Canadian Biography*, edited by Francess G. Halpenny and Jean Hamelin. Toronto: University of Toronto Press, 1979. http://www.biographi.ca/EN/ShowBio.asp?BioId=35896.

Wallenfeldt, Jeff. "Timeline of the American Revolution." *Encyclopædia Britannica*, n.d. https://web.archive.org/web/20220202193935/https://www.britannica.com/list/timeline-of-the-american-revolution.

Weis, Frederick Lewis. *The Colonial Clergy and the Colonial Churches of New England*. Baltimore, MA: Clearfield, 2010.

Wells, Charles Chauncey, and Steven Fanning. *New North Church: From Birth to Death in Early Boston*. Oak Park, IL: Chauncey Park, 2014.

Whitmore, William Henry. *Andrew Elliot, of Beverly, Mass., and His Descendants*. Primary Source ed. Charleston, SC: Nabu, 2013.

Wilson, Robert J. *The Benevolent Deity: Ebenezer Gay and the Rise of Rational Religion in Colonial New England, 1696–1787*. Philadelphia: University of Pennsylvania Press, 1984.

Wood, Gordon. "Religion and the American Revolution." In *New Directions in American Religious History*, edited by Harry Stout and D. G. Hart, 173–205. New York: Oxford University Press, 1997.

Worthley, Harold Field. *An Inventory of the Records of the Particular (Congregational) Churches of Massachusetts Gathered 1620–1805*. Harvard Theological Studies. Cambridge, MA: Harvard University Press, 1970.

Wright, Robert E. "Lessons from America's First Great Inflations." *American Institute for Economic Research*, April 26, 2022. https://www.aier.org/article/lessons-from-americas-first-great-inflations.

Youngs, William T. *God's Messengers: Religious Leadership in Colonial New England, 1700–1750*. Baltimore, MD: Johns Hopkins University Press, 1976.

Index

A

Adams, Amos, 40
Adams, John, 139, 143
Adams, Samuel, 139
African Americans, 107
Alger, William, 154
Ames, William, 15
Anglican church, 2, 4, 77, 122
anti-British sentiment, 2, 100–102, 117, 120–27, 136
Appleton, Nathaniel, 37, 67
Arminianism, 69, 71, 79, 93

B

Bailyn, Bernard, 5–7, 69–70, 78, 87, 98–101, 112, 119–20, 143
Baldwin, Alice, 3–4, 119
Baptists, 40, 48, 117, 147
Barnard, John, 35
Beattie, James, 86–87, 112
Belknap, Jeremy, 61, 134, 145, 147, 152
Bentley, William, 51–52
Bernard, Francis, 125
Bird, Jonathan, 1
Blackburne, Francis, 6, 116, 120
Boston, 10. British occupation of, 8, 49, 60–62, 125, 128–35, 153; history of, 51, 153; population of, 44, 48, 51, 107, 128, 153–55; and religious diversity, 48, 50, 154–55. *See also* early America
Boston Massacre, 126
Boston Tea Party, 124, 127

Botein, Stephen, 53, 57
Bowdoin, James, 95
Bradford, William, 38–39
Brattle, William, 16
Breck, Robert, 91
Bridge, Ebenezer, 21
Bridge, Thomas, 36
Bullfinch, Charles, 152
Bullock, Steven, 39
Bunker Hill, Battle of, 118, 129
Burgoyne, John, 139
Burlamaqui, Jean Jacques, 4, 100
Burt, John, 21, 51
Burton, John, 18

C

Calvinism (general), 5, 16–17, 70–71, 74–79, 93. *See also* Rev. Dr. Andrew Eliot: Calvinism of
Catholicism, 25, 65, 104, 115, 120–21, 154
Chandler, Samuel, 108
Chauncy, Charles, xi, 71, 90, 97, 136, 149, 152
Church of England. *See* Anglican church
church ministers' salaries, 53–57
civil disobedience, 100–102, 116, 120, 143
Clark, J.C.D. (Jonathan), 6–7, 69–70, 93
Clarke, Samuel, 70, 86–87, 90–92
Condy, Jeremiah, 116

Congregationalism, xi, 6, 8–9, 40, 48–55, 66, 70, 73, 77–79, 84, 93, 119, 122, 129
Cooke, Samuel, 101
Cooper, Samuel, 20, 95, 146
Counts, Martha, 101
Cromwell, Oliver, 87
Currency Act, 55
Cutter, William, 11

D

Dana, James, 136
Dartmouth College, 108–9, 129
Davenport, James, 69, 84
deism, 1, 88, 147
Dexter, Samuel, 147
Dudley, Paul, 106–7

E

Earle, Alice, 38–39, 57
early America: and churchgoing, 37–38, 48, 66–67; and degeneracy, 78–80, 103–4; and economics, 53–55; and ministry, 4, 8–9, 37–41, 44–46, 53–54, 130; and theological controversies, 2, 6, 15–17, 70–74, 78–79, 90–93, 152. *See also* Boston
Edes, Henry, 67–68
Edwards, Jonathan, 3
Eliot, Andrew Jr., 52, 58, 63–64, 95, 136, 139–41, 151–52
Eliot, Andrew Rev. Dr.: and antislavery views, 106–7; background of, 11–13, 19, 51, 66; biblicism of, 23–31, 76–81, 84–93, 97–104, 117–19; and British siege, xi–xii, 2, 6–8, 49, 118–19, 128–36, 146; Calvinism of, xi, 3–8, 22, 68–81, 84, 89, 93, 112–13, 119, 148, 155; character of, 44–46, 142–51; death of, 1, 45–46, 141–42, 145–48, 151; education of, 13–19; family of, 1, 8–13, 24, 51–64, 129–32, 139–41, 147, 150–51, 155; and financial means, 8, 19, 21, 32, 39, 52–60, 150; historical significance of, xi–xii, 2–3, 7, 53, 150–55; marriage of, 51–52; and ministry, 23–49, 53, 61, 80, 106–7, 113, 128–31, 136, 139–40, 146–48, 151; and ministry posts, 13, 20–23, 36–37, 51, 67–68; politics of, 97–105, 110–27, 137–44, 148–50; pragmatism of, 9, 46, 61, 69–70, 82–84, 114, 149; pastoral care of, 44–47; preaching of, 36–43; as reluctant revolutionary, xii, 2–9, 69–70, 101, 116–22, 126–28, 137–44, 149–50; scholarship on, 2–9, 69–70, 119; theology of, 3–8, 23–36, 41, 61, 68–80, 84–93, 103, 110–17, 148; and views on war, 2–9, 136–40, 144, 149–50; and vocational choices, 20–23, 94–96
Eliot, Andrew (father), 12
Eliot, Andrew (grandfather), 11–12
Eliot, Charles William, 151
Eliot, Elizabeth (daughter), 52, 129
Eliot, Elizabeth Langdon, 51–52
Eliot, Ephraim, 1–4, 20, 46, 52, 69–70, 106, 151–53
Eliot, John (ancestor), 11
Eliot, John (Harvard student), 17
Eliot, John (son), 52, 58, 60–62, 128, 131–32, 139, 142, 145–49, 151–52
Eliot, John F., 59
Eliot, Josiah, 52, 63
Eliot, Martha May, 151
Eliot, Ruth, 13
Eliot, Samuel (brother), 151
Eliot, Samuel (son), 13, 60, 62–63, 129, 131–34
Eliot, Sarah, 59
Eliot, T.S., 150, 155
Eliot, William Greenleaf, 151
Episcopalians, 48, 77–78

F

Fanning, Steven, 154
Fawcett, Bernadine, 63
Fenn, William, 68–70
Fiering, Norman, 16–17

Index

First Continental Congress, 127, 137–38
Fleming, Caleb, 116
Flynt, Henry, 17
Franklin, Benjiman, 85
Fuller, Arthur Buckminster, 154
funerals, 33–34, 38–40, 42–43

G

Gage, Thomas, 142
Gannett, Caleb, 147
Gay, Ebenezer, 136
Gilman, Nicholas, 21
Glorious Revolution, 104, 115
Gordon, William, 146–47
Great Awakening, xi, 2, 70, 82–83
Greenleaf-Eliot, Elizabeth, 62–63
Grotius, Hugo, 4

H

Halyburton, Thomas, 86, 88
Hambrick-Stowe, Charles, 38, 43
Hancock, John, 137–38
Hancock, Lydia Henchman, 137–38
Hancock, Thomas, 138
Harper, George, 45–47
Harrington, James, 121
Harris, William, 3, 110
Harvard College, 1, 3, 8, 13–21, 35–37, 52–60, 66–69, 93–98, 116, 119, 129, 141, 146–54
Hatch, Nathan, 89–90
Heimert, Alan, 5–6, 119
Helyer, Jonathan, 22
Hill, Alexander, 139
Hobart, Nehemiah, 13
Hobby, William, 69, 84
Holifield, E. Brooks, 3
Hollis, Thomas, 6, 78, 96–97, 109, 116–17, 120–26
Hollis, Thomas Brand, 6, 53, 117, 120, 137
Holmes, Nathaniel, 47
Holmes, Oliver Wendell, 150–51
Holyoke, Edward, 16–17, 20
Home, Henry, 112

Howe, John, 86–87
Humpage, Owen, 54
Hutchinson, Thomas, 2, 116, 125, 142–43

I

indigenous Americans, 107–10, 124
inflation, 53–57
Intolerable Acts, 127

J

Jackson, Joseph, 40
Jones, Alice, 59
Judd, Sylvester, 55

K

Keim, Alexander, 53, 153
Kent, Benjamin, 91
Kenyon, Clifford, 95
King George's War, 54
Kraus, Joe, 14–16

L

La Ramée, Pierre, 15
Langdon, Elizabeth. *See* Elizabeth Eliot
Langdon, Josiah, 51
Langdon, Samuel, 1, 147
Lathrop, John, 146
Leverett, John, 16–17
Lexington and Concord, Battles of, xii, 127–28
liberty, 1, 6–7, 45, 69, 77, 97–100, 110–17, 119–28, 143, 148–49
Lincoln, Abraham, 3
Locke, John, 5, 17, 69, 86–89, 99, 102, 112, 121
Locke, Samuel, 20, 96, 116
Louis XIV, 104
Lovell, John, 13
loyalism, xi, 2, 9, 142

M

Mather, Cotton, 33, 36, 57

175

Index

Mather, Increase, 35–36, 52, 57
Mather, Samuel, 130
Mauduit, Jasper, 108
Mayhew, Jonathan, xi, 7–8, 71, 79–80, 85, 90, 97, 101, 110–20, 123, 149
Middlekauf, Robert, 14
Mifflin, Thomas, 137
Miller, Perry, 15–16
Milton, John, 116, 121
missionaries, 4, 108–10, 148
Montesquieu, Charles, 4
Morison, Samuel Eliot, 16–17, 151
Murdock, Kenneth, 14

N

Native Americans. See indigenous Americans
natural religion. See John Locke, rationalism
New North church, 65, 69, 74, 106; changes at, 3, 21–22, 33–36, 47–48, 67–68, 83, 107, 146, 148–49, 151–54; inclusiveness of, 107; popularity of, 47–49, 146, 152–54; worship, 38
Newton, Isaac, 17
Noll, Mark, 3

O

Occom, Samson, 109
Old North Church, 33, 35, 48, 52, 146
Oliver, Andrew, 110

P

Parker, Daniel, 132
Parkman, Francis, 154
Pitt, William, 116
Pitt, William Elder, 121
Prentice, Thomas, 21
Presbyterianism, 83, 88
Prince, Thomas, 55, 81
Puritans (general), 3, 11, 15–16, 48, 71, 80, 90–91, 97, 104

Q

Quartering Act, 125

R

race. See African Americans; Eliot: anti-slavery views; slavery
Ramus, Peter. See La Ramée, Pierre
rationalism, 69–71, 84–89, 93, 152
Reformation (Protestant), 3, 39, 90, 104, 120
religious freedom, 77–78, 97, 110–17. See also liberty
Rexine, John, 13
Riccaltoun, Robert, 86, 89
Ridgley, Thomas, 92–93
Roberts, Joseph, 24–26, 44–46
Rogers, Daniel, 21

S

Salem witch trials, 11–12
Salter, Richard, 82
Schmotter, James, 54–55
Secker, Thomas, 77
Seven Years' War, 122
Sewall, Samuel, 36
Shain, Barry, 114
Shepard, Thomas, 67
Shipton, Clifford, 3–5, 12–13, 17, 36, 47, 52, 56, 67–69, 84–85, 93–95, 107–10, 119, 142
Sidney, Philip, 121
Simkovich, Boris, 59
slavery, 106–8
Smith, Aaron, 21
Smith, Isaac Jr., 118–19, 129, 131, 135–37
Spanish Armada, 104, 115
Sprague, William, 83, 85
Stamp Act, 3–4, 6, 94, 98, 102, 115, 120, 123–26
Stark, John, 139
Stiles, Ezra, 48
Stillman, Samuel, 147–48
Stout, Harry, 37, 41, 43
Sugar and Currency Acts, 122

Index

Symonds, Ruth, 13

T

Taylor, John, 90
Tea Act, 124
Tell, William, 116
Tennant, Gilbert, 83
Thacher, Peter, 21, 33–35, 42–45, 148, 152
Thayer, Ebenezer, 24
Tillotson, John, 17
Tindal, Matthew, 86, 88–89
Tories, 3. *See also* loyalism
Townshend Acts, 123–25
Townshend, Charles, 123
Trenchard, John, 121
Tucker, John, 101
Turner, Charles, 101

U

Unitarianism, 4, 69, 71, 93, 151–54
universalism, 16, 43, 71, 90, 97, 152

V

Vivion, Mary, 12

W

Wadsworth, Benjamin, 55
Walker Howe, Daniel, 71
Walter, Nehemiah, 21
Ware, Henry, 152
Washington University, St. Louis, 151
Washington, George, 137, 140
Webb, John, 22, 27–28, 33–37, 45–48, 51, 67, 74–76, 83, 103, 113, 149
Wells, Charles, 154
West, Samuel, 101
Wheelock, Eleazar, 108–9
Whigs, 2, 4–6, 70, 78, 97–99, 105, 119–21, 148
Whitefield, George, xi, 69, 82–84, 149
Willard, Joseph, 24
Williams, Nathaniel, 13–14
Winthrop, John, 95
Wolfe, James, 104
Wollaston, William, 86–87
Wolleb, Johannes, 15
Woodier, Grace, 12
Wright, Conrad E., 152

Y

Young, Joshua, 154
Youngs, William T., 19, 41, 44, 46

www.ingramcontent.com/pod-product-compliance
Lightning Source LLC
Chambersburg PA
CBHW062046220426
43662CB00010B/1674